A Short History of Malta

PRAEGER SHORT HISTORIES

BRIAN BLOUET

A SHORT HISTORY OF
MALTA

FREDERICK A. PRAEGER, *Publishers*
New York · Washington

BOOKS THAT MATTER

Published in the United States of America in 1967
by Frederick A. Praeger, Inc., Publishers
111 Fourth Avenue, New York, N.Y. 10003

Printed in Great Britain

Contents

7

Illustrations

PLATES

Plates 1a and 1b are reproduced by courtesy of Warwick Bray. Plate 2 Crown Copyright reserved. Plates 6a, 6b, and 8a are reproduced by courtesy of the Government of Malta. Plate 7b is reproduced with the kind permission of the Grand Priory in the British Realm of the Venerable Order of the Hospital of St. John of Jerusalem.

MAPS

9

Preface

Hardly a year passes without at least one book appearing on Malta. There are two reasons for this state of affairs. First, the islands contain so much of interest that they are genuinely worthy of attention. Secondly, Malta is a convenient and pleasant place in which to work and enables the urges to pursue scholarship and the sun to be satisfied simultaneously.

This book, however, does attempt to treat the Maltese islands from a fresh point of view. Most work on Malta's modern history has really been concerned with the activities of the islands' overlords: the knights of St. John and the British. Little attention has been given to the development of the Maltese landscape and society. Because the Maltese have lacked chroniclers they have tended to receive footnote treatment from historians concerned principally with greater powers. However, the physical environment of Malta and the Maltese people have played a profound part in the affairs of the overlords. In their turn the Maltese have adapted to the social and economic pressures which the knights and the British introduced into the islands. Naturally many of the social changes which took place will probably never be known to us in detail; on the other hand alterations in the size of the population, the distribution of the settlements in which the Maltese lived and the development of the local economy are comparatively well documented. This leads us to another point. The history of Malta is marked by several periods in which our knowledge of the islands is extremely limited. We know a great deal about Malta in prehistory, Malta of the knights, the British period and, to a lesser extent, the islands in late medieval times. We know virtually nothing about Malta under the Carthaginians, Romans, Vandals,

Byzantines and Arabs. As a consequence this book is, to a degree, unbalanced.

Very many people have assisted with its production; it is virtually impossible to record everyone who has helped but a number of persons deserve special mention. First of all my thanks are due to H. R. Wilkinson, Professor of Geography in the University of Hull, who directed my research into the development of Malta under the Order of St. John. His encouragement and careful criticism have had a great influence on all the work I have done on Malta. Many members of the same department including Dr. J. H. Appleton, Dr. J. R. Tarrant, R. Dean Esq., and especially A. J. Jowett Esq., were always ready to discuss and develop ideas relating to the islands.

At Sheffield University I have had valuable advice from Dr. Warwick Bray on prehistoric matters and Dr. Robin Jeffs, of the Department of Medieval History, read the greater part of the typescript, suggested many improvements and in discussion has contributed much to my knowledge of Malta.

In the Maltese islands themselves help has been continuous, encouraging and, above all, friendly. Joseph Galea, at the Royal Malta Library, gave unstinted help with the Archives of the Order of St. John; indeed the whole library staff, under the direction of Dr. Depasquale, made the collection of material much easier than it might have been. The library of the Royal University of Malta was also used extensively and again there is nothing to record but gratitude for the privilege of being allowed to use the University's collections of *Melitensia* and for the cheerful assistance given by the staff.

Dr. David Trump and Frans Melia at the National Museum were always ready to discuss archaeological matters and to invite the author into the field with them when they were visiting sites.

The Government of Malta through the Department of Statistics, the Tourist Board, and the Public Works Department has given considerable assistance. I am particularly grateful at being allowed access to the collections of topographical maps in the Public Works Department and for the help and advice given by Mr. Cassar and Mr. Zammit. The Department of Information must also be thanked.

Godfrey Wettinger first introduced me to the Archives of the Order and suggested some of the sources which were to prove extremely useful. Professor Lionel Butler, of the Department of Medieval History in the University of St. Andrews, has given me a great deal of valuable advice and encouragement. David Farley Hills, of the Royal University of Malta, has discussed innumerable points as the work has developed and has been a most helpful critic. Miss Anne Barwood of the University of St. Andrews provided much useful information.

Finally my thanks are due to Mr. and Mrs. David Farley Hills and Dr. and Mrs. Muscat Manduca and their family for unfailing friendship and hospitality during the course of many visits to the islands.

I

The Geographical Setting

The Maltese islands are not large; the whole group consisting of Malta, Gozo, Comino, Cominotto and Filfla occupies only 122 square miles which is rather less than the area of the Isle of Wight. The islands lack any important natural resources, the soil is not particularly fertile and for the last thousand years at least there has even been a shortage of water. Such a small, poorly endowed group of islands would seem to be of limited importance, and yet, ever since the archipelago was first colonized about 6,000 years ago, it has never been very far from the centre of events and has often played a critical part in them.

The reasons for this importance are basically positional, for the islands lie in the narrow channel joining the eastern and western basins of the Mediterranean. However, a good strategic position is not enough; Pantelleria, Lampedusa and Linosa are as well if not better placed than the Maltese islands and have failed to play any great part in history. The Malta group enjoys two important advantages over the islands just mentioned. Firstly, although the Maltese islands are comparatively small they are still big enough to hold a large garrison and its equipment, provided it can be supplied with foodstuffs from outside. This advantage still applies by modern standards and the Malta airfields have been developed, without great difficulty, to take the latest generation of fighters and bombers. The second great advantage which the islands enjoy is the possession of the Grand Harbour which has allowed Malta to develop as a major naval base in historical time. Again this asset was adaptable to modern warfare, for the Grand Harbour, together with adjoining Marsamxett, is deep water and capable of accommodating the largest fleets.

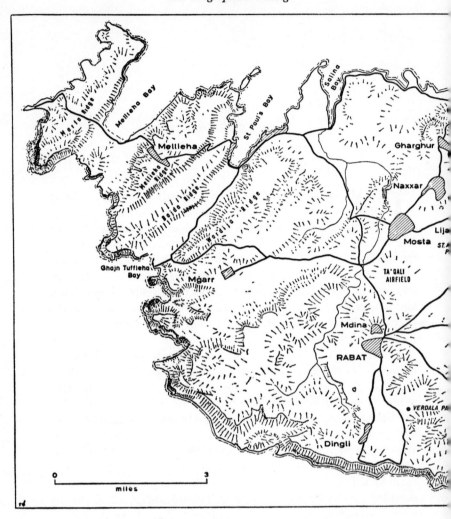

These potent strategic assets would have been of little value if the right political conditions had not developed. Sicily enjoys so many advantages as a base from which to control the central Mediterranean narrows that if Malta and Sicily are controlled by the same power then the former loses much of its strategic value; it becomes no more than an auxiliary base as a Sicilian overlord

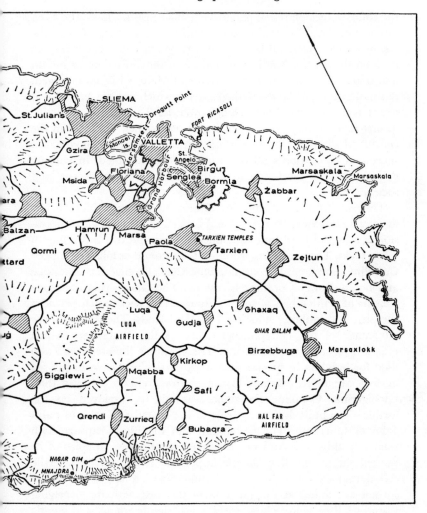

has no interest in doing anything with Malta other than keeping it out of the hands of a hostile power. Malta has tended to thrive, from a military viewpoint, when it has been held by a power other than that holding Sicily.

Position has been the key factor in Malta's history but other basic geographic facts like size, the nature of the islands' resources, the configuration of relief, particularly the coastline, have also been important. The resources of the group are such that, without the aid of a more powerful outside power, Malta could never impose itself on the central Mediterranean. From the limitations of wealth and population another characteristic of Maltese life has emerged. A small group of islands, with resources which are too small for it to act as the heartland of a major power, has been highly attractive to first-rate military powers wishing to secure their influence in the central Mediterranean. As a result the Maltese islands have had a succession of overlords all of whom have contributed, in varying degrees, to the development of the islands' rich landscape and society.

The rocks which make up the Maltese islands are basically in the form of a sandwich. At the top and bottom of the geological succession is a bed of hard limestone and between the two is a filling of softer rocks. The succession from top to bottom is as follows—Upper Coralline limestone, Greensand, Blue Clay, Globigerina limestone and finally Lower Coralline limestone. The Globigerina limestone consists of a thick bed of soft, easily quarried rock which provides the principal building stone used on the islands. The stone has the advantage of hardening on exposure to the atmosphere which makes it resistant to weathering. The Coralline limestones are also used for building in special situations, particularly close to the sea as they are more resistant to the corrosive effects of spray than Globigerina. Coralline limestone was widely employed on the fortifications built during the rule of the crusading Order of Saint John of Jerusalem. The Greensand and the Blue Clay are both relatively thin beds and outcrop over small areas. In spite of its limited extent the Blue Clay is important as not only is a fertile soil developed on it but, being impervious, a large number of springs are found at the junction of this bed with the overlying Coralline limestone. These springs are significant as a domestic water supply source and also because they are the basis of a rich zone of irrigation farming, producing excellent fruit and vegetables.

In areas underlain by Coralline limestone soils are generally thin and infertile but on the softer Globigerina limestone a deeper soil cover is normally developed.

The simple sandwich of rocks described above has been distorted by faulting. (A fault is a crack in the earth's surface along which

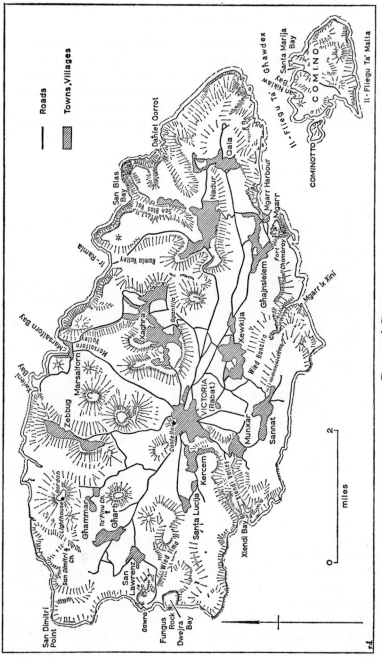

Gozo and Comino

Roads
Towns, Villages

miles
0   2

San Dimitri Point
San Lawrenz
Ghammar
Gharb
Zebbug
Marsalforn
Qala
Nadur
Dahlet Qorrot
San Blas Bay
Il-Ramla
Ramla Valley
Xaghra
Marsalforn Valley
Ta' Pinu Ch.
Lighthouse
San Dimitri Ch.
Qawra
Fungus Rock
Dwejra Bay
Xlendi Bay
Santa Lucija
Kercem
VICTORIA (Rabat)
Castello
Munxar
Sannat
Xewkija
Ghajnsielem
Wied Hanzira
Mgarr Harbour
Mgarr
Fort Chambray
Mgarr Ix Xini
Il-Fliegu Ta' Ghawdex
San Nikiaw Bay
Santa Marija Bay
COMINO
COMINOTTO
Il-Fliegu Ta' Malta

r.d.

movement, vertical or horizontal or both, has taken place.) North-western Malta has been shattered by a series of parallel faults which have thrown the rocks into a succession of ridges and depressions. The erosion of the ridges and the downwashing of debris into the depressions has led to the accumulation of a deep filling of soil in the latter. Between one fertile depression and the next is a bare,

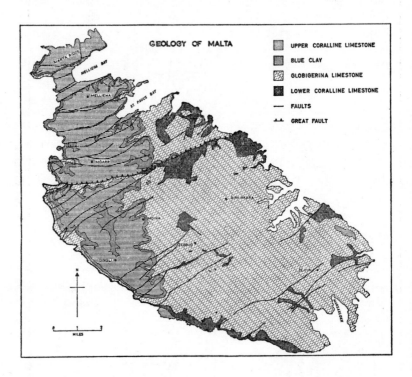

steep-sided, limestone ridge which makes communication in this part of Malta very difficult. Where the ridges and depressions run into the sea in the east, magnificent bays are formed which, being in a remote part of the island where communications are poor, have always been difficult to defend against raids by pirates intent on taking slaves or other booty. Such raids have been a hazard of life on the Maltese islands virtually throughout their history and north-western Malta has been particularly exposed to the danger.

The largest and most southerly of the series of faults mentioned above is known as the Great Fault and gives rise to a steep escarpment which in places exceeds two hundred feet in height. A relief feature of this size is an important natural defence and there has always been a tendency for the Maltese not to attempt the difficult and costly task of defending the more northerly coasts and to concentrate the defence works along the Great Fault. This has increased the isolation and vulnerability of north-western Malta and, in spite of its fertility, it has tended to be abandoned in unsettled times. Faulting has also been largely responsible for the high, sheer, cliffs which protectively wall Malta's western coast.

To the south and east of the Great Fault the relief of Malta is less varied than that found in the ridge and depression country of the north-west. The Rabat-Dingli plateau is capped by the tough Upper Coralline limestone and soils are generally poor, except where the agents of erosion have stripped off the limestone and exposed the underlying Blue Clay. The southern edge of the plateau has been serrated by a number of valleys and the intervening spurs provide good defensive sites for settlement. Mdina, the medieval capital of Malta, is on a spur of this type from which position it commands fine views of a large part of the island. The remainder of Malta consists basically of flat country sloping gently from west to east. However, this relatively smooth country has been cut into by a number of valleys, or *wieds* as they are called in Maltese, which are often of considerable depth. There is a strong tendency for the older Maltese towns and villages to be situated on spurs above the wieds.

Between Malta and Gozo in the Fliegu channel is the small island of Comino with its even smaller brother Cominotto. In area the two islands hardly exceed a square mile, they rise to no great height and, being composed largely of Coralline limestone, are infertile. Comino is important as it offers a site on which to build a fortress to command the straits separating Malta and Gozo.

Gozo, the most northerly island of the group, is second in size to Malta and, whilst it lacks good harbours and has therefore been of limited strategic importance, it is more fertile than Malta and has usually been able to supply a part of the larger island's food deficiency. Gozo's greater fertility is due primarily to the extensive outcrops of Blue Clay found on the island.

The major characteristics of the climate of the Maltese islands can be summed up as summer drought, mild rainy winters with, for a large part of the year, clear blue skies and a high light intensity. This, of course, is an oversimplification and, whilst summer conditions are normally settled, in winter the weather sequences can be very complex and almost as variable as those experienced over the British Isles.

In summer the Mediterranean region is dominated by high pressure conditions, and at Malta June, July, August and September all enjoy mean monthly temperatures in excess of 70° F. Even October has an average temperature throughout the month of 69° F. Fortunately the heat of summer is tempered by breezes which generally blow from a north-westerly direction over the whole Mediterranean. Occasionally this delightful summer climate is disrupted by an excessively heated airstream coming up from the Sahara desert to the south. Not only is the wind hot but, as it travels over the sea, moisture is absorbed rapidly and the air-stream becomes very humid. In these conditions it is difficult for the human body to cool efficiently by perspiring. In Malta this wind is called the *xlokk* and it produces a general enervation and even giddiness. The xlokk can wither in a short time the few crops that are raised in Malta during the summer using dry farming methods. Fortunately the xlokk does not occur frequently in its most highly developed form.

In the summer months then, the weather at Malta is very settled with continuously sunny days, virtually no rainfall, for even thunderstorms are rare, and there are normally pleasant sea breezes to modify the heat.

Summer usually breaks towards the end of September when colder air from the Atlantic penetrates into the Mediterranean and sets off the violent storms which mark the change from summer to winter. After these initial explosions the weather at Malta frequently cools and calms into what is known locally as Saint Martin's summer—October and November are pleasant, warm, sunny, showery months and they are busy times for the Maltese farmers. Throughout the long summer drought most plant life has lain dormant but now, with the first showers, growth begins rapidly. Few crops are produced in the islands during the hottest months except where irrigation water is available.

Winter conditions can be very variable since the weather is controlled by the relative positions of a number of air masses with widely differing characteristics. Over Europe there is normally a large cold air mass; the Sahara is covered by an extensive warm air mass; and depressions frequently penetrate into the Mediterranean from the Atlantic, whilst some depressions are generated in the lee of the Alps. The interplay of these various air masses determines the weather conditions over Malta and indeed the whole Mediterranean. If a depression, or low pressure system, passes to the north of Malta then warm southerly winds blow up from the relatively high pressure over the Sahara—sunshine hours are high and rainfall is low. Should a depression pass to the south then cold air may blow down from the high pressure system over Europe. These winds bring cold conditions and, whilst air frost at Malta is unknown, flurries of snow are not. When a depression passes close to the islands mild conditions with much cloud and rain result. Deep depressions can become the centres of violent storms. There are numerous variations of the weather patterns outlined above.

Just as the southerly winds have local names so do those blowing from the north. The *majjistral* blows from the north-west, the *tramuntana* from the north and the *grigal* from the north-east. The grigal is particularly important as it blows straight into the mouths of the Grand Harbour and Marsamxett and can restrict their use to shipping.

The average annual rainfall of the Maltese islands is 22 inches, most of which falls in short, sharp showers. Occasionally heavy down-pours develop, capable of causing great damage and washing the soil from the hillsides. To safeguard against this, farmers on the Maltese islands, and throughout the Mediterranean generally, carefully terrace slopes—but really violent storms can wash away the laboriously built retaining walls.

Maltese agriculture depends heavily on an adequate fall of rain during the winter months. The variable winter conditions are clearly not certain to provide a reliable fall each year. In some winters the depression weather predominates and the rainfall total is high. During the next winter season the predominant airstreams may be those coming up from the south and slight showers are all that result. In one year the rainfall may be as high as 40 inches, in the next less than 10 inches. In 1951 over 25 inches of rain fell in the month of October alone and yet October has also been a month of complete drought. The average rainfall of the Maltese islands has little meaning since great variation is encountered and catastrophic droughts do occur.

Very few streams on the islands flow for more than a few hours after the heavier winter showers. A small number which have their source at constant and plentiful springs do manage to trickle throughout the year over a short part of their courses. Water for domestic use throughout the islands is drawn from wells or the small number of perennial springs.

It would be useful to know for how long the present climatic conditions have prevailed for it is certain that the islands have not experienced a uniform climate throughout history. This is important because with such a delicately balanced water supply climatic changes would influence very greatly the possible activities of man on the islands. Probably during most of the Neolithic period and the Bronze Age conditions were wetter than today but since the late Middle Ages the climate has been very similar to that experienced today. There have been periods when the number of droughts has increased; for instance in the early decades of the eighteenth century hardly a year went by without the Grand Master of the Order of Saint John decreeing that prayers should be offered up for rain. On these occasions the knights of Saint John went in procession through the streets of Valletta in their striking black habit, emblazoned with a great eight-pointed cross, to the church of the saint thought most likely to intercede on behalf of the islands. Such droughts brought great hardship to the countryside but did not occur frequently enough to alter Maltese agricultural practice.

Today the Maltese islands have very few trees and most of the land is cultivated, except on the areas of bare Coralline limestone where only the hardiest plants survive. The islands possess very little woodland—a few citrus groves and ornamental plantations together with a small number of figs, olives and carobs which grow along the walls surrounding the fields. It has not always been so. When man came to the Maltese islands 6,000 years ago he came to a land well clothed with soil and natural vegetation. Man changed this. The vegetation has been stripped off and over large areas the soil itself has been exposed to erosion and washed from the hillsides, creating the barren limestone karst which is a feature over

24

parts of the islands today. With the disappearance of soil and vegetation the speed of run-off after rain has increased, and water finds its way more quickly to the sea and has less opportunity to sink into the islands. The effectiveness of the rainfall has decreased and aridity has increased.

These are some of the facets of the local geographical setting which have influenced life on the Maltese islands. However, whilst such factors have clearly been important in some respects, frequently changes taking place far from the archipelago have had a profound effect on the history of the islands. Again and again local life has become linked with the fortunes of great powers and thus with events taking place in a world setting.

2

Malta in Prehistory

The penetration of man into the central Mediterranean area was relatively late. In Sicily it was not until the Upper Palaeolithic period that clear traces of human occupancy occur; remains from the Lower and Middle Palaeolithic are lacking. In Malta no trace of Palaeolithic or Mesolithic cultures has yet been uncovered. However, it should be remembered that at the time when these cultures were represented in the area the sea-level may well have been considerably lower. Malta could have been considerably larger at the time and the subsequent rise in sea-level may well have covered the evidence of any Palaeolithic or Mesolithic occupation. If man did occupy the island at the time it is likely that he lived close to the sea shore, for in Sicily the hunting and gathering communities made considerable use of shellfish, etc., and their habitation sites showed a predominantly coastal distribution. The existence of pre-Neolithic man on the islands cannot be ruled out yet, although the number of persons involved would be small and they probably had very little influence on the development of the landscape.

Mesolithic culture in Sicily did not evolve, it was superseded by Neolithic culture brought in by colonists from other lands. The *Neolithic revolution* took place in the Middle East, in the areas now called Syria, Jordan, Anatolia and Iraq. Here for the first time man learnt to control many elements in his environment and escape the vagaries of a hunting and collecting economy. Plants and animals were slowly domesticated from the wild forms, a wide range of implements was developed and as a result it became possible to produce, and store, food surpluses. The production of food surpluses is really the breakthrough in terms of cultural evolution, for once certain members of a community can be freed from the necessity of

26

spending all their time producing food they can devote themselves to other pursuits: the production of tools, textiles, pottery, building and the priesthood. Armed with artisans, craftsmen, thinkers and visionaries a society has the basic ingredients of cultural development. The way is open for more specialized divisions of labour.

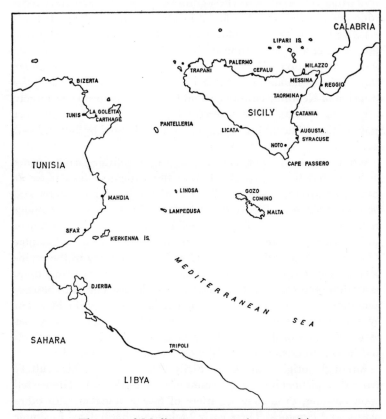

The central Mediterranean area (not to scale)

Changes of this type took place in several Middle Eastern areas in the eighth and seventh millenniums B.C. Wheat and barley were developed from wild cereals, a number of other plants were also domesticated. Ancestral sheep, goats, pigs and cattle were brought into captivity, tamed and eventually bred to suit the requirements of man.

From the centres of development in the Middle East Neolithic

27

culture spread out and occupied surrounding regions. The Neolithic colonization was essentially seaborne and it reached Sicily late in the fifth or early in the fourth millennium B.C.

It is generally recognized that the first Neolithic men to establish themselves on Malta probably came from Sicily for there are marked similarities between the earliest cultured phase of the Sicilian Neolithic (stentinello) and that found in Malta (Ghar Dalam). It is interesting to note that the colonization of Malta took place relatively quickly after the occupation of Sicily, long before there can have been any question of land hunger and overcrowding in the larger island. The explanation of this fact is relatively straightforward; the diffusion of Neolithic culture around the Mediterranean was largely a seaborne operation and covered a large area in a relatively short space of time. The diffusion was probably instigated by cultural and social forces as well as economic ones.

We do not know precisely at what date Neolithic farmers came to Malta but it seems probable that the settlement took place at some time around 3800 B.C. The colonizers found the islands well wooded, verdant, soil-covered and plentifully watered. The fauna included, amongst other species, wild boar and deer. It is worth noting here that the physical environment described in Chapter I has not been a static background to human activity in the archipelago. Vegetation, soils and climate have all altered, sometimes as a result of forces operating on a world scale, like climatic changes, sometimes changes in the environment have been brought about by the intervention of man. For example human activity has removed much of the natural vegetation and soil from the islands and helped to create many of the barren, limestone hillsides.

Although originating from Sicily Maltese Neolithic culture evolved on distinct lines. The community which developed depended upon farming, producing a variety of cereals together with other plants, and livestock. These early Maltese probably lived in simple huts grouped in small villages, the total population of the islands being quite small. There was probably no pressure on the available agricultural land and many areas in the islands remained wooded. The agricultural system was probably based upon a rotational scheme in which areas of land around the villages would be cultivated for short periods and then allowed to revert to woodland and scrub until fertility had been regained.

Table I

PREHISTORIC CULTURAL SEQUENCE[1]

Period	Phase	Approx. date	Landscape features visible today
NEOLITHIC	Ghar Dalam	3800 B.C.	
	Grey Skorba	3600 B.C.	Remnants of villages
	Red Skorba	3400 B.C.	
===?===	===?===	===?===	===?===
COPPER AGE	Zebbug	3200 B.C.	
	Mgarr	2900 B.C.	Rock-cut tombs
	Ggantija	2850 B.C.	Rock-cut tombs, numerous temples of several designs
	Saflieni	2450 B.C.	
	Tarxien	2400 B.C.	Tarxien temples
BRONZE AGE	Tarxien Cemetery	2000 B.C.	Cremation cemetery, dolmens
	Borg in-Nadur	1450 B.C.	Fortified villages. Cart-tracks (??)
	Bahrija	900 B.C.	Fortified villages

========= Arrival of new people from abroad.

The religion of the Skorba people was probably linked with fertility cults and it appears that eventually simple shrines were developed.

Life on Malta evolved relatively slowly for something like 600 years after the Neolithic colonization and it is probable that the landscape of the islands was little changed by man during the period. The wild fauna was thinned out by hunting, the woodland became sparser and the plant associations were altered but funda-

[1] The sequence has been drawn from work by Brea, Evans, and Trump (p. 240).

mentally the physical environment was not drastically altered. However, about 3,200 years before the birth of Christ new influences reached the islands (it is difficult to say whether or not a migration of peoples was involved) from Sicily and as a result a Copper Age level of cultural development was instituted. The islands became subjected to a more intensive utilization of the available resources. After a time the Copper Age people developed elaborate, kidney-shaped, rock-cut tombs which occupied a central place in their religion which was based upon fertility cults and ancestor worship. From this beginning in religious architecture there was an efflorescence which produced a most remarkable series of temples and tombs. It has been suggested that when the Maltese of the day started to build temples they attempted to reproduce above ground the essential forms of their religious architecture, which had been developed in the subterranean tombs. Below ground lobed tomb structures had probably developed naturally and the early temples are, in fact, of a similar form. As time passed the morphology of the temples became increasingly complex, acquiring a trefoil structure which was superseded by elaborate apses of varying number. Not only did the ground plan of the temples undergo development but they increased in size, the stonework became very elaborate, the interior fittings and decoration became highly sophisticated and clearly the temples reflect a society which is becoming technically highly skilled within the limits set by the resources available. The greatest part of this religious and technical evolution took place within the Ggantija phase of the Copper Age. The phase, of course, lasted several hundred years.

As yet no satisfactory explanation has been advanced as to why the inhabitants of the islands were able to develop the facility for building what are technically very refined temples. Some authorities have sought outside influences as the cause, others see the temple architecture as wholly the product of local society and environment.

Even more controversy has been aroused as to the place of the architecture in the prehistory of Western Europe. From the evidence available to us today it appears that Maltese megalithic architecture is older than anything similar that is known in the western Mediterranean and it has been suggested that Malta was the centre from which the style emanated. If this were so then the islands would hold a key place in the cultural evolution of prehistoric Western Europe.

Against this point of view is the fact that megalithic architecture elsewhere in the western Mediterranean shows very little sign of having been derived from the Maltese temples and as yet there is only limited evidence of cultural contact between Malta and the surrounding areas. In conclusion it is fair to say that there are great gaps in the evidence marshalled by both sides and until we have a fuller regional and chronological picture of megalithic architecture in the western Mediterranean, and adjacent areas, the controversy is unlikely to be settled satisfactorily.

Another great puzzle associated with the temples is just how they were paid for. The elaborate structures represent a considerable number of man hours in terms of construction, modification and upkeep. While we know that the rituals performed in the buildings were relatively complex, probably implying a full-time priesthood, there is no escaping the fact that the temples, in the context of their times, are a very considerable feat of construction and some authorities have wondered whether or not the islands had sufficient resources to finance their building. Various solutions to this problem have been advanced, although none of them is entirely satisfactory. It has been suggested that Malta was a 'magic island sanctuary' with a great part of the religious paraphernalia being paid for by gifts or fees extracted from pilgrims coming from other lands. This theory is open to the objection that if pilgrims did come to Malta then virtually no trace of them has been discovered in the islands, nor have many Copper Age souvenirs of Malta turned up in the lands from which visitors are supposed to have travelled.

Another theory is that the islanders traded widely to offset the limitations of their homeland. Again similar objections can be raised for little evidence has come to light to indicate strong and constant contacts between Malta and other lands in the Mediterranean. Yet this theory cannot be dismissed quite so easily. Firstly, there was some trade, the islanders needed hard rocks like flint and obsidian which could be acquired from Sicily and the adjacent islands. These imports must have been exchanged for something and it is difficult to know what the Copper Age Maltese exported. Imports were certainly not paid for with pottery, at least there is no sign of Maltese ceramics in the relevant regions. Malta has no raw materials which could be exported. Possibly the imports were paid for by the skills of the inhabitants. We know that the Copper

Age people produced textiles which were probably of a relatively high quality and might well have been sufficiently in demand to be used in bartering for raw materials. If the islanders were overcoming the deficiencies of the archipelago in this way they would be employing, at a very early stage, an adaptation to the local environment which has been used frequently throughout Maltese history; namely the development of high quality craft industries and the export of their products to pay for the many goods which the islands, with their scarce resources, have always had to import.

If textiles (or some other perishable product of a craft industry) were being exported in exchange for raw materials, why could not textiles also have been used to buy food from Sicily to support a population large enough to build the temple complexes? It is difficult to answer this question due to difficulties associated with identifying the source of textiles even if remains are found.

Theories of the type outlined above have been bandied about for some time although it is possible that the islanders built the temples unaided by food surpluses from other lands. Estimates have been made of the population densities which early forms of agriculture could support and if we apply these estimates to Malta we find that the islands could have fed a population of approximately 5,000 persons, in the Copper Age, if the greatest part of the available land was brought within the system of cultivation. Clearly this is a very broad and general estimate and the whole question is complicated by the fact that it is almost certain that sea-level at Malta in 3000 B.C. was not the same as it is today. If sea-level was lower then the area of the islands would be greater and *vice versa*. Apart from global changes in sea-level, which in itself is a highly complex topic, the central Mediterranean area is marked by crustal instability and there have been considerable changes in the height of the land areas within historical time. Changes of the order of 60 feet within the past few hundred years are being talked of. Now, if, for example, the sea-level at Malta was something of the order of 100 feet lower in the Copper Age than it is today, then large areas to the east of Malta would have been dry land and the food-producing potential of the islands would have been considerably larger. Conversely a higher sea-level would have had an adverse effect.

Assuming a population which numbered about 5,000 would it

have been possible for it to build, maintain and man the temples? There are about 30 known temples in the archipelago. If we assume that each temple was supported by a community of roughly 200 persons, approximately 50 able-bodied men would be available for the construction of each monument. In the case of most of the temples this does not seem to be an inadequate work force, if construction was spread over a period, and if the agricultural system of the day was producing reasonable surpluses. Of course, the work may not have been undertaken in this way, the temples may have been constructed by combining the resources of the whole island (monuments like Tarxien probably were) or by several communities banding together. The point is that, rough and ready though the above calculations are, provided the system of agriculture operating on the islands was reasonably typical of the times, the temples might well have been constructed by the islanders alone without invoking a great deal of special pleading in the form of magic island sanctuaries and the like.

Clearly a great deal of the above is simply speculation and it is true to say that we shall never learn the answer to many of the problems associated with Maltese prehistory until we know more about the basic environmental factors with which the early inhabitants had to contend.

What became of the temple civilization? Well, this story is surrounded by yet another great cloud of problems. There are possibly signs in the final (Tarxien) phase of the Copper Age that the society had lost its vitality and then, sometime after 2400 B.C. the civilization terminates and from the available evidence it appears that the islands were left uninhabited. This evidence may be suspect for in archaeology the next excavation is always liable to produce new material which alters the existing interpretation of events. When dealing with Maltese prehistory it should not be forgotten that the great bulk of our evidence has been derived from temples and tombs and may fail to reflect the full face of the society's existence.

What was the cause of the curtailment of the temple civilization? Invasion and warfare can be ruled out and we have to look for a natural cause of death, although when dealing with a society so bound up with religious cults it may be wrong to seek for rational solutions. The climate probably got drier after *c.* 2500 B.C.

c   33

The most likely sequence of events leading to decline is as follows. During the Ggantija phase, when temple building was at its most buoyant, it is likely that the population of the islands was increasing relatively rapidly, although it proved possible to step up food production as well. But there came a time when there was no more land to be brought into cultivation. The optimum intensity of land-use had been reached, the islands could support no more inhabitants. However, the population continued to grow in numbers and the society, unwittingly, got itself into a self-destroying situation. In a shifting agricultural system it is possible to keep food production increasing by shortening the periods of fallow, although this starts an accelerating cycle of depletion. The fallows are cut, the crop yields begin to fall, so that to raise productivity the rest periods are further curtailed, whereupon the yields drop again, and so on, until the fertility of the soil is exhausted. By this stage the agricultural basis of a society will have been destroyed and it must go into decline. Each year the number of deaths from malnutrition will increase rapidly, infant mortality will rise, diseases will take a heavier toll of the weakened population.

It has been suggested that there was a large-scale migration from the islands, but there are many objections to such an idea. Indeed the process of decay was probably not so suddenly obvious as to suggest to the inhabitants a quick, positive, response to the change in their environment. It is more likely that the process was spread over a period of years with the population becoming more and more depressed economically and mentally; incapable of finding a solution to their situation now that the fertility goddesses and ancestors had failed. No doubt a few persons escaped to Sicily; it has been suggested that some of the inhabitants got as far as Sardinia. Possibly a very small population survived, moved away from the temple sites, lived at a very low level and have simply left no ceramic evidence of their existence. There are many examples of societies undergoing deculturation in response to overharsh environmental conditions.

It is as well to add that the greatest part of the sequence of decline described above is pure speculation; a search for an explanation of some peculiar facts in the existing archaeological record. However, it is true to say, and this can be almost stated as a law, that every human group which has occupied the Maltese islands successfully has in the end outgrown the ability of the archipelago to produce food. In later times it was possible to organize large-scale imports of food; in the Copper Age it may well not have been so.

After the islands had been left abandoned, or very sparsely populated, for an undefined length of time, Malta was recolonized by a Bronze Age people who probably came from a region in the heel of Italy. There is nothing particularly noteworthy about these new Maltese, or the Bronze Age colonists who subsequently came to the islands. There is little sign of exceptional technical expertise, or wealth, and the islands were probably relatively thinly populated in comparison with the Copper Age. The first Bronze Age Maltese re-used the great Copper Age Tarxien temples as a crematorium and as a result they have been named the Tarxien Cemetery people. These inhabitants built for themselves a number of dolmens (megalithic structures consisting of a large, one-piece, capstone, supported by smaller rocks) in which, it has been postulated, cremated remains were buried.

The Tarxien Cemetery people enjoyed the use of the islands for many hundreds of years before, in about 1450 B.C., Malta was invaded by another Bronze Age group, the Borg in-Nadur people. These colonists, who probably came from Sicily, take their name from the Malta type site which is on a promontory above Marsaxlokk. The invaders apparently overwhelmed the Cemetery people and subsequently incorporated the previous inhabitants within their communities. The Borg in-Nadur people lived in warlike times and dwelt in fortified villages which are normally sited on hill tops. Warfare may have been the result of invaders attempting to establish themselves on the islands, or Malta may have been divided into a series of village territories and battles could have been fought between competing communities.

About 900 B.C. another group of settlers, the Bahrija people, did establish themselves in the islands; the new culture and that of the Borg in-Nadur people co-existed, although the relationship between the two groups is not well understood. Maltese prehistory closes at around 800 B.C. when the Carthaginians established themselves and began to have a cultural influence on the existing population.

Clearly the Bronze Age in Malta was less rich culturally and economically than the Copper Age. The islands were probably not capable of supporting as many people as previously. The existence of warlike conditions over large parts of the Bronze Age must have made agriculture less efficient and possibly resulted in a greater reliance on stock farming rather than arable, for it is possible to protect herds from raiding parties in a manner which is impossible with sown crops. Once again we have the import-export problem. We know that bronze was imported into the islands but we do not know how it was paid for. However, at some of the later Bronze Age sites there is a plentitude of paraphernalia associated with the manufacture of textiles. It has been suggested that textiles were used to purchase bronze, and other goods, from surrounding areas.[1]

There remains yet one more enigma of Maltese prehistory to be discussed: namely the so-called cart-tracks. It is hardly necessary to add that we are entering speculative realms once more. Bare rock, in many parts of the islands, is scored with parallel ruts which look very much like cart-tracks. They are almost certainly not cart-tracks. The distance between the ruts varies and wheeled vehicles would frequently become stuck if they attempted to use them. Clearly the tracks were part of a system of transportation but what age are they, what type of vehicle used them and what was transported? With regard to age we have very few clues apart from the fact that in several places Punic tombs are found cut into the ruts, indicating that the tracks were in existence at the time when the tombs were excavated. Thus the tracks are pre-historic. The ruts are noticeably absent around the Copper Age temples but they do correlate well with Bronze Age village sites. *A priori* there is a case for assuming the tracks are Bronze Age, although this condition is based on assumptions that could prove to be wrong.

What vehicles used or made the tracks? We have ruled out wheeled vehicles and sledges would find the ruts extremely difficult to negotiate. It has been suggested that the tracks were worn by slide cars which were towed by draught animals. Basically the car would consist of two shafts attached to the animal at the front, held together by a framework in the middle and resting on the ground at the rear. The rear ends of the shafts were probably shod

[1] In 1964 an excavation near Syracuse produced large quantities of pottery 'exactly like the Maltese ware from the Tarxien cemetery'. It has been suggested that the site represents 'a Maltese commercial settlement set up on the Sicilian coast'.

with stone in some way. The framework would be strong enough to carry goods, or a passenger, or both.

An obvious objection to this slide car theory is that a vehicle of the type outlined above could be dragged across exposures of Coralline limestone for years and hardly make a scratch, let alone ruts. In fact local limestones only become hard on exposure to the atmosphere and fresh outcrops are quite soft. If many of the hills, which today are barren limestone, were covered with soil at the relevant time then the whole process becomes more feasible and was probably very similar to the formation of conventional cart-ruts. The first time a slide car crossed an area it would cut into the top soil and on each subsequent occasion would tend to follow the same rut and to deepen it. Eventually the soft, protected, underlying limestones would be grooved by the shafts. After a time the ruts would become over deep and a new track would be created nearby; this would explain the duplication of routeways in some areas.

For what purpose were the slide cars used? Here we must immediately admit that we have no evidence to go on and that the patterns developed by the tracks are not all susceptible to logical explanation. We can simply say that the number and distribution of the tracks must indicate that they were used very frequently for a large number of daily tasks. Whether these tasks included an industry, arable farming, herding and warfare, or any combination of these activities, is impossible to say in the present state of our knowledge.

3

Carthaginians, Romans, Medieval Malta

By the year 1,000 B.C. the Phoenicians were trading in the western basin of the Mediterranean. It is difficult to believe that Malta was not touched at a very early stage by Phoenician activity in the area, although the earliest remains of these people found so far in the islands date only from the ninth century B.C. The Phoenicians established many colonies in the western Mediterranean and when their homeland in the Levant was overrun the area around Tunis, or Carthaginia, became the new heartland of their activities. The Carthaginians colonized the Maltese islands in the eighth and seventh centuries B.C.

In the eighth century B.C. Greeks started to trade with Sicily and southern Italy and eventually established colonies in the region. Although in succeeding centuries there was a clash of interests between the Phoenicians and Greeks in the central Mediterranean, which frequently led to war, there is some evidence of peaceful co-existence between the two parties in Malta. Many importations from the Hellenic world have been discovered in the islands but the Greeks do not appear to have enjoyed a great deal of influence; Malta was strongly controlled by Carthage and Punic culture appears to have put down deep roots.

From the fourth century B.C. the power of Rome increased in southern Italy and eventually came into conflict with that of Carthage. Malta lay in the zone of contact between the parties and began to acquire a value, not only as a refuge harbour and trading station, but also as a military base. What little evidence we have suggests that Malta had become, at the time of the First Punic War (262 B.C.–242 B.C.), a Carthaginian naval base. During the course of the war the Romans captured the island, burning and pillaging it in the process. The Carthaginians eventually regained possession but in 218 B.C., in the Second Punic War, Rome acquired undisputed control.

It is doubtful if the islands were ever thoroughly Romanized. Pottery styles continued to exhibit a strong Punic flavour long after Carthage had been destroyed. Diodorus Siculus, writing a century and a half after the start of the Roman domination, describes Malta and Gozo as Phoenician colonies. The account in the Acts of the Apostles of St. Paul's shipwreck at Malta in A.D. 60 describes the islanders as *barbaroi*, a term which indicates they spoke neither Latin nor Greek. It has been suggested that the Maltese of the day spoke a dialect of Phoenician. Some authorities would take this idea further and claim that the islanders were still speaking a basically Phoenician language at the Arab conquest in A.D. 870. The argument goes on to suggest that Arabic and Phoenician would be, fundamentally, not too dissimilar, which explains why Arabic was adopted so thoroughly in the islands during the Arab domination. Other authorities claim that at the Arab conquest the Maltese were speaking Low Latin. It is as well to bear in mind that we have very little detailed evidence relating to the period between A.D. 60 and the coming of the Arabs.

There is no doubt that Malta was highly prosperous for a long period under Roman rule. It is probable that the economy flourished to a degree which was not attained again until the Order of St. John started to develop the islands.

The picture of Roman Malta which we can reconstruct today is lacking in detail but the major aspects of the geography of the period are discernible. In the centre of the island, on roughly the site now occupied by Mdina and Rabat, stood the fortified capital; a relatively gracious town which was some three times as large as Mdina. In the Marsa area there were port facilities and possibly a harbourside town. The capital and the port were probably linked by a good road. We know that Gozo, too, had a central town in Roman times in the area now covered by the Castello. It is difficult to say what other settlements existed but the countryside was dotted with villas. The sites of many villas have been excavated and the remains found indicate that the agricultural system of the day was concerned principally with the production of wheat and olives.

From Cicero's impeachment of the rapacious Verres, a Governor of Sicily who misused authority to plunder the territory given to his charge, we know that Malta produced a number of luxury goods for export. Additionally the islands were renowned as the centre of a quality textile industry.

Malta still retains many relics of the prosperity of Roman times. Apart from the villas already mentioned, the baths at Ghain Tuffieha are in a reasonable state of preservation and there are some fine early Christian catacombs in Rabat. Indeed, until well into the seventeenth century, the streets of Rabat contained the remains of many Roman buildings, in eloquent testimony to the grace and affluence of a former time.

During the fifth century A.D. Roman power in the Mediterranean waned rapidly and the Vandals were able to found a kingdom in North Africa. The invaders quickly established a strong navy and began to raid Malta and Sicily. There is great doubt as to whether or not the Vandals occupied Malta and Sicily or simply used the islands as a source of plunder. In the course of the sixth century A.D. the Byzantines were able to gain control of Sicily and Malta. There is no concrete trace of the Vandals in the landscape and, until more extensive excavations have been undertaken, it will be impossible even to outline conditions in the islands during the Byzantine period.

By the middle of the ninth century A.D. the Moslems had expanded from their homeland in Arabia and conquered large areas in North Africa, Spain and Sicily. In A.D. 870 Malta was attacked and taken from the Byzantines. It is as well to admit, right at the beginning, that our knowledge of Malta under the Arabs is limited and most of what we claim to know is based upon inference as there are few written records. We have no real idea of the economic state of the islands when the Arabs arrived, or of the number, religion and language of the local population. Nor do we know whether the Moslems came simply as overlords or as colonizers as well. We can say with certainty, however, that the islands were profoundly affected, culturally and economically, by the two centuries of Arab rule. The Maltese language is basically Arabic, although even this fact is open to many interpretations. It could mean that Arabic-speaking migrants moved into the islands until they outnumbered the existing community, or it might mean that the language of the ruling élite was gradually assimilated by the whole population. In the latter case it would be expected that elements of the old language would have survived, particularly as place-names. There is little evidence of pre-Arabic word forms.

The question of religion is also complex. Apparently Christianity never died out during the period of Moslem rule but there is evidence to suggest that it became the religion of a minority. Whether this situation was due to defections, as a result of non-Moslems being liable to higher taxation, or to a large influx of migrants is again in doubt.

Economically the islands seem to have gained considerably from Arab rule. A few contemporary descriptions have come down to us and, although these are lacking in detail, they do give a general impression of prosperity. One Arab chronicler refers to Malta in the following terms; 'Malitah (Melita the Latin name for the island) . . . rich in everything that is good and in the blessing of God . . . well peopled, possessing towns and villages, trees and fruit.' This description, and others of the same period, provide a picture of well-being and verdure which is in marked contrast to the tales of poverty and aridity which characterize fifteenth and sixteenth century accounts of Malta. There is a certain amount of corroboratory evidence to suggest that the islands were better wooded with cultivated tree crops during the Arab rule.

The Arabs appear to have made considerable changes in the system of agriculture practised in the islands. The new rulers were highly skilled in the art of cultivation by irrigation and they introduced the *noria* (Maltese *senija*), an animal-powered device for lifting water from wells onto the land.

The Arabs brought a new range of crops into the western Mediterranean world. From Malta's point of view the introduction of cotton and citrus fruits was particularly important. Cotton, over a period of centuries, came to occupy a central place in the Maltese rural economy.

There appears to have been a great increase in central Mediterranean trade during the period in which the Arabs had domination over the area. Palermo, captured by the Moslems in 831, developed into an important centre of commerce. It seems that Malta, although not an important trading station, did benefit from the increased commercial activity in the region. There is also some evidence to indicate that the islands became a small centre of piracy and in general the Moslems were highly active as raiders on the coasts of southern Europe.

As to the size and distribution of towns and villages in the islands we have little knowledge. The Arabs refortified the old Roman capital and renamed it Mdina—the city. The Moslems are also credited with the foundation of the fortress which is today known as fort St. Angelo. After the foundation of the fort the small town, which is now called Birgu or Vittoriosa, probably begun to develop.

In sum it must be said that our knowledge of Malta under the Arabs is hazy and yet there is no disputing that the cultural and economic imprint of this period was deep. The most important legacy left by the Arabs was the Maltese language. In the normal course of events, had the Moslems continued to control the islands, the Arabic spoken in Malta would have evolved into a dialect in just the same way as Tunisian has. However, when the Arabs lost Malta the islands were eventually drawn into the European sphere of influence and made strong contact with the Romance languages, particularly Italian. Over a long period the Arabic spoken in Malta incorporated a large number of words from France, Spain, Italy and, more recently, Britain. As a result of this linguistic mixing Maltese has evolved into a separate language; although the islanders are still able to make themselves understood in Tunis, for instance, without too much difficulty.

The Moslem hegemony of Malta was terminated in somewhat peculiar circumstances. At the beginning of the eleventh century a group of Normans, who were returning from a pilgrimage, passed through southern Italy and on the way were invited to take up employment as mercenary soldiers. Over a period of years small bands of Norman warriors moved into the region until gradually they became extremely powerful and started to rule their former employers. Having gained control of the foot of Italy, the Norman warlords turned their attention to Sicily. In May 1061, a man revered in Maltese history, Roger the Norman, captured Messina. The victory was the first in a thirty year campaign which culminated in the Norman domination of Sicily. In the year 1091 Roger's fleet descended upon Malta and, by the employment of a ruse, took the islands without bloodshed from the Arabs.

At first the Christian reconquest did little to lessen the Moslem

influence. Few Normans can have settled in the islands and it has
been suggested that the Moslems continued to control affairs but
paid a tribute to the new overlords. Other sources of information
reinforce the picture of a Malta which remained essentially Moslem
for many years after the Norman conquest. The Bishop of Stras-
bourg visited Malta in 1175 and recorded that the island was inhabited by Moslems. In 1240 the population of the islands was
assessed for tax purposes. The original documents concerning this
assessment have not come down to us but a summary of the relevant
points does exist. There are, of course, great dangers in drawing
conclusions from secondary sources of this type but, as it stands, the
summary indicates that the Moslems outnumbered the Christians
and controlled most of the wealth.

During the course of the twelve-forties the Moslems were expelled
from the islands and Christians came to form the majority of the
population. Many Moslems no doubt renounced their religion
rather than leave their home country.

Other forces helped to lessen the influence of Islam in the islands.
At first the Normans developed the economic potential of Sicily
slowly but after 1130, the year in which Roger II became the ruler
of a kingdom which included Sicily, Reggio Calabria, Apulia and
Malta, the pace of economic expansion quickened. Eventually
Roger's 'income from Palermo alone was said to be greater than
that which the King of England derived from his whole kingdom'.
Malta could not be unaffected by prosperity in the neighbouring
island and increased trade probably led to stronger contacts with
the outside world, particularly Sicily and southern Italy. Under
the two Norman kings who succeeded Roger II, William the Bad
and William the Good, the islands continued to prosper. With the
death of Good King William (1189) the kingdom entered a confused period but once the Emperor Frederick II, who ruled from
1198 to 1250, was able to take a firm hold upon events Sicily became
the centre of a cultural and economic vitality which transformed
the central Mediterranean area into one of Europe's richest regions.
Frederick was a decisive, brilliant leader, a man of great learning
but also a fine administrator who appreciated the need for the
sound economic management of his domains. The Emperor
encouraged agricultural improvement, new industries were developed and the trade of the kingdom was carefully regulated. Fred-

erick had a considerable stake in Malta, as the royal lands there were extensive. Documents of the time relating to the islands show the Emperor taking an interest in cattle raising, pig breeding and enforced labour on the royal lands. Frederick also encouraged falcon breeding and planned the establishment of a camel breeding farm.

The impressive economic prosperity of the region was not to last. In 1250 Frederick died excommunicate and the Pope encouraged Charles of Anjou to exterminate the Emperor's dynasty and take over the Sicilian kingdom. The arrogant French impostors soon incurred the hatred of the Sicilians and in 1282 the islanders rose up and massacred every Frenchman upon whom they could lay hands. The Sicilians had previously been in contact with Aragon and upon the defeat of the French Sicily became part of the lands of the crown of Aragon. In the following year, 1283, Charles of Anjou attempted to use Malta as a base from which to recapture Sicily. His fleet was defeated in a sea battle which took place in the Grand Harbour and Malta, too, eventually became part of the kingdom of Aragon.

The years between 1090 and 1200 had probably not resulted in any great influx of Europeans and Christians into Malta. The Normans, even in Sicily, were few in number; they were rulers rather than colonizers. In the latter part of the twelfth century the Genoese established a trading station at Malta but the number of men involved must have been small. During the course of the thirteenth century several developments took place which helped to lessen Islamic influence. In 1224 part of the population of the rebellious town of Celano, in the Abruzzi, was deported to Malta. The number of people involved was probably not large but the migrants must have made an interesting contribution to the local life, particularly bearing in mind that within a relatively few years a start was made on expelling the Moslems.

During the thirteenth century the religious orders began to establish themselves in the islands. The convents were no doubt important disseminators of European culture and generally strengthened the position of Christianity.

Aragon exercised an important influence in Malta and Sicily. The foundation of the Maltese nobility dates from the early part of Aragonese rule and clearly this new element in society helped

44

to project certain aspects of Spanish culture into local life. The crown of Aragon controlled part of mainland Spain, Sicily, Sardinia, land in Greece, and several other areas which formed a 'western Mediterranean common market'. Aragon enjoyed lucrative trade links within the trading area and with North Africa. Malta benefited from the association with the Aragonese possessions and developed contacts with many lands.

Most of the communities which comprised the widespread kingdom of Aragon had a considerable degree of autonomy in the organization of their affairs. Malta was no exception. It is difficult to trace the growth of local administrative institutions but by the fifteenth century they had reached a relatively sophisticated stage of development. Collectively the administration was referred to as the *Università*. At its head was an official known as the *hakem*, (leader) or *capitana della vega* (captain of the rod). The hakem was the chief justice and the head of the *consiglio popolare*, a representative council which debated matters relating to the islands. The hakem was appointed by the King of Aragon or his deputy in Sicily. Beneath the head of the administration came four elected *giurati* and these men were responsible for the day-to-day conduct of affairs. Additionally there was a group of officials who were responsible for specific tasks. The *catapani* oversaw the marketing regulations and supervised weights and measures. The *marammero* was responsible for the upkeep of the walls and the *portolano* looked after the ports.

Now, whilst it would seem that the islanders had a deal of autonomy the position is not quite as it appears. From the correspondence which took place between the local officials and the Aragonese authorities it is plain that the former made administrative decisions within a carefully defined framework. Frequently the island was given in fief, as a reward to a supposedly deserving servant of the Aragonese crown. The noblemen who held the Malta fief were probably fairly rapacious; many were rebellious as well and involved the islanders in wars with the crown. The Università was able to exercise little influence upon events when such adventurers held sway. As a result of this situation the Maltese collected a goodly sum of money in 1428 and gave it to the crown on condition that the present incumbent of the fief was bought off and the islands not enfeoffed again. Another factor which limited independence was the manner in which the local nobility was at times able to control the internal administration.

The Università, which was based upon Mdina, did not administer affairs for all parts of the islands. In the fifteenth century Gozo operated a separate Università and dealt directly with the Aragonese authorities. There is also some doubt as to whether the Mdina administration was recognized in the town of Birgu. Birgu was in many ways a distinct element in medieval Malta. The inhabitants of the town lived largely by trading and many foreigners, particularly merchants and craftsmen, made their homes in the settlement. It is interesting to note that, alone amongst the towns and villages of medieval Malta, Birgu had a name which was basically Latin rather than Arabic in origin.

The rise of Christianity to take a central place in Maltese society, the creation of a nobility, the development of local government, the influx of migrants, particularly from Spain and southern Italy, together with the cultural influence of Iberia and Sicily, all these factors combined to bring about a marked change in the outlook and way of life of the islanders, during the course of Aragonese rule.

Economically the islands did not fare well in the Aragonese period. The dismissal of the Moslems must have had a disrupting effect upon the economy, whilst the troubles surrounding the Sicilian Vespers uprising (1282) resulted in Malta being fought over at least once. In the fourteenth century piracy became an increasing problem in the central Mediterranean. Indeed, most ports, including Malta, were involved in the activity to some degree. After a time the religious element became increasingly important and there was a strong tendency for the Moslems of North Africa to attack southern European shipping and *vice versa*. Being small and remote Malta could expect rather more than its fair share of raids. Additionally Sicilian and Calabrian pirates were always liable to visit the waters around the islands if the looting was poor on the North African coast.

During the fifteenth century the scale of hostilities increased. In 1412, 1422 and 1423 North African forces attacked Malta. In 1424 an Aragonese expedition, using Malta as a base, launched a reprisal raid at the Moslems. This provoked a counter attack upon the islands in 1429, which resulted in both Malta and Gozo being sacked. Three years later the Aragonese retaliated with a large-scale raid upon Djerba, an island lying close to the Tunisian coast. The attack may have salved Aragonese pride but it did little to repair the economy of the islands, which was still in ruins. In 1428 the Maltese had, as we have mentioned, made a large cash donation to the crown of Aragon, which probably consumed a large part of the islanders' savings. In the 1429 raid the economy was wrecked and agriculture damaged to such a degree that there followed several years of total sterility. During the fifteenth century the frequency of droughts appears to have increased and this exacerbated the problems of the countryside. Additionally the fact that cotton cultivation had become more important, at the expense of the olive, helped to increase aridity and the likelihood of agricultural failure.

The years of warfare disrupted trade and made it difficult to export the cotton crop and obtain essential food imports from Sicily. Population numbers almost certainly declined. We have no precise information but it would seem that, from a peak in the first half of the thirteenth century, the general trend of the population graph was downwards. Decline began with the expulsion of the Moslems, and although the fourteenth century may have been a period of moderate decrease the pace of depopulation quickened in the fifteenth century. The landscape reflected these demographic changes. Small villages and hamlets, which lay in coastal or exposed areas, were abandoned and the population tended to live in settlements sited well inland. The map on page 94 shows how few isolated settlements existed in 1436 and most of those which did stand in exposed situations were later abandoned. As villages disappeared, so the agricultural land which the villagers had formerly worked became less fully utilized. One area which was particularly influenced by the happenings was that isolated part of Malta which lay to the north of the Great Fault. Here many hamlets were abandoned and much agricultural land ceased to be worked.

By the middle of the fifteenth century the population appears to have become demoralized. The records of the Università are dominated by accounts of poverty and insecurity; one entry referring to Malta as 'a rock in the middle of the sea far from help and comfort'. After a time, through lack of spirit or lack of funds, the fortifications of Mdina and Birgu ceased to be properly maintained and many inhabitants of the former town abandoned their dwellings.

47

Plague was another factor which helped to decrease population numbers and depress trade. In 1492 the Jews were expelled and although their community was probably small it had no doubt made a contribution to the commerce of the islands.

The frequency of raids upon the islands seems to have decreased after the mid-point of the fifteenth century was passed. There is no evidence to suggest that any significant degree of economic recovery took place. The island which had been 'rich in everything that is good and in the blessing of God' had become, according to a sixteenth-century account, 'merely a rock barely covered with more than three or four feet of earth, which was stony and very unfit to grow corn'. The inhabitants 'were poor and miserable, owing to the barrenness of the soil and the frequent descents of corsairs . . . in a word . . . a residence in Malta appeared disagreeable indeed, almost insupportable.'

4

The Crusading Order of St. John of Jerusalem

At the same time as the Maltese were suffering persistent and unkindly attention from North Africa, the Order of St. John Jerusalem on the island of Rhodes was being subjected to increasing pressure from the Ottoman Turks. Several Turkish attacks in the latter part of the fifteenth century were beaten off by the knights of St. John, but in 1522, after a lengthy siege, the Order was forced to abandon Rhodes. Dislodged from their highly developed fortress in the eastern Mediterranean the knights retreated westward and, by a devious route, came to Malta in 1530. The islands became a military base in the fight to contain Ottoman expansion.

The Order of St. John had by this time a long and, for the most part, honourable history stretching over nearly four centuries. In the middle of the eleventh century there had been set up at Jerusalem, a city then controlled by the Moslems, a small charitable hospital which provided for the needs of Christian pilgrims visiting the Holy City. During the course of the first crusade, when the kingdom of Jerusalem was established by Christian knights, the importance of the hospital had rapidly increased. The institution acquired valuable gifts from grateful crusaders and many knights joined the community and helped to run the hospital. Peter Gerard, the then head of the hospital, petitioned the Pope that the institution might become a religious foundation with all members taking vows of poverty, chastity and obedience. The Pope was pleased to consent to this request in 1113. Gerard died in 1118 and was succeeded by Raymond de Puy. Under the rule of the latter the newly established convent evolved rapidly. The need to defend the kingdom of Jerusalem and the martial outlook of many of the monks, who had

D

49

had joined the convent as a result of the first crusade, made de Puy
suggest to the Pope that the brothers should be prepared, not only
to tend the sick, but also to defend their faith by force of arms.
Thus, by the middle of the twelfth century the Religion, as the
Order was frequently called, had established its two principal
functions as crusader and hospitaller. The constitutional evolution
of the Order from this point need not concern us here. Suffice it
to say that by the time the Religion reached Malta it consisted of
knights drawn from noble European families. The head of the
Order was an elected Grand Master and he, together with a council
of knights, was responsible for formulating the Order's policy. The
knights were drawn from many parts of Europe and belonged to
langues corresponding to the areas from which they came. A knight
from Aragon thus belonged to the Aragonese langue and normally
lived in the *auberge d'Aragon*. In 1530 there were eight langues:
Aragon, Germany, France, Italy, Castile, Provence, Auvergne and
England. The last named became defunct within a few years as a
result of the Reformation of Henry VIII.

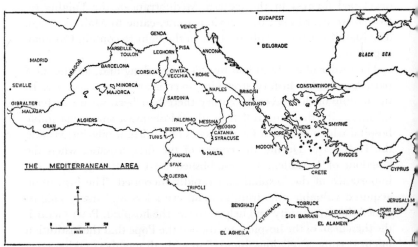

The Order was supported by incomes from a number of sources.
A new entrant paid a fee, or *passaggio*, and on death all the possessions of a knight, apart from the fifth, or *quint*, which might be
willed away, became the property of the Religion. Such gains were
referred to as *spoglie*. As a by-product of crusading the galley

squadron often contributed a great deal to the funds of the Order by way of booty. The earnings from this source were not normally large enough to pay for the upkeep and replacement of the navy. The Order's largest source of income came from the various estates and urban properties which it owned in Europe. Many of these assets had been given to the Order during the Middle Ages by pious persons who wished to offer material support to the crusaders.

Members of the Order might serve in the convent or they might remain in their home region and administer one of the Religion's estates, or commanderies as they were termed. Each year the commandery paid a percentage of its income into the central treasury at Malta. These payments were known as responsions. Under this system a diligent commander who increased the efficiency of his commandery would also raise his own income.

Although the Order was composed of members drawn from many regions of Europe, Frenchmen composed the largest single group and traditionally dominated the Religion's affairs. Something like half the income from the commanderies was drawn from estates in France.

In 1291 the crusaders were driven out of the Holy Land. The Order went first to Cyprus and subsequently, in 1308, took the island of Rhodes from the Byzantines. At Rhodes the Order built up a prosperous community: one of a number of small Latin states and trading stations which existed in the eastern Mediterranean and the surrounding lands. During the fourteenth century, however, as the Order developed Rhodes, the Ottoman Turks had been consolidating their possessions in Asia Minor and south-east Europe until they formed a terrestrial crescent about the small Christian kingdoms and outposts. With the accession of the Sultan Mehemmed II (1451–81) the Turks were ready to challenge Christian interests in the area. In 1453 Constantinople was taken, in 1459 Serbia was conquered, between 1458 and 1460 the greater part of the Morea was overrun; while the conquest of Bosnia was completed in 1464. Venice lost a number of possessions to the Turks and Genoa was forced to give up several trading stations on the Black Sea. In 1480 the Turks laid siege to Rhodes but they were beaten off with heavy losses. In the following year Mehemmed died and upon his death the Ottoman state was troubled, not only by a war of succession, but also by conflicts with other Moslem states. These conditions relieved the pressure on the knights of St. John.

In spite of the Order's position, far as it was from European support, the knights did not cease to challenge Turkish power in the region of Rhodes. The island's fortifications had been badly damaged during the siege of 1480 and by a subsequent earthquake. During the latter part of the fifteenth century and the early decades of the sixteenth century, the Order undertook a large-scale re-building programme which created on Rhodes an exceptionally strong fortress. At the same period, the galleys of the Order made many good captures amongst the shipping moving in Turkish waters. Of course, there had to be an end to such activities. The very success of the Order attracted to it unwanted attention, and, once Turkish power was fully and ruthlessly organized against Rhodes, the valour of the knights would be unable to turn or stem the tide. The expected blow came in the reign of Sulaiman the Magnificent. Sulaiman ruled from 1520 to 1566 and during this time he acutely embarrassed most of the other European powers, nearly shattered the Order of St. John, and came close to turning the Mediterranean into a Turkish sea. On June 24th 1522, a large Ottoman force was disembarked at Rhodes and preparations were made for an attack upon the fortress. A month later, towards the end of July, Sulaiman arrived to conduct the assaults. The knights, under Grand Master L'Isle-Adam, fought with their usual skill and courage and were able to inflict a series of reverses on their assail-ants. However, constant pressure by the huge attacking army had to prove successful in the end. The Turks were close to their bases; they had no need to withdraw at the end of the summer and went on grinding at the defences for six months. The knights were eventually forced to accept terms. The spirit of the Order did not break, the knights were prepared to go on fighting and retrenching until the last man died but the Rhodian townsfolk had had enough. Their leaders made it clear to the Order in December that they wished for a halt in hostilities before the town, and all those living therein, were consumed by the Turks. As there was clearly no chance of victory or of a Turkish withdrawal the Rhodian attitude was not unreasonable. The islanders could hardly be expected to uphold the honour of the Order with their lives if there was no prospect of any other conclusion to the battle than massacre, raping and slavery for men, women and children, respectively. The Order was forced to take notice of the wishes of the Rhodians, for it was almost impossible to maintain the defence once the morale of a large part of the defenders had crumbled. On December 21st the Order accepted a treaty which surrendered the fortress at Rhodes but allowed the knights to leave the island in the galleys. The rights of the Rhodians were also protected. The islanders were not to be enslaved. They retained their religious freedom and those who wished to leave with the Order were permitted to do so. Many Rhodians eventually found their way to Malta.

During the course of the long siege the Order had received very little help from Western Europe. The distances were so great that it would have been extremely doubtful if a relief force could have successfully attacked the Turks so close to their bases. In any case France and Spain, the most likely sources of help, were diverted by their mutual hostility at the time. Nor did any of the Christian powers established in the eastern Mediterranean even flex their muscles in anticipation of moving to the Order's aid. Venice was probably glad to see the Levant rid of the Order's disrupting influence. Occasionally the galleys from Rhodes were 'careless' in their search for Moslem prey and boarded Venetian vessels. Essentially Venice wished to preserve her trading interests within the Ottoman empire and all this latter-day crusading, which the Order indulged in, only made the Turks suspicious of all Christian interests within their sphere of influence. Then there were the Jewish trading activities which the Order molested and the Jews had a great deal of influence at Constantinople. It was widely rumoured that Sulaiman had borrowed heavily from Jewish bankers to finance the siege of Rhodes. The chroniclers might write of the shame of Christendom at not having succoured the knights as they fought to check the Moslem advance but many canny traders no doubt smiled benignly at the Order's discomfort and hoped that the removal of the knights would lead to more stable relations with the Turks. Already, to certain Christian interests, the crusading Order of St. John had become an anachronism.

On the night of January 1st, 1523, the Order's fleet sailed from Rhodes to the Venetian island of Crete or Candia as it was then called. January is not a good month for sailing in the Mediterranean and some of the ships were badly damaged during the voyage. At Crete the party rested and repaired the vessels before sailing on to the port of Messina on the north-east tip of Sicily. Here the knights settled briefly only to be driven on again by an outbreak of plague in July of 1523. The Grand Master moved the knights to Civita Vecchia which was reached on August 1st. In January 1524 the Pope granted Viterbo to the Order as a temporary base.

By now the realities of the situation were beginning to become clear to the knights. They had torn honour from defeat in the battle for Rhodes, yet they could not escape the political consequences of failure. The Order of St. John was an international body and, in a Europe which was becoming increasingly nationalistic, the knights were not going to be sympathetically received. During the next few years, from 1524 to 1530, the Order had to conduct a long and complex search for a new base.

If the Order wanted a new base in the Mediterranean then the man most likely to be able to help was the Emperor Charles V, who possessed a number of suitable fortresses on the islands and shores of the sea. Unfortunately Charles was at war with France and as the Order was predominantly composed of French knights he could hardly be expected to give up, without proper safeguards, a strategic position to an organization dominated by his enemies. An appropriate safeguard would have been an oath of fealty from the Order, but it was constitutionally incapable of binding itself to one Christian power against another. This was by no means the only difficulty as France was determined that Charles should not be allowed to extract any advantage from providing the Order with a base. The Emperor was known to be over extended in his defence commitments and for the knights to take over any of these, even if they provided protection against the Moslems, would ease the imperial position and make Charles better able to challenge France. Additionally Charles and the Pope became embroiled, and this embarrassed the negotiations for the Pontiff was the spiritual head of the Order. In 1527, if not wholly intentionally, Charles's forces sacked the Vatican.

The Order was prepared to accept a base in the western Mediterranean, if a suitable one was offered on reasonable terms, but failing this the recapture of Rhodes was a solution to the problems favoured by many knights. The Grand Master travelled indefatigably from one European court to another trying to gain support for an attack on Rhodes. He did receive a number of offers of help, including one of money from Henry VIII in 1528, but the aid offered was insufficient and the Order was forced to abandon the project.

As the years passed the power and resources of the knights were weakened, and the Grand Master came to realize that if the Order was not to become completely ineffectual a new base would have to be quickly secured. As early as 1524 Charles V had offered the Maltese islands. However, not only had the terms been constitutionally unsuitable but the islands could not be regarded as a generous gift. Malta was something of an embarrassment to the Emperor, since it was poorly defended and offered an aggressor a good harbour close to Sicily. A little later the Order sent a commission to look at the islands and a report was produced which was highly discouraging; the few fortifications Malta possessed were old and dilapidated, the islands produced only enough food for a few months of the year and large imports of grain from Sicily were necessary. Charles V also insisted that if the Order accepted Malta then it should take responsibility for Tripoli as well. The Order was being offered a barren, impoverished, ill-defended group of islands together with a Christian outpost in North Africa. Not unnaturally the knights negotiated very hard, either for a more suitable base, and this included the recapture of Rhodes, or for better terms. In particular the Order did not wish to be encumbered with the fortress at Tripoli which is about 200 miles from Malta and would involve a division of forces. The Emperor was not to be moved and, as the Order's position was getting no stronger, in the end it was forced to accept. In the spring of 1530 the Maltese islands, together with the fortress of Tripoli, were given in fief to the Order of St. John, but with the condition that the Religion should be free from all service customarily performed by vassals. This clause safeguarded the Order's neutrality; the knights were merely required to proffer an annual fee of one falcon. A number of clauses safeguarded the Emperor's interests. In the event of the Order's leaving, the islands could not be disposed of except by reference to Charles, or his successors. The admiral of the Order's galley fleet had always to be an Italian, to keep French influence out of a key position. The Emperor also reserved certain rights with regard to the nomination of the Bishop of Malta. Even after the transfer of the islands to the knights had been agreed a number of small difficulties arose relating to the Order's privileges in Malta and it was not until October 26th, 1530 that the Grand Master and the main body of the Order arrived at Malta in three galleys. The knights took up residence at Birgu.

The Maltese had hardly been consulted as the negotiations dragged on but they, or at least certain sections of society, had very definite views as to whether or not they wished the islands to pass to the Order of St. John. In 1428 the Maltese had paid 30,000 florins to Alfonso V of Aragon in return for a pledge that the islands would always remain directly subject to the crown and not be given out in fief. As soon as it was suggested that Malta might be a suitable base for the homeless Order, the Maltese despatched emissaries to the viceroy of Sicily to remind him of the pledge of 1428. The islanders were fobbed off with assurances that nothing had been decided and they were not to worry. When, however, Charles V assigned Malta to the Order, the Maltese again protested, only to find that they were too late to influence events. The deed of fief did attempt to safeguard the rights of the Maltese but clearly the islanders were not going to have much influence on the government of Malta once the Order arrived.

Soon after moving into Malta Grand Master L'Isle-Adam made the seven mile journey from Birgu to Mdina. At the city gates he was halted and called upon to declare that the Order would uphold all the rights and privileges of the Maltese. The Grand Master assented whereupon he was presented with the keys to the city. The ceremony was little more than a concession to good manners and once the Order started to take a firm grip on the affairs of the island the Università of Mdina was quickly divested of any real authority. The transfer of power was done very skilfully. The Order simply created a pocket Università at Birgu and this gave the knights control of the only part of Malta in which they were really interested —the lands lying close to the harbours. The Università of Mdina had been responsible for the collection of customs, managing the harbour and guarding the coasts. All these functions were taken away from the old body and the Order also set up its own law-courts. Of course, it was inevitable that the Mdina Università should slip into the background simply because it was impossible to have a division of responsibility on such matters as defence and law enforcement. The knights were masters of the island and the Maltese were not powerful enough to contest the issue.

There was never any violent trouble arising from the Order's take-over and the matter was eased by the fact that the knights took up residence in Birgu rather than Mdina. Birgu had always stood apart from traditional Malta and resented the authority of the capital. Its inhabitants tended to look outside the island and probably quickly grasped the advantages of the Order's arrival and welcomed the knights. Birgu became the seat of the Order's power and Mdina the retreat of traditional Maltese interests. The two parties were separated and friction avoided.

Almost certainly L'Isle-Adam accepted Malta as a transitory base and originally did not intend to spend long on the island. Malta's disadvantages must have become more apparent once the Order settled there. A large part of the island's foodstuffs had to be imported from Sicily and there was immediately trouble with the Sicilian authorities who claimed that Malta was no longer part of the kingdom of Sicily and, therefore, would have to pay the normal export taxes on foodstuffs. This problem was quickly settled in the Order's favour but nothing could alter the fact that Malta depended upon imported food. The island was almost completely under-developed militarily; the existing fortifications were old-fashioned and in need of extensive repairs. The local population was hardly large enough to provide an adequate force for the defence of the island and Malta was so lacking in natural resources and industries that everything from timber to nails had to be imported. In short, Malta had considerable inherent flaws as a potential base and if it were to be developed the costs would be exceptionally high, because so much, including at times labour, would have to be imported. And overshadowing all arguments was the problem of dependence. Without doubt Malta would be largely dependent upon Sicily and the Spanish viceroys; politically this might well prove disastrous. Above these problems members of the Order simply found Malta unpleasant. The Order's commission had stated that a residence in Malta would be extremely disagreeable, if not insupportable, particularly in summer. Life on the island had only confirmed this view.

The question of money was crucial. The battle to retain Rhodes had been expensive and the Order had lost the island together with a large number of revenue-producing properties. For nearly a decade the Order had wandered around the western Mediterranean;

this also had been costly and the Order probably could not afford to develop the defences of Malta. L'Isle-Adam wished either to retake Rhodes or obtain another base which was at least properly fortified. Little time was wasted and in the summer of 1531 the Order's galleys struck at the port of Modon in the Morea. The attack was successful and the town taken. Unfortunately a large body of Turkish troops was encamped not far from Modon and the Order's forces were compelled to withdraw, though with a great deal of plunder and many prisoners.

At the same time the Order continued its diplomatic efforts to obtain a new base. The Grand Master suggested to Charles V that Syracuse would be more suitable than Malta. Syracuse was a small, prosperous town set on a peninsula on the east coast of Sicily; it was almost entirely surrounded by sea, well-fortified, pleasant, and a centre of some importance. There were sound tactical advantages to be gained from the move; the forces of the viceroy and the Order could work more closely together and support each other, the knights would be less isolated, less liable to blockade, nearer to the mainstream of European life and, most important of all, close to relatively assured supplies of food. All these factors, besides making the Order more secure and effective, would reduce costs, cut out expensive transhipment to Malta, give the Order a ready-made defence system and a reasonable setting for the social life the knights prized so highly. On the surface it might appear that by going to Sicily the Order was dropping itself into Charles V's pocket and sacrificing its neutrality. In fact, provided suitable conditions were arranged, exactly the opposite would result. If the Order were given Syracuse and a stretch of surrounding country it would become a more self-contained unit than would ever be possible in Malta. The Order would have a domain in which little interference could take place, without physical intervention. In Malta, with so many goods having to be imported from Sicily, the Order could be put under pressure by political action alone— close, or threaten to close, the ports of Sicily to vessels trading with Malta and the knights soon came to heel. Action of this type was taken on a number of occasions during the Order's rule in Malta.

At this time Syracuse was the seat of the viceroy of Sicily and Charles V did not wish to lose the fortress, though the Grand Master suggested that the viceregal court might be moved to Palermo. Nor did the Emperor glow with enthusiasm when the Order suggested it might take possession of Gallipoli or Otranto in the heel of Italy. The Pope thought about giving the Order Ancona but the scheme came to nothing.

The problems generated by Malta were not the only difficulties the knights faced. There were forces at work in Europe, and within the body of the Order, which threatened to disrupt the Religion entirely. In the period between the loss of Rhodes and the gaining of Malta not only had it been difficult for the Grand Master to keep the knights together but certain European powers had glanced covetously at the possessions of the Order. If the Order was no longer an effective crusading power, was it entitled any longer to extensive possessions whose income was intended to finance military operations? This question provoked trouble in Portugal, England and Germany while France and Spain were both, to a degree, attempting to manipulate the Order for their own purposes. By and large the Order successfully combated these pressures although as a result of the Reformation in England the English langue was dissolved in 1540.

On August 22nd, 1534, Grand Master L'Isle-Adam died. The Order had the useful habit of finding a great leader at times of crisis and L'Isle-Adam had governed through many difficult years. He led the Order through the long and courageous defence of Rhodes, wrung reasonable terms from the Turks, and between 1523 and 1530 held the Order together in spite of the problems which confronted it. An able leader in war, L'Isle-Adam was also skilled at negotiation and he trooped endlessly round the courts of Western Europe trying to gain aid for the Order. His visit to England in 1528 won over Henry VIII at a time when he was thinking of taking control of the Order's possessions. L'Isle-Adam worked hard to bring about a reconciliation between Charles V and the king of France and achieved some success. However, when all was added up, L'Isle-Adam had too few cards in his hand to win much from the monarchs of Europe. He negotiated for nearly eight years to avoid committing the Order to what he felt was an unsuitable base at Malta. In the end he had to accept what the most powerful man in Europe, Charles V, wanted and it could be argued that the Order would have been in a stronger position if L'Isle-Adam had accepted Malta in 1524 instead of in 1530.

The events immediately following the death of L'Isle-Adam show what a precarious state the Order was in. The next Grand Master, Pietro del Ponte, never reached Malta and died in France eight months after his election. Juan d'Omedes, del Ponte's successor, did not come to Malta until fifteen months after his election. Clearly no one was really keen to accept the arduous post of Grand Master at the time.

The great web of uncertainty and tension which surrounded the Order's existence in the fifteen-twenties and early fifteen-thirties had important side effects in Malta. The knights wished to make their stay on the island a short one and were obviously reluctant to invest much money in fortifications and other buildings. This outlook persisted for nearly forty years and it led to grave weaknesses in the island's defensive system, which nearly cost the knights the Siege of 1565. Little building was done in the first years of the Order's rule. In 1530 L'Isle-Adam took up residence in the *Castello a mare* (fort St. Angelo). An existing house was converted into the Grand Master's palace and a number of private citizens, who had previously dwelled within the walls of the Castello, were instructed to removed themselves. Birgu, which spread out from the Castello gates, was largely unprotected when the Order arrived and some works were erected to fortify the landward side of the peninsula on which the town stood. Apart from this, and repairs to existing structures, the knights built no new fortifications, though the defences were known to be completely inadequate.

Very few public buildings were started during the first year of the Order's stay. However, the failure of the diplomatic and military attempts of 1532 to find a new base made the knights realize that they would probably have to remain in Malta for a few years and a modest building programme was started. In November 1532 the foundation stone for the infirmary was laid and at about the same time the langues started to build auberges for themselves in Birgu. Most of these building projects were sited in that part of Birgu which stood farthest away from the Castello. Here there were relatively few existing buildings and land was available for development. But the building of auberges and fortifications was on a small scale and a comparison between the large auberges erected a few years later in Valletta and the rather mean auberges in Birgu is revealing.

The knights knew that if Malta was to become a secure base for their naval operations their fortifications would have to completely dominate the Grand Harbour. Dominance could not be achieved from the existing defensive system which centred upon fort St. Angelo. The problem was this. Although St. Angelo and Birgu were surrounded on three sides by the sea, both were overlooked by higher ground to the south and, more dangerously, by Sceberras peninsula on the north side of the Grand Harbour. The adjoining peninsula, L'Isola, on which Senglea now stands, could also embarrass the defences of the town if properly used by an attacker. When St. Angelo had been built, many centuries before, the range of the existing weapons was so limited that they had been unable to exploit the surrounding higher ground. However, with the development of modern artillery the site of the fort became unsafe.

Sceberras peninsula, on which Valletta was eventually built, controlled both the Grand Harbour and Marsamxett by virtue of its height and position. Certainly Sceberras had many disadvantages; it was composed of rugged broken limestone, steeply walled by cliffs, the surface of the peninsula had been serrated by the valleys of small ephemeral streams, it lacked an assured water supply and there were no natural mooring places where vessels might tie up. In spite of these drawbacks the dominating position of Sceberras made it essential that the Order should have complete control of the peninsula. The most satisfactory way of commanding Sceberras would be to build a new fortress capital on the peninsula. The knights were aware of this fact right from the time they first came to Malta, and the commission which had been despatched to report on Malta's suitability as a base had commented on the matter. L'Isle-Adam admitted the idea was sound but the Order lacked the funds for such a project during its early years in Malta.

In 1541 the Order brought the military engineer Antonio Ferro-molino to Malta to advise on how best to improve the fortifications. Ferromolino examined the whole problem afresh but came up with the same solution: build a new fortress upon Sceberras peninsula. Hopes of a return to Rhodes or a move to a more congenial area still lingered with many knights, particularly the older and more powerful members of the Order, and it was decided not to attempt such an ambitious scheme but to improve the defences of Birgu and St. Angelo. The improvements included the erection of a cavalier (a fat masonry tower with provision for artillery positions on top) in St. Angelo, to gain parity for the defenders' artillery with any that might be deployed by an aggressor on Sceberras. The ditch which divided St. Angelo from Birgu was deepened to below sea-level and other improvements were started. As a result of Ferromolino's work the St. Angelo-Birgu defences were developed to the point where they were proof against anything but a major attack.

In July 1551 a Turkish fleet put into Marsamxett and landed a force which was estimated to number 10,000 men. As the soldiers came ashore they were ambushed by the Order's troops and then harried by a force of cavalry led by the dashing and corpulent English knight, Sir Nicolas Upton. Upton's skirmishing was highly successful but on the evening of the battle he died from his exertions. Having eventually got their force ashore the Turkish commanders positioned it on Sceberras peninsula but decided that it was too small to take Birgu and St. Angelo quickly. The Turkish army then moved to Mdina, looting and burning the countryside around Birkirkara and Quormi on the way. Mdina enjoys a good hill-top, defensive position although at this time the fortifications were weak and the garrison small. The commander of the town, by skilful use of his resources, was able to convince the Turks that the capture of Mdina would not be a quick and easy conquest. This show of determination was enough for the Turkish commanders were reluctant to commit their forces to a prolonged siege inland, in case a Christian relief fleet appeared off Malta and attacked the half-manned Moslem galleys. With these considerations in mind it was decided to attack Gozo, where the Citadel was known to be weak. The Gozo garrison did not hold out for long and after a few days it capitulated to the Turks. Contemporary writers estimated that when the Turks withdrew they took with them about 5,000 Gozitans. Many of these people were eventually ransomed but for a time the northern island was depopulated and it took one and a half centuries for the population to recover to the level of 1550.

The Order's cup was not yet full. The Turks now left the islands and sailed south to attack Tripoli. The fortress was inadequately defended and after a little fighting the commander was forced to surrender.

After the military setbacks of 1551 a commission was set up to examine the Malta defences and to make recommendations as to how they might be improved. The commission recommended that a new fortress should be built on Sceberras peninsula and suggested a course of action which amounted to a phased removal of the Order from Birgu to Sceberras. First, a star-shaped fort (St. Elmo) was to be built at the tip of Sceberras to hold the peninsula and the harbour mouths. At a later stage a town was to be laid out and the fort incorporated within its defences.

The building of St. Elmo lessened one of Birgu's major weaknesses and the commission also suggested that a fortress should be built on the adjoining peninsula of L'Isola. The fortress of St. Michael was erected on the landward end of the peninsula and prevented an attacker using it as a convenient gun platform.

St. Michael and St. Elmo were built during 1552 but no effort was made to start the new town on Sceberras; the Order's equivocal attitude to Malta was asserting itself once more even after twenty years on the island. In 1548 the idea of attacking Modon had been discussed again and when this was found to be impractical the Order seriously considered removing itself to Tripoli, leaving only a small garrison in Malta. The idea was still being discussed in 1551 when Tripoli was lost due to its half-defended condition. In 1554 Charles V offered the Order the fortress of Africa (Mahdia) and the proposal was taken up quite seriously and discussed at a high level, in spite of the obvious disadvantages of moving to North Africa. There is no escaping the fact that the knights of St. John did not like Malta and were prepared to consider almost any alternative to the barren, impoverished, island on which they unwillingly sojourned. Over and over again there are references in documents of the time to the aridity and sterility of the island and as Giacomo Bosio, the Order's great sixteenth-century chronicler puts it, 'everyone who had not previously been to the island marvelled that the knights could think of remaining there.' The general attitude of the Order is reflected by Sir Oliver Starkey, one of the last English knights and a man who served with great distinction during the Siege of 1565. A close friend and adviser of Grand Master Valette he wrote in 1560, when trying to claim a pension from a charitable body in Rome, 'I am at Malta of all places in the world'; only poverty was keeping Sir Oliver in Malta, hero though he proved to be. A few months before the Siege Starkey let it be known in England that he was prepared to renounce the Catholic faith if allowed to return to his homeland.

There was, however, at least one man of vision in the Order's high ranks—Jean de la Valette, who later became one of the Religion's greatest Grand Masters. By 1548 Valette was beginning to be heard in the Order's councils and some of his pronouncements show that he had a realistic view of the Order's position in the world, was aware that it must evolve a policy and cease drifting in the way that it had done for over twenty years. Valette could see that if only the Order could get its priorities right then the position of the knights in Malta might well become distinctly useful. In 1548 Valette spoke out strongly to the effect that unless Tripoli was properly fortified it must inevitably fall to the first determined attack made on it. He was soon proved right. In 1549, when the knights were seriously considering moving to Tripoli, Valette, with a clear sense of the strategic realities, opposed the change and stated that the Order should build a fortress town on Sceberras.

In 1557, after service as Governor of Tripoli and Captain General of the Order's galleys, Valette was elected Grand Master. According to Bosio, his first thought on attaining the office was to build a new town on Sceberras. Within a short time one of the foremost European military engineers, Bartolomeo Genga, was persuaded to come to Malta to design a new fortress. Unfortunately Genga died in Malta before work could be started on the town he designed. This setback did not halt the Sceberras project and by the early fifteen-sixties it had been widely accepted within the Order. In 1562 another well-known military engineer, Baldassare Lanci, came to Malta and drew up plans for the new town. In 1563 papal approval was obtained and all the major problems relating to finance, supply and the engineering of the project appear to have been largely solved. Quite why the Order did not press on with the building of the fortress is difficult to say but it appears that by 1563 the knights were fairly sure that a Turkish attack was imminent. In such circumstances it might be dangerous to start building in case the fortress could not be finished by the time the Turks arrived and had to be abandoned to them in a partially completed condition. Additionally the Order was becoming short of money again. During the latter part of the fifteen-fifties the Order's finances had revived, but now, as the Turkish threat to Malta increased, the knights were forced to spend heavily on war materials. Sulaiman was putting pressure on the Order without moving his forces from Constantinople and unwittingly postponing the building of defences which might secure its position in Malta.

Nor were the Turks alone in bringing pressure to bear on Malta: the North African pirates were becoming increasingly active in the western Mediterranean. Piracy had long been a profession on the Barbary coast and during the first half of the sixteenth century the business became increasingly highly organized. The two men chiefly responsible for this development were the Barbarossa brothers who came originally from Mitylene and started operating from Tunis in the early years of the sixteenth century. The brothers became a potent threat in 1516 when they took Algiers and were able to resist a Spanish attempt to remove them. A few years later the surviving brother Khair ad-Din, for one had been killed in 1518, requested and obtained recognition and help from the Turkish sultan. At this point the North African corsairs ceased to be merely a nuisance and became an extremely important factor in Ottoman efforts to push into the western Mediterranean.

The Turkish sea-threat and the rise of the Barbary corsairs altered Malta's strategic importance. Control of the central Mediterranean seaways was to be violently contested and in such a situation Malta becomes a key fortress.

Shortly after the knights took up residence on Malta, Sulaiman made Khair ad-Din admiral of the Turkish fleet. In 1534 the Turks, under the command of Barbarossa, ravaged southern Italy and also took Tunis. In the following year Charles V led a large Christian force against Tunis and recaptured it. However, the Turks and the corsairs were gaining an increasing number of successes. In 1538 a Turkish fleet won the battle of Prevesa and in 1541 a Christian expedition against Algiers ended in disaster.

The strategic situation was complicated by the way in which the French were prepared to co-operate with the Turks to gain an advantage over Spain. Negotiations between France and Turkey had been going on since the late fifteen-twenties. In 1536 France was granted commercial privileges within the Ottoman empire and when in 1542 war broke out again between France and Spain the Turkish fleet helped the French in combined operations. In 1543

Barbarossa burnt the town of Reggio and wintered in the French port of Toulon. The Order was in a peculiar position here for it was completely opposed to the Turks and yet a Christian country, France, which supplied a great part of the Order's members, was in an 'ungodly alliance' with the Ottoman empire. There is no evidence to show that the French knights seriously faltered in their loyalty to the Order but, in the early fifteen-fifties, Sulaiman was rumoured to have asked France for Malta, presumably being under the misapprehension that the Religion was a French organization.

Barbarossa died in 1546 but there were many able lieutenants left to continue his activities. Torghud (Dragut) became the best known of Barbarossa's successors and combined with the Turks for attacks on Christian powers. Pressure on Malta became increasingly heavy. In 1547 Dragut landed at Marsaxlokk and, although the attack was driven off with only small losses to the Order and the Maltese, the skirmish was the forerunner of several similar attacks. In 1548 and 1550 there were landings on Gozo. 1551 was the year of the powerful combined attack by the forces of Sulaiman and Dragut on the islands. During the same year Augusta, on the east coast of Sicily, was burnt and in 1554 a Turkish force landed on Malta and attacked Siggiewi. In 1560 the Order was involved in the catastrophic attack, by a combined Christian force, on Tripoli which ended in a complete victory for the Turkish fleet off Djerba. During the same year Gozo was attacked again, in 1562 the Order lost two galleys to the Moslems and in 1563 a Turkish force sacked Milazzo and Dragut again attacked Gozo. Some compensation was gained when the Penon, the fortress at Algiers, was taken in 1564 by a large Christian force and it is fair to say that the Order's galleys had been highly successful in their attacks on Moslem shipping.

During the early fifteen-sixties reports reached Malta from the Levant that a great Turkish force was being prepared for an attack on the island. By 1564 probability had become certainty and the Order made what preparations it could to defend the island. Early in 1565 Don Garcia de Toledo, the viceroy of Sicily, inspected the defences at Malta and La Goletta at Tunis for reports indicated that the Turks were about to attack both these key central Mediterranean fortresses. Toledo and Valette attempted to work out combined defence plans and the viceroy made generous promises of aid. Unfortunately the viceroy's military resources were limited and the assurances of help were made in anticipation of the reinforcements he hoped to receive from Spain. As events turned out, Toledo's requests received a very tardy response and the Order was very largely left to fight with the resources it had built-up prior to 1565.

In the spring of 1565 Valette had at his disposal the fortresses of St. Elmo, St. Angelo, St. Michael and the fortified towns of Senglea and Birgu. In the centre of Malta was the weakly fortified town of Mdina. On Gozo the Citadel, which had been strengthened since the attack of 1551, was also garrisoned. These positions were manned, according to Bosio, by about 9,000 men, consisting of knights, imported soldiers and Maltese. The greatest part of the force was concentrated in the harbourside fortresses and only small contingents were placed in Mdina and the Gozo Citadel. All the available cavalry was stationed in Mdina.

5

The Great Siege

On May 18th, 1565 a Turkish armada of about two hundred vessels arrived off Malta. Appearing on the eastern horizon, the fleet closed with the island before sailing around its southern tip to reconnoitre the west coast for anchorages. The first night was spent anchored in a small bay on the north-west coast. At first light on the following day the fleet turned south again, apparently having decided that of the available anchorages and landing places Marsaxlokk was the best. The Turkish decision to put their army ashore at Marsaxlokk made any but a cursory Christian opposition to the landing impossible. The great horseshoe bay has a coastline of six and a half miles and easy landings can be made along a large part of the shore. The Turks would have been able to engage the Christians over a relatively long front and take advantage of their greater numbers. In a limited landing area there is the possibility of allowing a few thousand of the opposition ashore before launching a crushing counter-attack which cuts the advance party to pieces before it can be reinforced. The form of Marsaxlokk precluded this manoeuvre and Grand Master Valette, lacking any important artillery positions along the shore, allowed the landing to proceed without serious resistance.

For the next three days the Turks burned, pillaged and killed. A number of peasants had failed to get within the fortified positions as there had been so many alarms in the past few years that they decided to ignore this one. Their mistake proved costly to them and to the rest of the islanders for it allowed important numbers of livestock to fall into the hands of the Turks. During the first few days after the Turkish landing there was some skirmishing but the Order could not afford a full-scale engagement away from the fortified positions and its cavalry was hindered by the unsuitability of the Maltese countryside.

The story of the Siege has been told and retold so often that today it is extremely difficult to distinguish the facts from the fictions. In the years immediately succeeding the Siege a number of accounts of events appeared, some of them eye-witness, and since that time chroniclers and historians have used the material over and over again to write new descriptions of the Great Siege. By the eighteenth century Voltaire could say with justification that nothing was so well known as the Siege of Malta and yet there are very many aspects of the story which are far from well known. We have a plethora of accounts written by Christians but of the Moslem side of the story we know very little. Were there really as many Turks as the Christians claim, were Turkish losses really so huge and were the commanders of the Turkish force split by internal jealousies? All these questions and a number of others have only been partially answered and, when we know more of the Turkish view of events, accounts of the Siege may have to be modified in some respects.

It is well to remember that the story of the Great Siege, which has come down to us, has been written by Western Europeans glorifying their own military prowess. There is something of the flavour of a morality play about the European chroniclers' descriptions of events. The Turks are frequently represented as a vast, brutal, barbarian horde impervious to fear and innately evil. Against this force for evil stands a small band of Christian knights, led by a man who epitomizes the knightly virtues of chivalry, courage and devotion. And of course good triumphs over evil, the courage and devotion of a few well-led, intelligent knights overcome the bestial Moslem hordes who are portrayed as being ill led and lacking in chivalry.

The story has become stylized and few have questioned it, both because it makes such a good story and because the knights of St. John had a vested interest in appearing as the saviours of Christendom. The Siege story increased their renown and made European monarchs more kindly disposed towards them. It is noticeable that the Maltese, who made up the bulk of the Christian fighting force, are given very little praise in the majority of accounts.

To say these things is not to deny that great feats of arms were done during the summer of 1565 but simply to say that the story has been rather overtold. As has been said of one chronicler, 'his appetite for the marvellous sometimes carries him into the miraculous.' In particular, care must be taken when reading the statements of omnipotent chroniclers who, without any reservation, confidently give us detailed accounts of conversations amongst the Turkish commanders as they try to plan their campaign against the Order. Certainly renegades from the Turkish army brought some information, but would such men be allowed an ear at the councils of the war lords? The great majority of renegades were men of lowly position who probably brought no more than camp gossip.

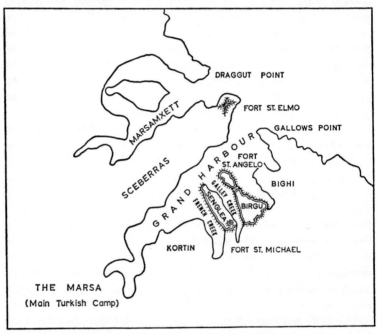

The fortifications around the Grand Harbour, 1565

On May 21st a short battle ensued between the two sides close to Birgu and it appeared that the Turks were about to invest the Order's major fortified positions. Apparently to the surprise of the defenders, on May 22nd the attackers started to move their forces onto Sceberras peninsula in preparation for an attack upon St. Elmo.

It has generally been assumed that the Turks should have attacked the Birgu-Senglea positions first, at the same time sending off small forces to capture Mdina and the Gozo Castello, which were expected to provide footholds for any relief force coming from Sicily. The decision to attack St. Elmo has been represented as a very bad tactical error and the chroniclers give the following reason for it. The Turkish admiral Piali was jealous of the power placed in Mustapha as general commander of the expedition and did his best to make the enterprise difficult. Accordingly, when Mustapha suggested an immediate attack on the Birgu-Senglea positions, Piali insisted that St. Elmo be reduced first in order that the Marsamxett could be made available to his fleet. As Piali was the son-in-law of the Sultan, Mustapha was forced to acquiesce. This may well be so, although it could immediately be asked 'Why, if Piali was so powerful, did he not gain the command of the whole expedition in the first place?' In fact, the decision to attack St. Elmo can be justified on tactical grounds without invoking dissensions amongst the Turkish commanders. First, whilst Marsaxlokk is an adequate anchorage weatherwise during the summer, in the event of a Christian fleet coming to relieve Malta it was a very bad one. The entrance was too wide to give any real protection and the Turkish fleet might have been pinned to the coast of Malta without any room to manoeuvre. The Turks were obviously worried by this fear as they manned artillery positions at Marsaxlokk to give some protection. Secondly, supply problems would clearly be eased if the Turkish army, which established its main camp at Marsa at the head of the Grand Harbour, and the fleet were in close proximity. Thirdly and crucially, the best way to attack the major positions may have been by getting control of Sceberras which was a superb gun platform from which to bombard the Birgu-Senglea defences. The Order's military engineers had been pointing out since 1530 that the major weakness of the Birgu defences was the way in which they were commanded from Sceberras. From Sceberras artillery could hamper movement within the town and fire onto the defenders' side of the fortifications. Artillery positions here would not only significantly increase the firepower which could be brought to bear on the defences but would be especially effective in demoralizing the defenders.

The decision to attack St. Elmo, then, may have been taken as a result of sound tactical reasoning. Where the Turkish command was possibly in error was in underestimating the difficulties of subduing St. Elmo and in mismanaging operations against it.

The chroniclers usually represent St. Elmo as a small weak fortress, containing only a few, inadequately supplied men. This is far from the truth. St. Elmo had been completed some twelve years before the Siege and had been designed by a military engineer who knew his job. More than this, it had been specially built to deny an aggressor unhampered use of Sceberras. St. Elmo was a modern fort, with outworks and well supplied with artillery positions on the landward front; and if the normal garrison was small, several hundred men were put into it once the Siege started. A few hundred determined men, stiffened with a strong cadre of the finest fighters in Europe, in a modern fort surrounded on three sides by the sea could pose a number of problems to an attacker for, however powerful the aggressor, he could only bring a small part of his strength against the fort at one time. It was true that St. Elmo lay on the lowest part of the peninsula and was overlooked by higher ground, but even so attacking the compact fort involved considerable difficulties. Any troops deployed along the Grand Harbour side of the peninsula were exposed to the fire of the artillery mounted in St. Angelo. And whilst an attack could be launched downhill, just before the fort was reached there was a shallow col and 300 yards of open ground which the St. Angelo artillery commanded. By controlling this ground the St. Angelo guns protected St. Elmo from complete Turkish investment and allowed the fort to be supplied by sea with fresh men and materials. Finally, the fort was on a knoll of higher ground at the tip of the peninsula and was built into the solid rock. This last fact is most important as it made difficult the use of mining techniques by which fortresses were frequently made untenable. As far as is known no serious attempt was made to mine St. Elmo.

Attacks on the small fort could only be developed over a limited front and in the face of strong artillery supporting fire from St. Angelo. The Turks attempted to counteract these problems by building an earth and rock wall along the top of Sceberras to protect the troops. In addition strong artillery positions were erected to engage the St. Angelo and St. Elmo guns.

There was considerable concealed strength in the position of St.

Elmo and it may be that the Turks did not become fully aware of this until they were committed to operations against the fort. In the present state of our knowledge it is impossible to say whether the Turkish commanders undertook the attack on St. Elmo for internal political reasons or as a result of hard tactical thinking. What is certain though is that a good case could be made out for attacking the fort. Sceberras peninsula was the greatest weakness in the Birgu-Senglea defences, as the Order well knew, and it is reasonable to suppose that in attempting to take St. Elmo the Turks were attempting to exploit this weakness. The Turkish commanders may have underestimated the cost but then no one, least of all St. Elmo's garrison, dreamt it possible that the fort would defy the Turkish force for a month.

On May 22nd the Turks started to place their artillery in preparation for the attack upon St. Elmo. The building of the positions for the guns took a considerable time as did the construction of the wall and trenches. Fighting was spasmodic during this period of preparation (these lengthy preparations are hardly the action of a commander about to attack a small, weak fort) and when heavy fighting broke out it was initiated by the Christians. In the early morning of May 29th the garrison of St. Elmo sortied. The Moslems in the forward trenches were taken unawares and a general panic ensued which quickly transmitted itself to a large body of the army. Eventually the Turkish commanders restored order, brought up fresh troops and pushed the garrison back within St. Elmo. In the confusion the Turks established themselves in some of the outworks of the fort. A few days later, again due to negligence on the part of the defenders, the Turks gained control of the remainder of the outworks which fronted the fort. The attackers were so encouraged by this success that they attempted to take the main body of the fort by escalade. Not enough preparatory work had been done to allow this, for the ditch surrounding St. Elmo had not yet been filled in and the scaling ladders were found to be too short. There followed a general massacre which gave the defenders some good match practice in the use of boiling pitch, wildfire and a particularly potent refinement that had been developed in the weeks of hectic preparation which preceded the coming of the Turks. The new weapon consisted of a hoop amply bound with cloth and soaked in incendiary chemicals. The missile could be quickly ignited and when cast from the walls onto the besiegers usually ensnared a small group and quickly set fire to the flowing dress of the Moslems.

The Turkish losses on this day, according to the chroniclers, were high, some putting the figure at 2,000 dead, others being content with a mere 500. The defenders' losses were in the order of 100 dead including 20 knights.

At the beginning of June the great corsair captain Dragut arrived from the North African coast with 1,500 of his followers. Dragut Reis was a master of all the arts of war and his arrival was as much a fillip to the Moslems as it was feared by the Christians. According to the chroniclers Dragut immediately upbraided the Turkish commanders for their tactical failings, particularly their having attacked St. Elmo. He took the view that the fort would die automatically on the demise of the parent positions. However, having started operations against St. Elmo it was not commensurate with the dignity of the Sultan for the Turks to break off the engagement. Dragut went on to scold the commanders for their inadequate handling of operations against the fort. The truth of such statements is difficult to corroborate but it appears that the bombardment of St. Elmo became, to a degree, more systematic after Dragut's arrival. New batteries were erected on the promontory since named Dragutt point, another battery was built between St. Angelo and the open ground fronting St. Elmo, and on Gallows point, today called Ricasoli point, yet another artillery position was set up. St. Elmo was now engaged by artillery on three sides and the erosion of its masonry was quickened.

Several breaches appeared in the walls and the fort's garrison came to the conclusion that honour was satisfied, they had put up a good fight and the time had now come for them to be withdrawn from a position which certainly must fall. Not only did the walls contain substantial breaches but the Turks were well established, together with some artillery, in the captured outworks. Snipers were lodged in a number of positions around the fort and the garrison, far from dying a glorious death in battle, were scuttling about behind hastily developed shelters and steadily suffering an unpleasant hole-in-the-corner extermination.

On June 5th Chevalier Medrano, a knight of unimpeachable courage, was despatched to represent the view of the defenders to the Council of the Order. Medrano was given a sympathetic hearing and most councillors agreed that St. Elmo should now be abandoned. Not so Grand Master Valette. He realized how valuable was the time the Order was gaining by the survival of the fort, and such was the standing of the Grand Master that the Council supported his views.

Medrano returned to St. Elmo to deliver the decision of the Council. The garrison was astonished at being called upon to defend a position which was clearly going to fall within a short time. A statement was drawn up and signed by over fifty knights. It declared that they were prepared to die for the Order but not in the miserable way they were at present falling: if the Grand Master would not withdraw them then they would sally forth, engage the Turks and die honourably in battle.

Valette reacted to this situation with subtlety, despatching a commission of three to inspect the St. Elmo works. One member of the commission was strongly convinced that the fort could hold out for some time longer. He offered to assume command and take a relief force into St. Elmo. The relief force was raised by calling for volunteers and such was the spirit of the garrison that more men came forward than there were places in St. Elmo. Valette now sent a short, incisive note to the knights in St. Elmo informing them that they were relieved from the duty of holding the dangerous post and were to return to the safety of the Birgu.

To be withdrawn from a post of danger and replaced by other men was a dishonourable stain which no knight could live with. The knights in St. Elmo called upon the Grand Master to allow them to remain in the fort. After a further exchange of letters Valette agreed, having placed upon the garrison the obligation to wipe a stain from their honour.

Midway through June the Turks became convinced that if St. Elmo was ever going to be taken it would have to be sealed off completely from reinforcement and supply. The Moslems had surrounded the fort with artillery positions, breached the walls, lodged snipers in the outworks; and yet as long as fresh determined men could be ferried into St. Elmo each night the breaches were always held against the Turkish general assaults. More than this, they were often beaten back with large demoralizing losses. The Turkish command decided to extend the trenches right down to the edge of the Grand Harbour and cover the landing places used by the boats sent over from St. Angelo each night. The construction of the new works along the exposed shore entailed great loss of life. During this phase of the battle Dragut was mortally wounded by a flying splinter of rock thrown up by a cannon ball. The new works were completed by June 19th, the fort was sealed and re-inforcement ceased—it was now only a matter of killing off the garrison that remained. For the next three days the Turkish artillery pounded away and then on the 22nd a general assault was launched. Somehow the defenders found the courage and determination to throw the Turks back again; but it was the end and the garrison knew it. That night they prayed and had their sins absolved. The next morning the wounded and the dying were carried to the breaches and propped up ready to die, sword in hand.

On the morning of the 23rd the Turkish commanders unleashed their great baying horde and yet again it faltered, staggered and withdrew only to reform and sweep into the fort, casting aside the last tattered remnants of Christian chivalry. A few Maltese soldiers escaped by swimming across the harbour to St. Angelo, a small group of knights were fortunate enough to fall into the hands of Dragut's corsairs—men who knew the value of a live knight on the ransom market—but the remainder of the garrison was slain. Then heads were struck from dead or dying knights, and their bodies, scored with bloody ironic crosses, were lashed to timbers and floated out into the harbour whence they drifted down to Birgu and the sorrow of their comrades. The carnage was removed from the water and with full honours the remains were buried in the Order's conventual church.

Then similar senseless anger burst forth amongst the Christians. The Turkish prisoners were cut down and their heads stuffed into cannon barrels and discharged into the enemy ranks. From this point neither side took prisoners.

It had taken the Turks just about a month to subdue St. Elmo at a cost, according to the chroniclers, of 8,000 men including Dragut, their most talented commander. The Moslems also lost their arrogance and confidence in victory. The story goes that Mustapha, looking from the ruins of St. Elmo across the water to the Birgu-Senglea defences, cried out: 'What will the parent cost when the child has been purchased at so fearful a price!' Already the seeds of defeat must have been in his mind and in the body of his army which had taken such a dreadful beating from the small St. Elmo garrison. As the Turks moved their main forces away from Sceberras, around the head of the Grand Harbour, to take up new positions in front of Birgu and Senglea the lust for Christian blood and victory had been blunted by the hardships of the past month. No doubt, too, the problems of organizing and supplying such a large force were beginning to make themselves felt and contributing to declining efficiency.

The Christians had lost 1,500 of their fighting force including about 130 knights, yet they had fought a delaying action so startling and heroic that the whole garrison was now fired with enthusiasm which, since the brutality that marked St. Elmo's fall, was stiffened by fanatical hate.

Knights of St. John courted honour. They lived to kill Turks or die a hero's death and now they were defending Christendom, set on a stage eagerly watched by the whole of Europe—it was an opportunity to reap honour that came to few, and no knight could ask for more.

With the fall of St. Elmo on June 23rd the Turkish fleet entered Marsamxett and Mustapha brought the main body of his forces round to attack the Birgu-Senglea positions. During the siege of St. Elmo the defences of the two towns had been greatly strengthened and the defensive system carefully organized. A bridge had been built between Birgu and Senglea to allow reinforcement of either garrison by the other if one should be particularly hard pressed.

Mustapha directed that the Turkish trenches should be cut from Kortin to Bighi and Birgu and Senglea thereby completely enclosed. However, before this operation was completed a body of about 700 men, 50 knights and some Spanish infantry, were sent from Sicily and put ashore in the north of Malta on June 29th. This relief force was able to slip through the still incomplete Turkish lines and into Birgu.

The building of the Turkish works was completed in about two weeks and on July 15th an assault was commenced on the fortress of St. Michael. The attack was a combined operation involving a simultaneous assault on the land and French Creek flanks of the fort. The French Creek flank was to be attacked from the sea and the Turks had got a large number of boats into the Grand Harbour, by dragging them overland from the head of Marsamxett for the purpose.

Early in July the Turks too had received reinforcement when a son-in-law of Dragut, called Hassem, had come up from Algiers with 2,500 men. These Moors, eager to display their prowess to the Turks, were chosen to spearhead both the land and sea attacks. Hassem led the land assault and his lieutenant was at the head of the flotilla of vessels which were to attempt the landing in French Creek. For a time the attack neared success; both the land and sea assaults made slim lodgements on St. Michael's walls. Each side now called up reinforcements. The Order's reserves came across the bridge from Birgu, whilst the Turks despatched nearly 1,000 janissaries, in 10 boats, to add power to their seaward attack. Unfortunately for them the janissaries exposed themselves round the point of the Senglea peninsula and were promptly blown out of the water by one of the St. Angelo batteries, which was mounted almost on the water line. Nine of the 10 vessels sank immediately and most of the janissaries involved were killed. This salvo decided the battle, and those Moslems who had gained a footing were flung down from the fortifications of Senglea and St. Michael.

On the day Christian losses were estimated at two to three hundred and those of the Moslems at two to three thousand.

For the Turks two weeks of preparation and planning had come to naught and they had taken yet another beating accompanied by heavy losses. Mustapha now drew off and for the next fortnight his artillery pounded the fortresses of the Order, in preparation for a simultaneous attack on Senglea and Birgu.

By the beginning of August a number of substantial breaches had been opened in the walls. Heavy Turkish attacks were now developed day after day and, although the attackers' losses were large, so long as Christians were being killed the fortresses must ultimately fall through want of defenders. In this period both sides had their successes and near successes. Once the Turks charged into a large breach on the Birgu land front only to find that a secondary wall had been built inside the first line of defence. The attackers were caught in the narrow space between the two walls whilst the defenders poured down a torrent of boiling pitch, scalding water and inflammable substances well laced with shot. The Turks behind thought their comrades were streaming into the town and eagerly pressed forward to share in the blood-letting and pillaging. They simply hastened the death of their fellows: the more that pressed forward, the more were slain. Finally the terror of those in the breach communicated itself to those outside and as flight began the defenders sallied and slaughtered the laggards.

Twice the Turks were on the point of grasping victory only to have it torn from them by the courage and resource of the Order's heroes. Quite early in August, Mustapha saw his forces cut their way deep into a breach at St. Michael and plant their standards on the ramparts. Birgu was heavily engaged and at last it appeared that superior numbers must prevail. Then suddenly all was confusion at the rear of Mustapha's army; a Christian relief force had arrived from Sicily and was attacking his base at the Marsa. The smoke and flames rising from the burning camp could probably be seen. The retreat was sounded, the army about-faced and marched to the Marsa to meet the attack. At the burning camp the Moslems found no one but a few dying camp servants and guards. At the height of the battle the cavalry from Mdina had come down on the ill-guarded camp, butchered the wounded, burnt the tents and supplies; and those Turks who escaped the massacre had fled into the rear of their army and bruited the tale which led to Mustapha calling off his nearly victorious men.

On August 18th, the Turks should have won the Siege. On that day, having mined a large section of one of the Birgu bastions, the Turks exploded a charge beneath it and brought a large section down. The garrison was taken unawares and the Turks started to move into the town. News of events reached Valette who led a counter-attack with such élan and ferocity that the attackers were beaten back. The Turks attacked again that night and were thrown out once more.

This was really the last defeat of the Turks. Their army was now dispirited, its numbers were much reduced and the survivors had to be driven into battle. Time was running out. By the end of August, unusually early, Malta's implacable summer weather was beginning to break; there were a number of showers and Piali was probably thinking it was time to get the fleet back across the thousand miles of ocean to Constantinople.

Barring outside interference the Turks, given time, could still win; but their time had gone. And then, on September 6th, the Sicilian viceroy put 9,000 troops ashore at Mellieha, a bay in the extreme north of Malta. The viceroy's fleet thereupon went back to Sicily to ferry more men across.

Mustapha ordered a general embarkation on September 8th. This was a hasty action undertaken before he was in full possession of the facts.[1] The relief force was small enough to be defeated by the Turkish forces if they were properly organized. When Mustapha realized this he put the army ashore again at St. Paul's Bay and marched it inland. But his soldiers turned and fled before the first charge of the fresh troops and many were massacred, on the shore of St. Paul's Bay, as they tried to scramble into the boats waiting to take them out to the fleet.

The great question mark which hangs over the Siege is, why was help so long in coming to the small garrison? The blame is usually laid with Don Garcia de Toledo the Sicilian viceroy, who is constantly represented as a vacillating, pusillanimous and incompetent commander. This is certainly an unfair judgement. Even by the end of July the viceroy had only about 30 galleys against the 180 in the Turkish fleet. Don Garcia scratched round all summer to raise 15,000 troops and this force was not enough to ensure victory even if he had enough shipping to get it to Malta in one trip, which he had not.

The knights of St. John at Don Garcia's court railed that some help should be sent, saying that they and those who would venture forth with them should go to Malta to die with the fraternity; but such fine, courageous, sentiments were tactical nonsense. Don Garcia had no alternative but to wait until the Turks were so weakened that his small force would bring victory. Had he sent out his fleet loaded with troops in mid July and had it been intercepted by Piali's naval force, Don Garcia would have lost the greater part of the resources he had for the defence of Sicily. Even if the troops had got ashore they would probably have been defeated. It is worth noting that Mustapha felt he could defeat the relief force put ashore in early September. Don Garcia was in the unfortunate position of having too few forces to meet his defence commitments. The knights never appreciated the point but the viceroy had to look on Malta in just the same way as they had

[1] Here, once more, we are taking the word of the chroniclers. Mustapha may have been attempting a complicated manœuvre, the object of which was to keep the Christian forces divided and to attack the relief force on its flank or rear.

Tarxien Temples. (a) This picture gives an impression of the elaborate nature of the fittings within the temple. Note the paved floor, spiral decoration, altars, and niches

(b) In contrast to the early temples the stonework at Tarxien is of a very high quality. Note the size of the blocks and the skill with which they have been fitted together and dressed. During their active life the temples were roofed, probably with timber

Prehistoric 'cart-tracks' on the Upper Coralline limestone. The man-made fields have been constructed at a later period

looked on St. Elmo: the small fortress bloodily sacrificed to give the main positions more time. In terms of Philip II's empire Malta was a small outlying fortress; Sicily was a major position and no competent viceroy could be justified in sallying out to Malta with his forces. In fact the choice was not in Don Garcia's hands for under the viceregal system operated by Philip II all important decisions were referred back to Spain.

Don Garcia was not at fault in this matter and events proved his course of action to be the correct one. But what of the rest of Europe —where were the fleets of France and Venice? Why was it that in four months only 15,000 men could be assembled in Sicily? These questions must be answered before Don Garcia is arraigned.

Philip was very hesitant in replying to Don Garcia's requests for reinforcements. Additional forces were gathered in Sicily, but slowly, and the commanders were instructed not to take any risks. The king was heavily involved in other regions and he did not wish to commit many forces to the central Mediterranean.

In May of 1565 the Seville fleet, commanded by Àlvaro de Bazán, transported reinforcements to Oran and Malaga. When this mission was completed Bazán took the force on to Genoa, Civita Vecchia and Naples, picking up troops at each port. By early August Bazán had joined Toledo in Sicily and the combined force amounted to about 90 galleys and something over 10,000 troops. Toledo and Bazán evolved a battle plan which did not expose the fleet to great risks. The best 60 galleys were to be selected and 150 infantry were placed aboard each vessel. The fleet would then sail as quickly as possible to Malta, disembark the troops and return to Sicily. The speed of the operation should prevent the Turks from concentrating their fleet and a sea action would therefore be avoided.

On August 25th the force set sail for Malta but ran into a storm and suffered damage and dispersal. The fleet returned to Sicily and it was some time before it was reorganized for another attempt to reach Malta.

The sacking of Don Garcia from his viceregal post shortly after the Siege was lifted is frequently quoted as evidence that he was regarded as incompetent. In fact, as the knights strove to gain every ounce of credit for the victory, the Order mounted a campaign against Toledo who at first had received considerable praise in Europe for his handling of events. Philip II was probably quite happy to see Don Garcia's reputation destroyed, for this shuffled the blame for the delay in relieving Malta from him onto the viceroy. What had really happened was almost certainly well known in Europe at the time. A report reached the English court from Madrid early in September 1565 to the effect that Philip had 'lost a great deal of reputation by not succouring Malta'. Don Garcia's position was also undermined at Philip's court by an anti-Toledo party.

Another important problem associated with the Siege is the question of how many Turks were in Malta during the campaign. The estimates of the chroniclers are probably exaggerated, for it is doubtful if the Turks were capable of transporting an army of thirty to forty thousand troops from Constantinople to Malta in 1565. In 1557 the French estimated that the Turks could get an army of 12,000 men from Turkey into the western Mediterranean. Intelligence reports circulating in Western Europe in the spring of 1565 suggested that the Turks were to bring fifteen or sixteen thousand men to Malta. The estimates of an army of thirty to forty thousand men start to appear after the Turks had landed in Malta. In short, the estimate of the number of the Turkish troops which gained general credence was the estimate of the defending army and armies are notoriously prone to exaggerate the number of their opponents.

However, even if the Turkish army only numbered something like 20,000, including the corsairs who came from North Africa during the campaign, it must be remembered that the attacking force consisted of trained men whilst the defenders were very largely Maltese peasants and townsfolk.

There are a number of reasons why the Christians won and the Moslems lost the Siege. First, there is no doubt that the knights were superb, highly trained fighters, as indeed they should have been for their lives were dedicated to crusading. They lived in a community in which the finest virtue was courage, where life was steeped in a mystique of nobility and the service of Christ. It was not enough for a knight to die for the Order and Christ, he had to die courageously and honourably. So strong was the fear of being killed by the Turks in a corner, a highly dishonourable way to perish, that few knights stayed away long from the Siege fighting, even after being severely wounded. For such men there was no time, even in the longest battle against the highest odds, when a knight became disheartened; he went on fighting hard until he won or was killed. There could be no thought of surrender, defeat or flight. This may sound high flown but quite simply these were the standards of the society in which a member of the Order lived. The great desire for honour and the fear of dishonour kept the knights fighting long after they should have been demoralized and their example must have influenced the remainder of the garrison.

The brilliant leadership of Grand Master Valette had much to do with the Order's success. Valette has been lionized by the chroniclers, but even when the extravagant praise is discounted there emerges a picture of a man who had an extraordinarily complete grasp of the techniques of warfare and the ability to apply his knowledge throughout the stress and confusion of a long campaign. The thoroughness of Valette's defence preparations, the way in which he appreciated the advantages of delaying the Turks at St. Elmo even when it involved sacrificing many lives, and his skill in using the Order's meagre forces all build into a picture of an impressively resourceful man. Above Valette's tactical insight and courage of decision was his sheer personality as a war lord. Valette did not drive, he led, and all men knew that when it was necessary Valette, too, would die, and die well, for his Order. When the Turks brought down a great section of the Birgu land front by mining and fought their way into the town, Valette met the first confused fugitives from the battle with calm words, picked up his pike and strode towards the breach. All those around at once rallied at this example and, led by the Grand Master, they achieved one of the most important victories of the Siege. The Turks had the defences down, they were in the town and their superior numbers now must surely tell. Once more they were defeated by men fighting far above themselves, inspired by a heroic warrior leader. As one chronicler puts it, Valette had the ability, 'by his speeches as well as example, to animate his men, and thereby prevailed upon common soldiers to fight and behave themselves like so many officers and as men who were inspired with a true sense of glory'.

In the spring of 1565 there were about 9,000 men-at-arms in Malta. Of this number over 5,000 were Maltese and their contribution was decisive. Although only poorly trained they rose brilliantly to the occasion under Valette's leadership. Maltese women and children, too, played an important part and a large number of local inhabitants were killed in the fighting. The great majority met their deaths, not as a by-product of the battles, but as a direct result of them. Maltese women helped rebuild the walls, carried food to the warriors and aided the wounded. Towards the end they were frequently taking an active part in the fighting. The Maltese contribution is frequently passed over but with an apathetic or cowardly local population the Siege could not have been won.

In spite of the great courage displayed by the Christians the Moslems should still have won. The blame for failure must lie with the Turkish commanders. Apart from the supposed jealousies between Mustapha and Piali there was a lack of constancy in the Turkish tactical planning and a hideous waste of manpower that, in the end, demoralized the army. The misjudging of the strength of St. Elmo and the failure to cut off the nightly inflow of reinforcements into the fort were errors which cost the lives of hundreds of men.

The Turks outgunned the Order and, due to the local relief, their artillery batteries commanded many of the knights' positions. Theoretically the Turks had only to pound the defences to pieces and then use their superior numbers to gain victory in the breaches. Continually the Turkish army was put into attacks before the fortifications had been sufficiently damaged, with the result that men were needlessly sacrificed. To name just one instance, in the first assault on St. Michael two to three thousand Moslems were estimated to have been killed, including nearly 1,000 janissaries and a large number of the 2,500 fresh troops brought from Algiers. After this defeat the Turks held off for a fortnight having decided that the fortress required further bombardment.

There was also a lack of attention to detail about the Turkish campaign which proved costly. Allowing the small reinforcement from Sicily to slip into the Birgu early in July was a bad error. No serious attempt was made to invest Mdina which, together with Gozo, formed a most useful communications link with Sicily. If this could be ascribed to oversight then the use of Mdina as a cavalry base, from which the Turkish rear was continually harried, should have made the oversight obvious. The failure to contain the forces in Mdina is even more puzzling when we consider the terrain over which the Order's cavalry commander had to conduct operations.

Malta is divided into innumerable small fields surrounded by dry stone walls. No body of cavalry could cross country of this type or avoid using the roads and paths to a large extent. The Marsa was flat and suitable for more orthodox cavalry work as were some of the depressions in the north of Malta. But around Mdina it should have been possible to seal most of the routeways. The cost of tactical errors of the type listed is bound to be high and they almost certainly cost the Turks Malta.

The Siege of Malta was an important battle in European history but not a decisive one. The Turks had to take Malta before they could safely threaten Sicily and southern Italy, and even if Malta fell they still had many stiff battles ahead. In this sense the victory of the Order's forces did not save Western Europe but it prevented her being greatly discomfited.

Had the knights in Malta at the time of the Siege been annihilated it would not have been the end of the Order of St. John of Jerusalem. The knights fighting in Malta were only the flower of a rich and powerful organization which had its roots deep in European soil. If the Order in Malta had been destroyed the wealth of the Religion, which lay in its extensive European estates, would have remained and there would still have been enough knights in Europe to resuscitate the organization.

If to Europe and the Order 1565 was not a supremely critical year, to Malta it was the foundation year of her modern history. Had the Turks won the Siege, Malta would have been left a deserted battlefield. As it was, the Order won and stayed. During the next two and a half centuries the knights of St. John spent lavishly on fortifications, ordnance establishments, new towns, palaces and villas. The Maltese prospered on this spending and on the spending necessary to maintain the high standard of living which the knights enjoyed. During the Order's rule the number of Maltese increased fivefold, new trades and industries were developed and the islands became the home of one of the most prosperous communities in Europe. All this sprang from the victory of 1565.

6

Malta under the Order of St. John

T
he Order and the Maltese had won a great triumph in 1565 but many problems remained to be solved before either party could gather the rewards of victory.

Much of the countryside of Malta was a wilderness and many of the towns and villages had been extensively damaged. Large numbers of Maltese had been killed in the fighting, although the size of the death roll is in doubt. Contemporary writers estimated that about 7,000 Maltese were killed but this figure appears to be excessive and there is no evidence to sustain it. In fact an examination of parish records suggests a rather different story. Baptismal registers are not well preserved in Malta for the Siege year. At a few parishes the records are missing entirely and even where they are preserved the registers are usually incomplete for the years 1565 and 1566. Incidentally, the fact that there was a widespread failure to keep parish records in the year after the Siege is evidence in itself of the serious way in which the life of the island had been dislocated. When in the years 1567 and 1568 parish priests were once more able to make complete records it would be expected, had a large proportion of the population been killed off in 1565, that many fewer baptisms would be recorded. In most cases, the figures for 1567 and 1568 do not differ significantly from those for the years before the Siege. There are good reasons for thinking that the 1567 and 1568 figures have not been inflated by the postponement of baptisms during 1565 and 1566. First, a child would be baptized as quickly as possible by any priest that was available in times of danger and uncertainty. Secondly, the number of baptisms increases steadily in the years after 1567 whereas a fall could be expected if a large backlog of baptisms had been worked off. Similarly there would be a falling off if the 1567 and 1568 figures simply represented an after-war increase in births.

The position is complicated by the fact that we do not know how many Maltese moved in and out of the islands before and after the Siege. Nor do we know how many Maltese there were at the beginning of 1565; 20,000 seems to be a reasonable estimate. If the population of Malta was 20,000, a death roll of 7,000 during the Siege would have accounted for roughly one third of the people living on the islands, and completely altered the population structure. The evidence available today does not indicate that the population was massacred in this way during the fighting in 1565.

The evidence relating to the number of knights killed during the Siege is much clearer and it appears that just under half those taking part were slain.

Although estimates of the number of Maltese killed in 1565 may be inaccurate, there is no doubt that a great deal of damage had been done to the island and that there was widespread hardship amongst the inhabitants.

The Order's problems were more complex. The Religion had sustained heavy losses of materials and manpower. The fortifications were largely in ruins and the monetary cost of sustaining the Siege had been high. In these conditions the old dissensions broke out again and many knights were in favour of abandoning Malta now that the Order's few possessions on the island had been wrecked and the return of the Turks might confidently be predicted.

Even Grand Master Valette, who had wished to make Malta the Order's home, seems either to have had doubts about the advisability of remaining on the island or to have been not fully in control of the situation. As soon as the Siege was lifted the Grand Master had asked the Pope to provide a military engineer capable of planning a new town for Sceberras peninsula. However, by the time the man chosen for the job, Francesco Laparelli, reached Malta, in December 1565, he found that many of the possessions of the Order were packed ready for removal. As the Order was in an uncertain and disorganized condition Laparelli worked quickly. He examined Sceberras and was impressed by the peninsula's defensive and strategic possibilities. Within the space of a few days Laparelli placed the plans for the new city of Valletta before the Council of the Order. Although the knights vacillated, Laparelli collected workmen and materials and traced out the line of the fortifications for the new town. Laparelli's initiative was effective and on 28th March, 1566, Grand Master Valette laid the foundation stone of the city which bears his name. Although the decision to build Valletta helped to steady the knights it did not immediately quell all discussion as to whether or not the Order should remain on Malta. The arguments about this problem were only a symptom of deeper, underlying, tensions. Ever since the knights had come to Malta there had been a long record of drunkenness, gaming, wenching, brawling and disobedience. Now if incidents of this type might be expected in a community containing many lively young knights, the outbreaks of unruly behaviour had frequently amounted to direct disobedience to the Grand Master and the statutes of the Order.

In 1533, as the result of a duel between a Frenchman and an Italian, fighting broke out between members of the langue of Italy and the French langues. Shortly the Iberian knights joined in on the Italian side and the convent was engaged in an internecine war. Although the fighting did not last long the authority of the Grand Master was completely ignored for a time and L'Isle-Adam was unable to stop the outbreak of lawlessness. And if this incident could be put down to an outburst of nationalist feeling at a period of strain what was to be made of the widespread disregard for the vow of chastity? Not that breaches of this kind were particularly frowned upon by the order at the time, for the statutes issued during the rule of Grand Master Sengle (1553-1557) allowed any knight, found to be living in sin, nearly six weeks to make more seemly domestic arrangements. Nevertheless this aberration in knightly behaviour reached unusual proportions. By 1551 Malta was well known for the large number of prostitutes found there and before the Siege special arrangements had to be made to transport the ladies to the safety of Sicily. Their return was quickly facilitated after the battle and as the renown of Malta was now widespread, consequent upon the great victory, large numbers of travellers and 'adventurers' came to the island. The influx increased the instability of the convent and led to a marked increase in disreputable behaviour. Lawlessness reached a peak during the rule of La Cassière (1572-1581). The Grand Master attempted to curb the excessive licentiousness and rowdy living within Valletta and ordered that all concubines were to be removed from the city. The promulgation of this edict raised many members of the Order to fury. The Grand Master was arrested and, to the accompaniment of the jeers of the women he had attempted to persecute, La Cassière was transported to fort St. Angelo and imprisoned. An attempt was made to install Romegas, one of the Order's most renowned naval commanders, as Grand Master but the Pope intervened and both Romegas and La Cassière were called to Rome to justify their conduct. Eventually La Cassière was reinstated but the whole episode has yet to be fully explained. There are many more factors involved in the incident than the unpopularity of La Cassière, which may well be cloaking more profound political intrigue. At the time there was a great deal of trouble between the Order, the Bishop of Malta and the Inquisitor of Malta on the treatment of heretics, of whom there were apparently a number amongst the knights. There was also friction over the degree of jurisdiction the Bishop and the Inquisitor had over the Maltese.

It was against this background of lawlessness, disregarded vows, suggestions of heresy and conflict within the island that Valletta was founded and built. The building of the city gave work to large numbers of Maltese at a time when many of the islanders were practically destitute. The foundation of Valletta made it more difficult for the knights to abandon Malta and this was important for it gave the Order roots and a policy at a time when it might well have fragmented under the stress of events.

Fortunately for the Order and the Maltese the convent settled down after the La Cassière incident. Of course, the quarrels and the wenching continued but widespread outbreaks of lawlessness were generally avoided.

The Growth of Population

When the Order of St. John came to the islands there were probably something like 20,000 people living on Malta alone. The population of Gozo was estimated to be 5,000 persons and Comino was uninhabited. Throughout the Order's rule the population grew steadily in numbers, although at times setbacks occurred due to war, famine and disease.

Initially only a few hundred knights came to Malta but they brought with them servants, soldiers and attendants. Over the succeeding years many Rhodeans, who had depended upon the Order for a living, made their way to the island together with various other people brought in to help the knights develop their organization in Malta. This influx not only added several thousand persons to the population but also helped to make Malta more prosperous; for those who came generally had money to spend.

The early years of the Order's rule were marked by some drastic changes in population numbers. In 1550 the islands suffered a bad harvest and in the resultant famine many Maltese died. In 1551, before the attack of the Turks, some 3,000 non-combatants were transported from Malta to Sicily and, it was estimated by contemporary writers, about 5,000 Gozitans were taken prisoner during the course of the raid. In the following year, when the forts of St. Elmo and St. Michael were being built, labour became so scarce that workmen had to be imported from Sicily.

As uncertainty increased, in the years before 1565, many Maltese moved away from the islands and went to live in Sicily, to avoid further molestation by the Turks and Barbary corsairs. Certainly a large number of non-combatants were evacuated in the weeks immediately before the Siege.

Many Maltese were killed in the fighting of 1565 and most of those who had gone to Sicily to avoid this fate did not return until attracted back during the period of high prosperity occasioned by the building of Valletta. The construction of the new city absorbed vast numbers of labourers and at the peak of activity there were approximately 8,000 persons working on the fortifications alone. A chronic labour shortage developed in the late fifteen-sixties and workmen had to be brought in from Sicily and Calabria.

Our knowledge of the number of people living in the islands during the sixteenth century is not precise, partly because events led to the killing and migration of large numbers of people, and partly because little effort was made to count the population of the islands. Censuses only date from the end of the eighteenth century but before this time, in various parts of the world, reasonably accurate estimates of the size of populations were made. In Malta, from 1590 onwards, estimates of population numbers were made at irregular intervals. The mechanism of estimation was probably as follows. In Roman Catholic countries the parish priests have records, not only of births, deaths and marriages but also of the 'state of the souls'. In the *status animarum*, as the record was called, a tally was made of all those living in the parish together with a note as to whether or not each parishioner had attended mass and confession during the year. The possession of this record meant that the parish priests had a fairly accurate count of the number living in their parishes and good estimates of the total population could be made simply by enquiring of each priest how many souls he had in his care.

There are numerous reasons why it is important for an administration to know how many persons it controls, but in Malta the making of population estimates was connected with the importation of Sicilian grain. The islands had long enjoyed the right to import grain from Sicily free of the normal export taxes. The Sicilian authorities controlled the quantity of grain allowed to Malta under this system very carefully, because Sicily lost the export dues which were normally collected and it was necessary to prevent Maltese merchants obtaining cheap grain for resale. Before the authorities would agree to any expansion of the grain allowance they had to be thoroughly convinced that the population of Malta had increased. Thus it was necessary at intervals to take estimates of the number of persons living in the islands. On occasions the count was supervised by enumerators sent from Sicily.

The population of Malta grew very rapidly after the Siege and by the late fifteen-eighties the increased numbers were beginning to give rise to concern. In 1590 a population estimate was made and there were found to be nearly 30,000 persons living in the islands, apart from the Order and its followers. The Sicilians were warned that unless the grain allowance was increased there would be death by famine during the following year. In the event the whole region suffered poor harvests and 1591 was the year of a great southern European famine. As the Maltese started to die of hunger the Order considered the possibility of sending part of the population to Sicily, but the plight of that island was no better than Malta's. The famine continued into the following year when plague broke out as well.

By 1594 normal conditions had returned and the Maltese were soon increasing rapidly in numbers. In 1614 there were found to be nearly 40,000 inhabitants and in 1632 the 50,000 mark was topped. Some authorities question these figures and doubt whether so high a rate of population gain was possible. Such growth is feasible assuming an annual increase in population of about 2 per cent. A growth rate of this magnitude would be high in the early seventeenth century, although recently some Latin American countries have augmented their numbers by about 4 per cent per annum. Of course, the increase does not have to be accounted for solely in terms of Malta; it is probable that many people moved into the islands during the period of very rapid growth.

From 1632 to 1670 little increase took place in the number of the islands' inhabitants; a slight decline was even recorded during the famine years and war scares of the sixteen-forties. In 1676 a virulent plague broke out in the congested towns around the Grand Harbour and it was only by enforcing strict quarantine regulations, which amounted to a virtual ban on movement around the islands, that the disease was eventually contained. In the course of the epidemic thousands of Maltese died; one estimate placed the death roll at 8,569. The great majority of deaths were in Valletta, Birgu, Senglea and Bormla. The 1680 estimate of population revealed that the islands contained fewer inhabitants than they had done in 1632.

From 1680, until the end of the Order's rule, the population of the islands increased at a steady rate without experiencing anything like the surge of numbers which took place in the late sixteenth and early seventeenth centuries. This is in contrast to much of Western Europe which tended to experience more rapid population growth in the eighteenth century than in the seventeenth.

In 1760 there were estimated to be about 66,000 persons in Malta alone and by 1798 the islands probably contained about 100,000 inhabitants.

Naturally not all parts of the islands increased their population at the same rate. Some areas experienced rapid growth and others suffered decline. The most striking contrast was between the harbour towns and the rural areas. The number of persons residing in the harbour area increased very rapidly and part of this growth was due to people migrating from the rural areas where population gain was consequently less.

Gozo, after the near depopulation of 1551, increased the numbers of its inhabitants very slowly in the late sixteenth and early seventeenth centuries. In the eighteenth century the pattern changed and by the time the Order left the population of Gozo was probably in the region of 10,000 persons.

The Growth of Towns and Villages

During the rule of the Order of St. John the population of the Maltese islands increased from some 20,000 to about 100,000 persons. The increase in population was accompanied by alterations in the size, structure and distribution of the settlements in which the Maltese lived. Before we can examine these changes we must first go back to the late Middle Ages to discover just what the settlement pattern of the islands was like before the Order arrived.

We know very little about the development of Maltese towns and villages prior to the fifteenth century. There are occasional references to individual settlements in documents of the thirteenth and fourteenth centuries but, as yet, no complete picture of the distribution of towns and villages before 1436 is available. Until that year, Malta had a very simple ecclesiastical organization and was divided into two parishes; one parish was centred on Mdina and the other on Birgu. In 1436 an additional 10 parishes were created and these were centred on the principal rural settlements of the day. The settlements then existing are shown on the accompanying map and a number of interesting features are apparent from it. None of the settlements, apart from Birgu, lie near to the coasts and only one settlement, Mellieha, exists to the north of the Great Fault. The reason for this distribution is related to the unsettled times which developed in the fourteenth and fifteenth centuries. It is known that a number of villages and hamlets, lying close to the coasts or in the remote northern part of the island, were abandoned in this period. Mellieha did not survive for long after 1436 due to the attentions of corsairs.

During the rule of the Order three themes dominated the development of the settlement pattern of Malta. First, there was a continued reluctance to occupy the coasts and the northern part of the island. Secondly, the large rural settlements, like Quormi, Birkirkara, Zebbug and Zeitun, grew considerably in size. The smaller villages experienced very little growth and a number became extinct. Thirdly, there was the foundation and development of several new towns around the Grand Harbour and Marsamxett.

The Order was never able to make the coasts and the remoter parts of the islands really safe places to live. Until the latter part of the eighteenth century a Turkish reprisal raid was always to be

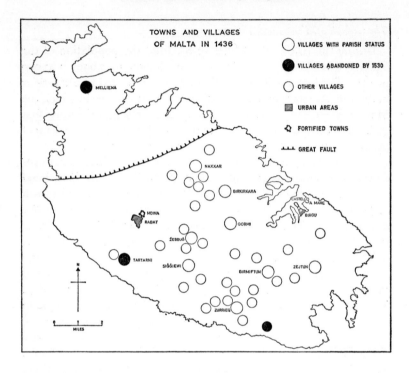

feared. In 1614 a Turkish force came ashore at Marsascala and ravaged the village of Zeitun. A Turkish attack was expected in the sixteen-forties, the sixteen-seventies and appeared to be a certainty in the seventeen-twenties. Added to these fears of a large-scale attack on the island, Barbary vessels were continually sighted in the waters around Malta, many of them captured vessels plying between the island and Sicily, and occasional raids were made on the remoter areas, particularly Gozo. In such conditions it is hardly surprising that very few Maltese felt secure enough to live in exposed areas unless there happened to be some particularly strong incentive for doing so. The existence of rich farmland, particularly if irrigation water was available, was a good incentive and a number of families moved into northern Malta. Here there are numerous spring-watered valleys where it is possible to develop highly profitable, irrigated smallholdings. However, even with this incentive no

94

settlement large enough to be described as a hamlet developed in the area. Northern Malta is divided into compartments by a series of barren limestone ridges and these tend to isolate the area and make it difficult to defend, particularly as there are so many good bays to facilitate the entry of the quick piratical thrust.

In the heart of the island the larger villages prospered under the rule of the Order. They grew considerably in size and increased the range of services which were offered to the surrounding countryside. By and large it was the villages which had been created parish centres in 1436, with the exception of Mellieha and Tartarni, which showed the most rapid rate of growth. Although many other settlements attained parish status in the late sixteenth and early seventeenth centuries few grew at the same pace as the old established parish centres. The old parochial nuclei were already providing services for the surrounding areas and it was predictable that they should capitalize, in most cases, on their initial advantage.

During the rule of the Order the Church came to play an increasingly important part in the life of Maltese society. Churches became larger and highly ornamented, while religious festivals were marked by more elaborate services. Naturally it was the larger villages which could provide best for this increasingly expensive complexity.

The old parish nuclei were the centres from which the defence of the countryside was organized and this gave the villages concerned status and made them safer places to live in.

The growing importance of the old established villages like Quormi, Birkirkara, Zebbug and Zeitun is reflected in their population figures. The population of Quormi increased from about 2,000 at the end of the sixteenth century to nearly 4,000 in 1766. The population of Zebbug increased in a similar manner. There were 2,000 people living in Birkirkara in 1614; by 1766 the figure was 3,900. Zeitun lost population as a result of the Turkish attack on the village in 1614. There were under 2,000 people living in the village after the raid but by 1766 the population had reached nearly 6,000.

By contrast the number of persons living in the new parochial units increased very slowly, if at all. Attard was created a parish in 1575, but there were no more people living in the village in 1766 than there had been at the end of the sixteenth century. Gharghur

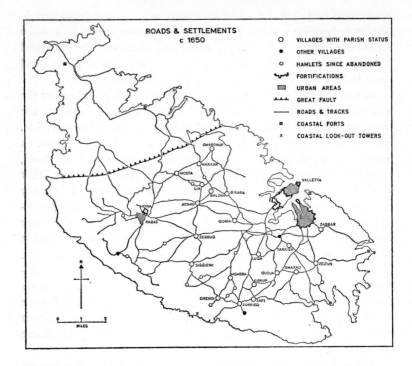

ROADS & SETTLEMENTS
c 1650

O   VILLAGES WITH PARISH STATUS
•   OTHER VILLAGES
o   HAMLETS SINCE ABANDONED
⌣ FORTIFICATIONS
▨ URBAN AREAS
⊥⊥⊥ GREAT FAULT
— ROADS & TRACKS
⊠ COASTAL FORTS
× COASTAL LOOK-OUT TOWERS

became a parish in 1610 when there were 700 people living in the village; in 1766 there were 800 inhabitants.

There were a few exceptions to these generalizations. Siggiewi, an old parish centre, grew very little in size because of the rather remote position of the village. The population of Mosta, created a parish in 1608, grew so rapidly that the village became larger than the mother parish centre of Naxxar. Growth at Mosta was stimulated by the Order's making a large number of land grants to people wishing to build houses in the village. Zabbar, which became a parish centre in 1615, experienced a rapid increase in population due to the proximity of the settlement to the Grand Harbour.

Many small villages and hamlets died out during the rule of the Order. In general terms any village with less than 200 inhabitants, at the beginning of the seventeenth century, was subsequently abandoned. Over a dozen small settlements suffered this fate as figure 9 shows. The sites of these villages are distinguishable in the

Part of Marfa Ridge in northern Malta. When Man first came to the islands the Upper Coralline limestone exposed here was probably soil covered. Subsequently the soil was removed to produce a barren ridge. In the nineteenth century an attempt was made to rehabilitate the area and the small fields visible here are a relict of this partially successful colonization

Jean de la Valette. Grand Master of the Order
of St. John of Jerusalem from 1557 to 1568

landscape today. Normally the name of the former settlement still exists and is prefixed by the word *hal* or *rahal*, which means village in Maltese. The old church is usually intact, as are the roads which formerly served the village, the small fields which lay immediately behind the settlement and the wells and cisterns belonging to the houses.

The disappearance of so many small villages and the increase in size of the larger rural centres concentrated the settlement pattern of the countryside. The causes of this concentration have not been adequately explained and there are probably a number of factors involved. During the late Middle Ages fear of corsairs was an important factor but other social forces seem to have been operating as well. During the rule of the Order the settlements which were abandoned were not sited in exposed positions and factors other than fear must have brought about decline. The smaller villages were simply not able to offer a sufficient range of services to a society which became more and more developed economically, and they succumbed to competition from centres that could offer such services.

The whole structure of the rural settlement pattern of Malta changed during the rule of the Order. In 1436 there were probably 38 separate hamlets and villages on Malta; by 1798 there were only 24. Most of the 24 were large, compact centres, which offered marketing and other commercial facilities to the surrounding countryside.

The concentration of the settlement pattern in Malta is interesting, not only because it reflects the changes which were taking place in Maltese society at the time, but also because it may well turn out to be a phenomenon of widespread occurrence in the western Mediterranean. A similar sequence of events is known to have taken place in the coastal plain of Bas Languedoc.

The evolution of the settlement pattern of Gozo has followed a different course to that of Malta. Very little is known about the villages of Gozo in the late Middle Ages as most of the smaller island's pre-Order documents were destroyed or captured during the Turkish raid of 1551. It seems, however, that during the fifteenth century Gozo, like Malta, was characterized by a wide scatter of settlements and population. Within this dispersed pattern the nuclei of larger settlements were developing but in 1551, when the Turks captured a great part of the population of the island, many settlements must have been abandoned. By the middle of the seventeenth century there had been a partial recovery in the numbers of people living on the island; and with the building of a series of coastal look-out forts, which helped to secure the better landing places, villages started to develop. In 1678 the village of Xewkija became a separate parochial unit and, by the end of the century, Gharb, Sannat, Xaghra, Nadur and Zebbug had attained a similar status. As a result of the later establishment of Gozitan villages they differ in form from rural settlements in Malta. One of the most important determinants of form in Malta was probably fear, and the villages are compact and narrow-streeted.

On Gozo the rural settlements developed principally in the eighteenth, nineteenth and twentieth centuries when the worst fears of raiding had passed. As a result the villages have broader

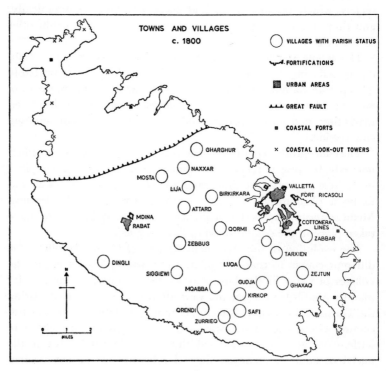

streets and straggling open plans. The fear of raiding will not explain all the morphological differences between Maltese and Gozitan rural settlements. The two groups of villages were established in widely differing times and their development must have been influenced by differing social and economic conditions.

The most striking change in the settlement pattern of the islands, which took place during the rule of the Order, was the establishment of a group of new towns around the Grand Harbour and Marsamxett. The installation of the Order on Malta made such a development almost inevitable for the knights had come to the island to exploit its strategic position and the fine harbours. During the latter part of the Middle Ages these assets had been put to limited use, largely because Malta was part of the Sicilian kingdom. Aragon, which controlled Malta and Sicily, had a negative interest in the island. There were plenty of good, easily supplied bases in Sicily free from the problems which Malta's lack of resources involved. The Aragonese wished to keep the islands out of the control of hostile powers and they were not vitally interested in developing them as a military base. Once the Order started to use and defend the Grand Harbour it was natural that the settlements lying in the surrounding area should become increasingly important.

When the Order came to Malta the towns then existing were miserable. Mdina, the capital, had been partially deserted at least since the middle of the fifteenth century and the Order's exploratory commission reported that the majority of the houses in the town were empty.

At the tip of one of the peninsulas which project into the Grand Harbour stood the small *Castello a Mare* and the unfortified town of Birgu. Neither Mdina nor Birgu was well suited to the needs of the Order. As a capital Mdina was impotent, for the town could not control the island from its withdrawn defensive site. Mdina had all the strategic limitations of a keep. By elimination the knights of St. John had Birgu forced upon them as their first Malta capital and, unfortunately, this was a town beside the harbours rather than a fortress dominating them. The Castello and Birgu had grown up before the invention of modern artillery and neither was sited with any consideration for the range of sixteenth-century weapons. At a very early stage the Order's military engineers pointed out that if the knights wanted a secure Malta base they would have to build a new fortress on the Sceberras peninsula. The Order was reluctant to commit itself to Malta and, by way of compromise, settled in unsuitable Birgu.

Of course, the town was quite unfitted to the Order's needs and extensive alteration and development was necessary. The Grand Master was housed in the Castello (fort St. Angelo), which was refortified and re-equipped. Within Birgu new buildings were erected to accommodate the knights, their followers and institutions. Auberges were built together with a hospital and various establishments for the armament industries. A start was made on a system of fortifications for the old town. The medieval street plan of Birgu survived this phase of rebuilding.

The pace of development within Birgu was such that in 1562 the Order was obliged to issue regulations to control building within the town. The regulations were enforced by a body known as the *officio della casa* which had the power to censor the design of any proposed building. The officio della casa was the first of a series of commissions which operated as planning control bodies and thereby shaped much of the urban growth which took place in Malta under the Order.

The regulations issued in 1562 also attempted to create a *collachio* in Birgu. At Rhodes the knights of St. John had lived within one area of the town, known as the collachio, and had been segregated from the local population. The 1562 regulations defined a collachio within Birgu and a number of restrictions were placed upon lay persons, in an effort to remove them from the area over a period of years.

Even with the redevelopment of Birgu there was insufficient housing space within the town and it seems that a small unplanned suburb, named Bormla, started to grow up beyond the walls and glacis. (A glacis was an open space left outside the walls of a fortified town on which building was not allowed in order to prevent an attacker enjoying a covered approach.) By 1565 Bormla was a well-established and thriving settlement.

In 1552 fort St. Michael was completed on the peninsula adjoining Birgu and shortly afterwards Grand Master Sengle (1553–57) gave out building lots in the area to promote the growth of a town. The settlement which grew up was called Senglea, after the founder, and during the Siege the inhabitants played an important part in the fighting.

The towns of Birgu, Senglea and Bormla (the Three Cities) were all very heavily damaged during the battles of 1565. In the case of Bormla part of the settlement was knocked down by the defenders before the conflict started, to deny the attacking force cover. What remained of the town lay in the no man's land between the opposing armies and received further damage during the fighting. After the withdrawal of the Turks a great deal of repair work was undertaken on the buildings and fortifications in the Three Cities, although the amount of reconstruction completed was naturally overshadowed by the establishment of Valletta.

The foundation stone for Valletta, the new capital city and fortress of the Order, was laid in March 1566. After much discussion and obstruction Francesco Laparelli's plans for the new works had been approved and the Sceberras peninsula adapted to the needs of the Order. The encircling cliffs were cut back, sheared and topped with walls. On the land front of the fortress great squat bastions were carved out of the solid rock and a moat excavated. It was intended that the moat should be cut down to a sufficient depth to allow the sea to wash through between Marsamxett and the Grand Harbour (plate 5a) but the work was never completed. Additionally it was intended that a sea-filled moat should be excavated around the other three sides of the city but, although work on the project appears to have been started, completion was never seriously pursued.

Sceberras had something of a hog's back form and efforts were made to modify its shape before the laying out of the street plan of Valletta. Two large excavations were initiated on the north side of Sceberras with the object of providing sites for a shipbuilding yard and a shelter pen, or *manderaggio*, for the galley squadron. For a variety of reasons these alterations to the physical geography of the peninsula were never completed. Levelling the surface of the peninsula proved too great a task in relation to the Order's resources of money and manpower, particularly as the new defences had to be completed quickly in case another Turkish force attacked the island. The failure to level the surface of the peninsula meant that the street plan had to be laid on uneven land and this gave rise to Valletta's 'cursed streets of stairs!' which caused Byron such discomfort.

For a time the excavations for the shipbuilding yard and the galley pen proceeded quickly. Indeed all building stone used in Valletta had to be cut from the manderaggio. Unfortunately, as the digging neared sea-level, a limestone of tougher quality was encountered which was unsuitable for building work. As a result the cutting of stone ceased and, because it had become clear that the costs of moving the galley squadron from its existing base at Birgu would be extremely high, the Order never completed the project. A move to Valletta would have obliged the galley squadron to operate from Marsamxett rather than the Grand Harbour and, as the former enjoys much poorer shelter, difficulties would have arisen in rough weather.

The need to complete the Valletta fortifications in the shortest possible time prevented resources being used to erect buildings within the new town for a number of years. In 1566 the rectilinear street plan was laid out but by the time Grand Master Valette died, in 1568, there were very few permanent buildings within the walls. Even when the Order moved into the new capital, in 1571, there was little accommodation available and the building up of the streets did not really begin until about this point.

When the Order undertook fortress building in Malta it usually imported European technicians to supervise the work. The building of Valletta was no exception and the city came to reflect many of the current European town-planning ideas. Valletta is a typical, if grand, example of the rectilinear fortified towns which were laid out in many parts of Europe in the sixteenth century.

Shortly before his death in 1570, from plague in Crete, Laparelli had served on the commission which drew up the regulations that governed the erection of buildings within Valletta. The regulations were published in 1569 and they carefully controlled the early development of the city.

The preamble to the regulations announced that Valletta was to be divided into two parts, one of which was to be called the collachio and occupied by the Order to the exclusion of all other persons. The inclusion of this regulation was a concession to papal pressure but enforcement was never attempted. Segregation was difficult to achieve alongside the Order's crusading activities, high living standards and the need to defend Valletta efficiently. When the knights started to erect buildings in Valletta they did so in most parts of the town without any attempt to segregate themselves from lay persons.

The omission of a collachio gave rise to a voluminous correspondence between the Vatican and Valletta but although the Order constantly promised compliance it always contrived evasion.

The remaining regulations were more specific and by and large they were adhered to. There were to be no gardens or courtyards fronting buildings, nor were projecting stairways or other works allowed. These regulations prevented any impediment of the thoroughfares and produced some uniformity within the streets. When a site was purchased building had to start within six months and the house to be occupied at the end of one year. Additionally, when a site was taken up the commissioners enforcing the regulations decided how much money was to be spent on the structure to be erected. The specified sum had to be spent within three years. This regulation could be used to ensure that building works were of a high standard and there were certain streets where sites could be acquired only if the buyer was prepared to erect a *palazzo*. The Order owned all the land within the Valletta fortifications having bought it by compulsory purchase in 1566. Building sites were sold at a fixed price by the commission and no site could be resold without its permission.

Anyone building on a corner site was obliged to ornament it and this work, together with the decoration of doorways, had to be supervised by a master mason appointed by the commissioners.

Each house was required to make connection with the sewers which were to be laid beneath the streets, and must be provided with a cistern for the storage of rainwater. The lack of water on Sceberras had caused difficulties from the day work started on Valletta and the water supply problem was not overcome until 1614 when Grand Master Alof Wignacourt (1601–22) built an aqueduct from a group of springs near Mdina down to the capital. The aqueduct would have been vulnerable in a siege and it was always necessary to keep the cisterns in good repair.

The penultimate regulation required that all building stone be cut from the manderaggio, and finally it was decreed that sites were to be allocated 'according to the resources and social position of those who will build'.

The regulations above provided the necessary powers to guide the building of an elegant city. From the start there was a strong emphasis on building at a high standard and an attempt was made to produce a unity of design within the new fortress capital.

Early in 1571 Grand Master del Monte, who had been elected to the Mastership of the Order on the death of Valette in 1568, decided that, although the auberges in Valletta were not yet complete, it was time for the convent to move into the new capital. Many knights were against the move fearing the discomfort they would suffer, but del Monte was not to be restrained. At the beginning of March it was decreed that on the eighteenth day of the month the Order would undertake a ceremonial removal from Birgu to Valletta. On the appointed day the Grand Master, accompanied by the Council of the Order and all the knights, went in procession from the palace in St. Angelo to the church of St. Lawrence on the Birgu marina. Here a solemn mass was sung and after the service had been completed all the knights, together with the people of Birgu, now called Vittoriosa to mark the victory of 1565, accompanied the Grand Master along the marina to the place where the flagship of the Order was moored. When del Monte had been escorted aboard, the knights and the citizens of Birgu boarded the galleys and any other vessels that were available. Then amidst much cheering, sounding of trumpets and firing of salvos the convoy cast off and sailed across the Grand Harbour. On reaching the opposite shore the Grand Master and his followers disembarked and mounting the steps from the small quay passed through the del Monte gate into Valletta. Singing a *Te Deum* the procession moved through the skeletal city to the church of Our Lady of the Victory, the site where five years earlier Valette had laid the foundation stone to the Order's new capital. As del Monte entered the church all the artillery in the city fired a salute.

When the celebrations had run their course del Monte retired to his new, half built, palace in the centre of Valletta. The Order was now firmly, if uncomfortably, settled in Malta.

When the Order moved into Valletta there were few completed buildings within the city but in the next few years new works shot up all over the site. The Order erected seven auberges, the Magistral palace, a treasury, a conventual church, the hospital and a bakery. At least half a dozen churches were built in the first few years and there were innumerable private building projects. The Maltese architect, Girolamo Cassar, was responsible for most of the buildings put up by the Order at the time. As a preparation for the work he had gone to Italy where he had acquired a number of Renaissance and Mannerist techniques. However, his work continued to incorporate the influence of Maltese vernacular architecture.

In 1582 a visitor to Malta recorded that the new capital was now largely built-up and there were few vacant sites remaining. By 1590 nearly 4,000 people were living within Valletta. The Maltese appear to have had very little reluctance about moving into the new town and there were several reasons for this. The need for security was undoubtedly one of the most important; the whole island knew that Birgu and Senglea had nearly succumbed in 1565. Besides, who could say that Birgu and Senglea would not be cut off and abandoned in any subsequent siege, if the Order found it necessary to concentrate upon the defence of Valletta? Then there were the social and economic pressures. Many persons made their livings in the service of the Order and found it more convenient to live close to their employers. Socially there was the desire to live in the new capital, alongside the rulers of the islands, and, more simply, genuine enthusiasm for the whole project.

The foundation and laying out of a town are only the first stages in the life history of a viable new settlement. In subsequent years its size and the range of services it performs will increase. The fabric of the town will adjust to new social and economic pressures although adjustment will probably be strongly influenced by the original framework of the settlement. Valletta is no exception and, although the city was shaped, in its broad essentials, during the latter part of the sixteenth century, a number of important structural and functional changes took place in the remainder of the Order's rule.

There were two forces of prime importance which shaped the later development of Valletta. First, there was the rapidly increasing population of the islands and here growth was strongly concentrated in the harbourside towns. Secondly, the knights took increasingly seriously their title of Sovereign Military Order and Valletta came to reflect these growing pretensions of grandeur. The city eventually became, with the suburb of Floriana, a microcosm of the great baroque, absolutist, capitals which developed in Western Europe. In the latter part of the eighteenth century an English visitor to the island, Patrick Brydone F.R.S., having seen the buildings and society of Valletta described the city as 'an epitome of all Europe'.

To the original group of public buildings the Order added a theatre, library, custom house and an administrative building for the Università of Valletta and the Three Cities. The law-courts were rebuilt and the conventual church and Magistral palace enlarged. The functions of a number of these buildings indicate the growing complexity of the state.

Many of the more sumptuous private dwellings were erected in the eighteenth century and the urban landscape came to reflect the growing attention which the Order paid to ceremony, administration and gracious living. Allied to these forces were a number of others. The increasing prosperity of the islands sustained the demand for commercial buildings and provided the means by which many lay persons were able to construct fine houses. During the seventeenth century Grand Masters were not content to rule well and munificently but also wished to endow the Order permanently in a way which would ensure its future well-being and the remembrance of their Mastership. Sixteenth-century Grand Masters like del Monte (the palace), La Cassière (the conventual church), Verdalle (Verdala palace and the fief of Marsa) and Alof de Wignacourt (the aqueduct) had been content to erect public works during their life-times and perhaps leave a goodly sum to the Order on death. Many seventeenth-century Grand Masters, including de Paule, Lascaris, Niccolo Cotoner and Carafa, besides indulging in lavish spending during their lives, set up foundations the incomes from which were to be applied, in perpetuity, to strengthening some aspect of the Religion's organization. De Paule and Lascaris both instituted foundations to provide galleys and, in the case of the latter, to ensure that sufficient money was always available to keep the island well stocked with grain. The investment work of these foundations was, as a rule, skilled and on a relatively large scale. Virtually all funds were invested in Malta and not only did this put money into the economy of the islands but the investments frequently provided the infrastructure for economic expansion: workshops, wharfs, warehouses and shops.

Grand Masters preferred to invest their capital in Malta rather than abroad because, apart from the administrative advantages, the Order was becoming increasingly embarrassed by the pressure that could be brought to bear on it by powers threatening to sequester the European estates. For instance, in 1645, the Venetians confiscated the property of the Religion within their jurisdiction as a reprisal for actions by privateers operating from Malta. The property was eventually returned but the point had been made. In the seventeenth and eighteenth centuries the French were able to apply considerable diplomatic pressure largely because so much of the Order's property was in France. The very wealth of the Order frequently attracted rapacious interest. The kings of France occasionally levied taxes on the Religion's estates, whilst the popes came to regard some of the Italian commanderies as being at the disposal of the Vatican. Above these difficulties there were an immense number of problems in administering hundreds of scattered European estates which varied in form and profitability. A resident member of the Order was responsible for each property or group of properties but many commanders were lax in paying responsions to the central treasury. There were numerous wrangles as to the proportion of the income to be retained by the holder of the estate and the amount to be sent to Malta. Some commanders avoided paying responsions altogether if it were possible and by the mid-seventeenth century abuses were widespread. Against such a background it is hardly surprising that a trend developed towards local investment. If Maltese property prices were possibly a little high in relation to yields, from the Order's peculiar point of view, there was a much higher degree of security.

A large part of the wharf and warehouse development undertaken around the Grand Harbour was financed by the foundations set up by Lascaris, Cotoner and Manoel. The *fondazione* Cotoner was big enough to redevelop a whole block in Valletta with a high yield, high density structure consisting of dwellings, warehouses and shops.

Away from the central group of streets, in which the Order dwelt and conducted its ceremonial life, one of the strongest forces shaping the development of the town was the increasing number of people coming to live within the walls and this altered, often fundamentally, the original conception of the city. Population densities became increasingly high, land which originally had been left free of buildings was taken over for housing and slums developed in the least favourable areas.

Once the Order moved into Valletta the expansion of the town was very rapid. In fact, growth seems to have got somewhat out of hand and a rather larger area than had been envisaged in the plans was built-up. The glacis which fronted fort St. Elmo was consumed; the hospital, which had been erected in an open space, was soon surrounded by streets of houses, several of the working areas left behind the fortifications were built over and even the abandoned quarry, which was to have become the Valletta shipyard, was filled with houses. In 1590 there were well over 3,000 Maltese living in the city and by 1632 nearly 9,000. The pressure continued to grow and with it a number of slum housing areas developed on land which was highly unsuitable. The old manderaggio quarry became a warren of shanty buildings inhabited by the lowest orders of society. Between the manderaggio and the shipyard slum the Ghetto valley developed into an unsavoury area. Similar slums sprouted at the back of St. John's cavalier, above the del Monte gate and between the slave prison and the hospital, to say nothing of the overcrowding that characterized existing lower-class housing.

By the middle of the seventeenth century the Order had become uncomfortably aware of the problems of urban overcrowding and in 1666 it was decreed that no more people from the countryside were to come and live within Valletta and the Three Cities. After the issue of the decree the growth of urban population slowed but did not cease. In any case the damage had been done and in 1676 the consequences were punched home when the great *peste* swept through Valletta and the Three Cities.

When the commission which drew up the building regulations for Valletta decided that sites would be allocated according to the position of the purchaser in society, it pretty clearly had in mind a town divided into a series of well-marked zones, at least as regards social structure. Certainly it was intended to produce a central group of streets which were flanked by the Order's more important buildings like the auberges, churches, treasury, palace, etc., and thus concentrate all the more important business of state and archi-tectural features in one area. Within this area there were subsidiary groupings of buildings, the most important being the placing of the Magistral palace, treasury and chancery around Palace square on Kingsway, or *strada San Giorgio*, as it was known during the time of the Order.

In the sixteenth and seventeenth centuries ideas on the zoning of urban functions were not rigid. Having excluded the lower orders of society from property ownership in the smarter streets, the governing classes were quite prepared to hire out premises to shopkeepers and tradesmen in such areas. Building styles made provision for this profit motive. Many of Valletta's finest buildings incorporated shop, warehouse or workroom space in the ground floor of the façade, and this arrangement led to the concentration of many commercial facilities in the same streets as the institutional and administrative buildings. Merchant street and Kingsway were the principal Valletta shopping streets in the seventeenth and eighteenth centuries, just as they are today. During the Order's rule, Old Bakery street (*strada Forni*), the third important street in the central group, was essentially residential and contained few shops and public buildings.

There were a number of industries in Valletta and little effort seems to have been made to segregate them. The Order's foundry (*ferraria*) stood at the head of Kingsway, just inside the main gate. The Valletta gunpowder factory (*polverista*) was housed in Merchant street, until a series of explosions led to the removal of the industry, in 1665, to a site in Floriana. The Order's great bakery was sited more discreetly, as was the mint, but by and large the small industrial establishments and workshops of numerous bakers, shoemakers, barbers, tailors, carpenters and silversmiths were scattered throughout the town. Naturally, irksome private enterprise was not allowed to disturb the peace and dignity of the Order or its members. There were, apparently, provisions for the removal of noisome trades if they disturbed the upper classes.

Throughout the seventeenth and eighteenth centuries the fabric of Valletta was constantly adjusting to the social and economic forces of the time. The knights were proud of their Order and their capital and they spent lavishly on both. As time went by, however, the form of spending underwent a marked change. It is true to say that until about the middle of the seventeenth century large-scale urban development was principally concerned with providing for the Order's primary functions as hospitaleers and crusaders. In the latter half of the seventeenth century and throughout the eighteenth century development was predominantly undertaken to provide commercial and recreation facilities and to house the administrative machinery of local government with which the Order became increasingly concerned.

In the seventeenth century fort St. Elmo was strengthened twice, great outworks were set outside the original walls to Valletta and efforts were made to complete the cutting of the sea-filled moat which had been planned for the land front. Grand Master Lascaris had every slave on the island, and many freemen, hewing out stone but in the end the task proved too much for even that Master's ruthless drive. During the sixteen-forties a second line of fortifications was built across the Sceberras peninsula, about 600 yards in front of the Valletta walls. These fortifications were known as Floriana lines after the engineer who designed the works. Fortification building was equally vigorous on the south shore of the Grand Harbour. In 1638 work was started on the Margerita lines which enclosed the town of Bormla. In the rule of Niccolo Cotoner (1663–80) the famous military engineer Antonio Maurigio Valperga was brought to Malta to design the vast Cottonera lines. The foundation stone to this project was laid in 1670 and eventually the new fortifications not only invested the Three Cities and Margerita lines but also enclosed a large shelter area, in which the inhabitants of the villages might take refuge in the event of an attack. The scheme included the construction of fort Ricasoli, named after a knight who contributed particularly generously to the cost of Cottonera lines, at the mouth of the Grand Harbour.

During the latter part of the seventeenth century St. Angelo was greatly improved after a number of new works were added to the fort on the recommendation of Don Carlos de Grunenberg, the king of Spain's military engineer in Sicily.

In the course of the seventeenth century a string of forts and look-out stations were constructed around the coasts of the islands.

During the sixteen-sixties the Order's hospital, or *sacra infermeria*, was enlarged and close by two like establishments were erected: a hospital for women and another for incurables.

Although the majority of Valletta's churches were constructed between the foundation of the city and about 1620, many were later enlarged and refurbished. Nearly every early church in Valletta was subsequently adorned with a baroque façade. The one notable exception was the conventual church of St. John which, externally, has maintained its original simple severity. The Order's principal church did, however, undergo some development. Late in the sixteenth century a sacristy was added and to balance this an oratory was later attached to the south end of the façade. Until the mid-seventeenth century the interior of St. John's had matched the exterior in austerity. Then in the rule of Niccolo Cotoner (1663–80) the Neopolitan artist, Mattia Preti, was commissioned to decorate the interior. Preti clothed the walls with elaborate sculptured work and covered the ceiling with a sumptuous series of paintings which depicted the life of John the Baptist.

Another important ecclesiastical event took place earlier in the seventeenth century. The Bishop of Malta, and his curia, moved from Birgu into a new palace in Valletta which had been started in 1622. The move is an indication that by this date Valletta was recognized as the island's foremost urban centre and was not simply regarded as a fine, disconnected setting for the Order's stately living.

During the eighteenth century, in contrast with what had gone before, development within Valletta had a much more worldly form. In 1731–2 the Manoel Theatre was erected in what is now known as Old Theatre street. Later in the same century a large library was built, the palace was richly embellished by Grand Master Pinto (1741–73) and, in the central streets, large numbers of existing houses were knocked down to make space for palatial homes. The effect of this last type of development was to emphasize further the contrast in population densities between the central area and the surrounding neighbourhoods.

As the trade of the Maltese islands expanded, an increasing floor area, within the towns lying around the Grand Harbour, was given over to warehousing. In Valletta the warehouses were concentrated on the Grand Harbour side of the town, predominantly along the marina but also within that part of the city lying at not too great a distance from the waterfront.

Prior to the mid-seventeenth century the waterfronts of Valletta were little utilized and there was only one small quay beneath the del Monte gate (plate 5a), which served as a mooring place for boats plying between Valletta and the Three Cities. The del Monte quay stood in a man-made amphitheatre in the rock which had been cut in order to set the fortifications back from the seashore. The set-back of the fortifications was apparently not initiated to provide space for a quay. Plate 5a shows that it was originally intended to ring the walls of Valletta with a sea-filled moat. Such an obstacle was more effective than the sea alone for it prevented war machines being sailed alongside the city walls. There are signs that the quarrying of the moat was started in various sections around Valletta but nowhere was it completed. Thus in the early seventeenth century the walls of Valletta were fronted by a stone apron which proved suitable for the development of mercantile facilities. Seemingly it was Grand Master Lascaris (1636–57) who first began to exploit these possibilities at Valletta. He built a line of warehouses from the del Monte gate to a spur of rock which projected from the landfront of the city to the edge of the Grand Harbour. When this development was complete Lascaris drove a tunnel, *la mina del Lascaris*, through the spur to the foreshore beyond where he built a wharf, which still bears his name, and another row of warehouses. Niccolo Cotoner (1663–80) extended the wharf and erected more warehouses. The succeeding Grand Master Gregorio Carafa (1680–90), who was also building up a portfolio of investments for his *fondazione*, built more warehouses as did Ramon Perellos (1697–1720). Manoel de Vilhena (1722–36) extended the line of warehouses along the Grand Harbour flank of Floriana and Grand Master Pinto (1741–73) added an extensive group of sumptuous storehouses. This completed a zone of warehousing which extended from the del Monte gate to Floriana lines. A large custom house was erected just outside la mina del Lascaris to serve the area.

The Marsamxett harbour, in spite of its disadvantages, was not entirely neglected by shipping. Manoel island, as it came to be known, was used for most of the Order's rule as a quarantine station by people and goods coming from suspect lands. As trade increased so did the number of quarantine warehouses on the island. A small number of warehouses were also erected on the Marsamxett marina of Valletta.

The rapid growth of Valletta, in the latter part of the sixteenth century, had an adverse effect on the surrounding towns. For a while Birgu, Senglea and Bormla were depressed but, with the revival of the island's economy and the increase in population, all the urban areas around the harbours began to grow speedily. From the time the Order failed to complete the Valletta manderaggio and arsenal, allowing the galley squadron to remain based upon Galley Creek (between Senglea and Birgu), the functions of the capital were split between the two sides of the Grand Harbour

A late sixteenth or early seventeenth century plan of Valletta. The
street plan and the built-up area are accurately shown. However, a
number of features which were part of the original plan, and never
completed, are also included. The sea-filled moat, the galley pen and
the shipbuilding yard are all well shown. Notice the generous spaces
left behind the fortifications and around St. Elmo

A later (seventeenth century) plan of Valletta which illustrates the
way in which the city spread into the extremities of the fortified area.
The zones of later growth are usually overcrowded slums

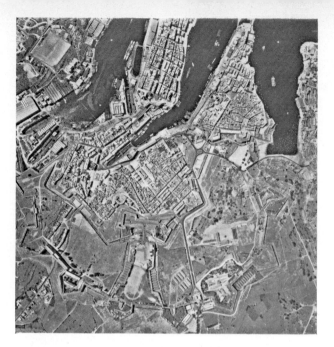

Part of the Three Cities—Birgu, Senglea and
Bormla—from the air. The fortifications enclosing
Bormla are Margerita lines which in turn are
invested by Cottonera lines

Valletta and its supporting fortresses—St. Angelo,
Ricasoli, Manoel and Tigne—from the air

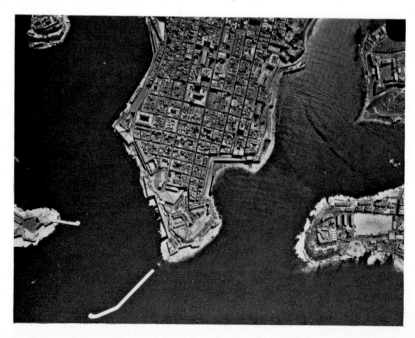

and the two areas developed in a complementary manner. However, in the late sixteenth century, this development must have been far from obvious. When, in 1571, the Order moved the convent from Birgu to Valletta, the Three Cities must have suffered by the removal of the auberges and several service industries. The Order's hospital moved to Valletta in 1575. With the upsurge in economic activity in the early seventeenth century the population of the Three Cities began to increase rapidly. Growth was not equally shared between the towns, as an examination of table II will show, and Senglea was the first town to start increasing its population rapidly. The town had been laid out in the fifteen-fifties in an area which had once been a park and pleasure ground for Claude de la Sengle. The first buildings erected in the town were menial but during the seventeenth and eighteenth centuries many inhabitants of Senglea made sizeable fortunes from piracy or in trade and the town was extensively redeveloped as booty was transferred into real estate. Senglea benefited in other ways from the increased maritime activity. By the beginning of the eighteenth century Galley Creek, and its shores, was no longer large enough to contain all the shipping activity associated with the Three Cities and Grand Master Vilhena's foundation built a mole along the Senglea shore of French Creek. Subsequently, on the apron of rock separating the sea and the fortifications, warehouses and ship-repairing facilities were developed. Eventually parts of the town became grossly overcrowded and slums grew up on the periphery of the original gridiron street plan. Even today, after the extensive rebuilding occasioned by the bomb damage of World War II, many unsavoury dwellings remain within Senglea.

By the beginning of the eighteenth century Senglea had become the most economically buoyant of the Three Cities. Aesthetically, too, it was in great part more attractive than Bormla or Birgu. During the first half of the eighteenth century Birgu could be described as being 'not very well built' and the settlement epitomized all the problems of urban congestion which afflicted parts of most Maltese towns and town-villages, during the Order's rule. Birgu's entwined medieval pattern of streets had survived the intense period of redevelopment which followed the arrival of the knights and now caused considerable difficulties.

The numbers of people living in Birgu apparently grew very

Table II

ESTIMATES OF POPULATION IN THE MALTESE TOWNS LYING
CLOSE TO THE GRAND HARBOUR

	Valletta	*Birgu*	*Senglea*	*Bormla*	*Floriana*
1575	—	—	—	1,200	—
1590*	3,397[a]	2,568	1,602	1,288	—
1614	10,744[b]	2,551	2,709	1,396	—
1617	11,185[b]	2,811	3,019	1,543	—
1632	8,601[a]	3,063	4,049	2,778	—
1658	9,219[a]	3,192	3,730	2,662	—
1670	—	3,000	3,750	2,877	—
1674	12,144	—	—	—	—
1680†	8,038[a]	1,900	3,138	2,400	—
c.1741	—	3,600	—	—	—
c.1772	20,780	3,766	5,539	7,112	—
1829	21,631	4,566	5,102	9,429	5,666
1861	25,162	6,414	6,887	11,120	7,871

* Famine and plague in early 1590's
† Plague in 1676.
[a] Maltese only—excluding the Order, slaves, men on galleys.
[b] Maltese, slaves, men on galleys, excluding members of the Order.

slowly at the end of the sixteenth century and in the early years of the seventeenth. However, as the Galley Creek area expanded its maritime activities the town attracted more inhabitants. Population growth in the whole area started to become excessive and in 1634 the Order commanded that no more private houses were to be built in Senglea and Birgu. Now whilst this measure might prevent new building it did not stop the overcrowding and subdivision of existing properties. Subdivision was commonplace and in 1645 even the old Birgu hospital of the Order was partially divided to provide living accommodation.

In 1666 the Order again attempted to check increasing congestion

in the harbour area by prohibiting any further movement of population into Valletta and the Three Cities. These measures were only
partially effective and in any case the population already living in
the towns continued to increase in number.

The problems posed to defence, trade and public health by
overcrowding are obvious and it is not surprising that in the 1676
plague excessively overpopulated Birgu suffered a higher death
rate than any other settlement in the islands.

On Birgu's Galley Creek water front stood most of the buildings
associated with the construction, repair, provisioning and administration of the Order's navy. Economically these activities were
the mainspring of life in the town.

It seems probable that Bormla, or Cospicua as it is also known,
grew up in the early years of the Order's rule, after the outward
growth of Birgu had been curtailed by the construction of a landward line of fortifications. The existence of the suburb could clearly
be an embarrassment to the defenders of Birgu and Senglea and as
we have seen Bormla was badly used both before and during the
Siege. The settlement seems to have recovered fairly quickly from
its razing for by 1575 there were estimated to be 1,200 people living
in the town. The Order's military engineers continued to be worried
by the presence of Bormla outside the walls until the sixteen-forties
when the building of Margerita lines solved the problem.

Part of Bormla impinged upon the head of Galley Creek and
shipping activity, in various forms, was one of the main sources of
livelihood to the inhabitants of the town.

Shortly before the Order forbade the building of private houses in
Birgu and Senglea, a more constructive attempt was made to ease
overcrowding in the Grand Harbour area. In 1626 Grand Master
de Paule decreed that a new town should be laid out to the west of
the Three Cities. Although inducements were offered, in an attempt
to attract inhabitants, there seems to have been little eagerness on
the part of the Maltese to take up building lots on the new rectilinear street plan, probably because Paola, as the town came to be
known, was a little too far from the existing centres and unfortified.
Paola is now a large and prosperous settlement but its growth has
taken place very largely in the nineteenth and twentieth centuries.

A more successful attempt was made by the Order to lay out a
new suburb in the eighteenth century. In 1634 Paolo Floriani came

to Malta and after examining the Valletta defences suggested the building of a new line of fortifications across the neck of the Sceberras peninsula. Work on the project, Floriana lines, had not progressed far when it was discontinued in favour of the Margerita lines around the Three Cities. It was decided to strengthen the existing landfront of Valletta, demolish that part of Floriana lines which had been built and sell off the stone. However, in 1640 the Floriana scheme was reappraised and the project restarted. It was mentioned that Valletta might be able to expand into the area between the two lines of fortifications, although nothing was done to further the idea at this stage. Pressure on housing within Valletta continued to increase and in 1672 the Council of the Order decided that a suburb should be built within the Floriana lines. Shortly after this date the island was visited by plague; thousands died and by the time the epidemic had been controlled there was no need to build a new town to cope with the problems of urban overcrowding. By the second decade of the eighteenth century the population had revived and with it proposals for the building of new suburbs. In 1717 a planned extension to Bormla was laid out and in 1724 the Floriana suburb proposal was examined by a commission from the following viewpoints: were new houses needed? Would the project be profitable to the Order and the Maltese? Would the efficiency of the fortifications be impaired? The commissioners were quickly satisfied on the first two points and after 'mature consideration' it was felt that with proper precautions the effectiveness of the fortifications would not be prejudiced.

The building of Floriana probably started very soon after the commission reported in 1724. By 1728 the gridiron street plan had been laid out and at least one block of the suburb built-up. The parish church was started in 1733 and by 1766 20 blocks of the new town had been completed. Some indication of the numbers living in the suburb in the latter year is given by the fact that 400 Floriana men were on the roll of the militia at the time.

Floriana still displays many features which are associated with the eighteenth-century urban landscape. The entrance to the town is spanned by a great triumphal archway, the thoroughfares are wide and the existence of barracks, monuments and gardens all help to give Floriana a general air of spaciousness.

The north shore of the Marsamxett underwent a relative neglect during the Order's rule. The buildings on the quarantine island were all that existed in the area until the eighteenth century was well advanced. Previously proposals had been made for fortifying the island but it was not until the rule of Manoel de Vilhena (1722–36) that a fort was erected. Work started in September 1723 and was completed in 1732. While fort Manoel was being built proposals were made for a fortress on Dragutt point, at the mouth of Marsamxett opposite St. Elmo. The scheme included a plan for another new town to be incorporated within the defences. The building of the works was delayed until the end of the eighteenth century and then only fort Tigne was built.

In contrast to the rapid and extensive urban growth which took place around the harbours the older, inland, urban centres of Malta and Gozo failed to prosper. The rise of Valletta, the growing control of Malta's affairs by the Order and the establishment of another Università based on the harbour towns, all helped to strip Mdina of status, population and function. Neglect bred neglect and as the old city's fortifications crumbled many Maltese moved to safer quarters. Late in the sixteenth century the Order attempted to halt decline and depopulation by exempting all who lived in Mdina from military service. The concession brought little response, the outflow continued and early in the seventeenth century several monasteries moved out of Mdina down to Birgu. One such establishment justified its move by describing Mdina as an uninhabited ruin.

In 1644, when a Turkish attack was feared, the old capital was still indefensible, and the Order decided to abandon it and bring the garrison and artillery down to the harbour towns. At this point the Maltese asserted themselves; they insisted that their old capital be maintained and after an affray, involving some of the Order's soldiers and a number of Maltese women, Mdina was eventually repaired.

Malta felt the outer ripples of the 1693 earthquake which caused such extensive damage in Sicily. Hundreds of people were killed in Syracuse and Catania, whilst the town of Noto was destroyed. Damage to the towns around the Grand Harbour was limited, the cupola of the church of the Aragonese langue fell in, the Gesu church in Merchant street was badly damaged and overall the effects of the quake were confined to individual buildings. However, at Mdina a large section of the town was severely shaken. The

Norman cathedral, which must have been very similar to the great
Sicilian Norman churches, collapsed and many buildings in the
town were damaged or destroyed. All this was a heavy blow to a
town which was not in good health. A new cathedral was built
between 1697 and 1702 by the Maltese architect Lorenzo Gafà,
who was also responsible for the Gozo cathedral and many other
fine churches in the islands. In general a great part of Mdina seems
to have remained unrepaired and early in the eighteenth century
talk of abandoning the town was again in vogue. The old capital
survived until the mastership of Manoel de Vilhena (1722–36) who
took a great deal of interest in the affairs of the Maltese and the
Università of Mdina. During Manoel's reign a large section of
the town was rebuilt. Between 1723 and 1728 the fortifications were
remodelled and repaired, a number of small alterations were made
to the street plan of the town and a whole series of new public
buildings were erected. The Bishop constructed a new Mdina
residence and a seminary while the Grand Master had Vilhena
palace built. At the same time the *Banca Giuratale* and the *Corte
Capitanale* were erected for the civil administration. Although this
phase of rebuilding revitalized the town to a degree and restored
some functions to it, Mdina never regained its former importance.
To this day the town remains a quiet, charming backwater containing a number of interesting medieval houses and some fine
eighteenth-century buildings.

During the Order's rule the fate of the Gozo Castello was similar
to that of Mdina and it too went into decline. In fact large numbers
of medieval hill towns in the Mediterranean area have gone into
decline since the end of the sixteenth century.

To the knights the defence of Gozo was a perpetual problem and
it was never completely overcome. Repeatedly, during the early
years of the Order's rule, Gozo was raided and numbers of its
inhabitants were carried off into slavery. Apart from the great raid
of 1551, when a large proportion of the population was removed,
there were attacks in 1560, 1563, 1572, 1574, 1582, 1598 and 1599.

The medieval capital of Gozo—the Castello—had a site which
in many respects was similar to that of Mdina. Like Mdina the
Castello had its Rabat and was the seat of a Università. Under the
Order Mdina and the Gozo Castello followed a similar history:
both went into decline, lost status and were to a large extent

abandoned. Unlike Mdina the Castello has remained almost deserted to this day and the walls contain only Lorenzo Gafà's fine cathedral, a few public buildings and the tumble-down ruins of former ages.

During the rule of the Order the idea of abandoning the Gozo Castello was frequently canvassed along with proposals to build a coastal fortress for the northern island. In 1643 Marsalforn was selected as the site for the new fortress town but the Order failed to find the money, or rather there were more pressing needs elsewhere. The proposal was still current when Valperga visited the islands to design Cottonera lines. Valperga was transported to Gozo and after reviewing the possibility of a new fortress at Malsalforn rejected the idea.

In the seventeen-twenties, Chevalier de Tigne designed a small fortified town to stand on Ras-el-Tafal overlooking the channel separating Malta and Gozo. Again the scheme was held up by lack of money and it was not until 1749 that the project was financed. In that year Chevalier Chambrai offered to meet the cost of the works as designed by de Tigne. Work was started very quickly but the fortifications were not completed until 1761. The fortifications having been built, a rectilinear street plan was laid out and building sites were put on sale to the public. There was, however, no great rush for places in the proposed town, probably because the need to live at inconvenient, if secure, sites had by this time disappeared. Fort Chambray failed to become a town.

The knights of St. John were not exclusively concerned with towns and town houses and a number of imposing country villas were erected during their rule. In the Mastership of Valette (1557–68) a small hunting lodge was built in what is now known as the Boschetto or Buskett valley. Over the next two hundred years many knights were attracted to this valley where ornamental gardens, woodlands and game enclosures were laid out. The possibilities for hunting on Malta were extremely limited but the island was a fine centre for hawking. The Maltese archipelago is a staging point for bird migrants moving between Europe and Africa so that, no matter how successful the predators, stocks were always plentiful in spring and autumn. Besides this Malta had long been recognized as a centre of falcon breeding and the annual fee which the Order agreed to pay to the Spanish crown was one Maltese falcon.

It was to take advantage of these opportunities that Grand Master Valette built a hunting lodge and stables at the Boschetto. These simple facilities sufficed until the rule of Verdalle (1581–95) when Girolamo Cassar was instructed to design a fortified summer palace, Verdala palace, close to the hunting lodge. When de Paule (1623–36) gained the mastership of the Order he expressed displeasure with Verdala palace as a country residence. Apparently de Paule was a highly sociable man and the prospect of living, for even part of the year, seven miles and well over an hour's carriage journey from Valletta did not please him. The Grand Master already owned a small country house near Attard and he determined to enlarge this to become the palace of San Antonio. The new residence was surrounded by intricate formal gardens, large groves of citrus fruits were planted and fish were imported from Sicily to stock the ponds. The palace subsequently became the residence of the British Governor and now houses the Governor General of the Maltese islands.

The knights not only built powerful defences around the towns, they also erected a comprehensive chain of forts and look-out stations in the outlying parts of the islands.

When the Order came to Malta the coasts were almost entirely unprotected by defence works. Before the Siege the knights did take steps to erect fortifications at Marsaxlokk and some towers were erected at the most convenient crossing points on the Great Fault. The fault was a fine natural defence and at first the Order did not attempt to defend those parts of Malta lying to the north. After the Siege, although the need for coastal defences was felt, all the available funds were absorbed by the fortifications being erected around the Grand Harbour. The coasts were guarded by small, organized groups of Maltese who gave the alarm as best they could, but there were no prepared positions which might have been used to repel an attacking force. It was not until the seventeenth century that the systematic erection of coastal works started. With money left for the purpose by Grand Master Martin Garzes (1595–1601) a small fort was built at Mgarr in Gozo to guard the landing place and the Comino channel. In the rule of the next Grand Master, Alof de Wignacourt, a series of substantial coastal forts were built at some of the larger bays around the islands. Fort St. Lucian was erected at Marsaxlokk and almost immediately proved its worth, for when a large Turkish force attempted to make a landing at the bay, in July 1614, it was driven off. The invaders then made another attempt at landing, this time at Marsascala. Marsascala was unprotected and the Turks got ashore to ravage the countryside around Zeitun. After this episode the fort of St. Thomas was built at Marsascala. Another fort was erected on the south shore of the Grand Harbour on the site which is now occupied by fort Ricasoli. Coastal fortresses were also built at St. Paul's bay, Comino and probably at Marsalforn. The small island of Comino had been deserted since the arrival of the Order but once the fort was built a small number of farmers settled there, cleared the scrubland and created patches of arable land.

After the period of war scare, associated with the Turkish attack of 1614, the islands became more settled but during the sixteen-forties there were again intense, and well founded, fears of a Turkish attack. It was at this period that the landfront of Valletta was strengthened and the Floriana and Margerita lines were started. Grand Master Lascaris also decided to make the coastal defences more complete by building a series of fortified look-out towers. This policy was continued by Lascaris's successor, Grand Master de Redin (1657–60), who built 13 towers at his own expense. In all, during the period from Wignacourt to de Redin, nearly 30 coastal towers and fortresses were built. Today they are still a characteristic sight in the coastal landscapes of the islands.

During the great war scare of the sixteen-seventies, consequent upon Venice's loss of Crete, defence preparations in Malta took the form of Cottonera lines and no new coastal fortifications were erected.

About 1720 the Turks were again expected; 'not a siege, but an incursion and devastation of the countryside', as a document of the day put it. The coastal defences were carefully inspected and it was decided that they could be further strengthened by the building of redoubts and batteries. A large-scale building programme was initiated and today the remains of many of these fortifications are still visible, even if they have not stood up well to sea spray and vegetation. The coastal fortresses and look-out towers tend to be in relatively good repair for many were incorporated in the British defence system for the islands and were thus preserved.

After the redoubt-building spree some quaint methods of coastal defence were developed. In 1723 a project for throwing large stones into the sea, at Gozo's more accessible bays, was started with the hope that if ships tried to disembark troops the bottoms would be torn from them.

During the seventeen-forties the *fogazza* was introduced into the islands. This device consisted of a carefully shaped pit cut into solid rock close to a landing place. The excavation was filled with powder and all kinds of missiles. When ignited the fogazza showered the coast and, it was hoped, any attacking force with lethal debris.

The defence of that part of Malta lying to the north and west of the Great Fault was always a problem. The area was very accessible from the sea; the coasts were difficult to defend, as each bay outflanks the last and communications within the area were poor. The standard solution to these problems has been to abandon the northern parts and concentrate the defences upon the Great Fault. Along the crest of the fault are the relics of several sets of defensive works. There are the remains of a Roman tower, the look-out towers built by the Order in the sixteenth century and Victoria lines, which were originally built by the British in the nineteenth century but greatly improved at later dates. The British project was anticipated by the Order for, about the year 1730, a discontinuous line of defences was erected along the crest of the fault.

Industry, Trade and Finance

When the Order of St. John came to Malta the economic outlook was bleak. The islands did not produce enough food to feed the inhabitants, and corsairs were causing direct damage to the economy and disrupting the sea routes to Sicily. The population of the islands was declining in numbers and the economy was decaying. The arrival of the Order altered the situation and the knights contributed to the economic development of Malta in a number of ways. First, the Order eventually created a relative security and the islands became a safer place for investment. The Order secured, for instance, the base of the *corso* and piracy once again made a contribution to the economy. Secondly, the large sums the Order spent in Malta provided work and frequently capital for the Maltese. Thirdly, the Order set up industries which were essential to the running of its military machine. These industries gave rise to supporting manufacturing activities so that the Order's war machine impinged upon the whole economy of the islands.

From the Order's viewpoint, Malta had many disadvantages as a base. Food supplies were insufficient, there were no raw materials on which to base the essential industries of war, the population was too small to provide an adequate army and the local market was so limited that it was difficult to warrant the production of many goods. All these things—food, soldiers, raw materials and many manufactured goods—had to be imported. Due to these shortcomings Malta never became, completely, the base of the Order. The galleys were partially based upon Sicily where the Order had a supply base to which the squadron normally went before starting a mission.

In view of the lack of resources any economic development of the islands required large imports and large amounts of foreign currency. Now the Order had just these external sources of wealth which the islands needed. The Religion's European properties were investments which each year yielded a percentage of their earnings to the Order's central treasury in Malta. It was very largely these sources, and the private fortunes of individual knights, which paid for the food imports, the new towns, fortifications and fleet of the Order. Malta, although basically poor in resources, was drawing a form of subsidy from Western Europe in return for the use of the island's strategic position and fine harbours.

In the first decades of their rule the knights were aloof and disinterested overlords but as time went by they became increasingly involved in the regulation of the local economy. There was more than one reason for this. First, being so heavily dependent upon imports could be politically and strategically embarrassing. Secondly, during the seventeenth and eighteenth centuries European powers became increasingly concerned with the detailed administration and control of their states, and as the Order normally reflected European practice it started to attempt to regulate the Maltese economy.

It is not possible to dispute that a great economic expansion took place in the islands between 1530 and 1798. Nor is it easy to claim that the knights were not responsible for the advance. The Order was by far the largest and most important economic unit in the islands and it follows that the economic health of the archipelago was regulated, to a very large degree, by the financial structure of the Religion. The Order's treasury records have not yet been fully investigated but certain general underlying trends are well known.

In 1554 the income of the Order was some 63,000 *scudi* per annum, a *scudo* being valued at approximately one shilling and eightpence. Expenditure in the same year was running at about 111,000 scudi, due to the very high defence budget. The Order would be able to cover the deficit from other sources. In the rule of La Cassière (1572–81) revenue had risen to 124,000 scudi per annum and although expenditure had increased as well to 120,000 scudi it was no longer exceeding income.

In 1583 the Order imposed a general tax upon its property with the result that income was increased to 151,734 scudi per annum. A breakdown of expenditure for the same year reveals how the Order was spending its income. Nearly 5,000 scudi p.a. was being consumed by St. John's conventual church, over 11,000 scudi p.a. was spent at the hospital, over 8,000 scudi p.a. on the palace, 3,431 scudi p.a. on charity, 40,200 scudi p.a. on feeding the Order and 97,535 scudi p.a. was spent on the galleys. In addition expenses were incurred outside Malta on the maintenance of ambassadors, receivers and other officials resident overseas. Clearly much of the Order's expenditure in Malta found its way to other lands. A large part of the money spent on food went to Sicily, although even this provided the Maltese shipping industry with trading opportunities. Similarly much of the expenditure on the galleys was consumed abroad; by the supply base at Augusta, purchases of food, timber and ships from foreign yards. The drain of funds out of the islands was in good measure caused by the lack of local resources.

The Order's revenue continued to increase in the seventeenth and eighteenth centuries. In the Mastership of de Paule (1623–36) the average yearly income was 269,116 scudi. Expenditure was very slightly higher. The major sources of income at this time were prizes taken by the galleys (12,000 scudi), property of deceased knights (33,000 scudi), entry fees to the Order (25,000 scudi), ransom and sale of slaves (7,000 scudi) and responsions from the European estates (213,000 scudi). Expenditure was, proportionately, pretty much the same as that undertaken in the late sixteenth century.

By 1780 income had reached 1,364,174 scudi per annum, with

expenditure running at a marginally lower level. The sources of income had remained very much the same although by this time the foundations set up in the seventeenth and eighteenth centuries were making a significant contribution to revenue. The pattern of expenditure had, however, altered slightly. The maintenance of ambassadors and receivers abroad had become the third largest item of expenditure after the galley squadron and the fortifications. Although spending on representatives abroad reflected the Order's pretensions of grandeur it also served a number of useful functions. Increased trade involved the need for more diplomatic representation and the receivers were an essential link in the financial structure of the Order and Malta. The receivers were responsible for transferring responsions to Malta and for making payments for goods purchased by the Order outside the islands. The receivers also functioned as the branches of a bank, the head office of which was the treasury in Malta. Knights and merchants could pay funds into the treasury at Valletta and withdraw them from one of the receivers against a bill of exchange.

The late eighteenth-century accounts show very little sign of the wasteful expenditure which is often attributed to the Order during the last years in Malta. What is more, in spite of the Order's political decline, its financial position was healthy, until the French commanderies were confiscated in 1792. The act of sequestration robbed the Order of one-sixth of its income.

There has been a deal of discussion concerning the amount of money that the Order put into the Maltese economy. Ransijat, who was in charge of the Order's finances towards the end of the eighteenth century, estimated the figure at £164,000 per annum at the time he held office. W. H. Thornton, one of the early British financial administrators, estimated the figure to be £185,000 per annum during the late eighteenth century. Thornton's analysis was more detailed and reliable than that of Ransijat. £185,000 per annum is probably a fair estimate of normal, official, local expenditure in the late eighteenth century. However, the calculations neglect extraordinary spending by the Order and its members. Exceptional expenditure could be financed from the Order's huge assets against which loans might be raised. Special demands could be, and were, laid on the European estates and, as long as there was a real threat from the Turks, donations were squeezed from European powers, whilst knights were never loath to help the Order financially in times of need. Such sources supported the many years of budget deficit in the mid-sixteenth century. The building of Valletta could never have been begun on the Order's income, but with contributions from Western European powers, the mortgaging of property, gifts in kind, loans of labourers, and the financial assistance given by knights, the work was successfully undertaken. The building of Valletta probably refinanced the Maltese economy which had been wrecked by the Siege of 1565.

A great part of the Order's building programme was not financed out of income but from the donations of members. It is unnecessary to list the many impressive structures built with money provided by knights but the works of Alof Wignacourt can be quoted as an outstanding example. Wignacourt was Grand Master from 1601 to 1622 during which time he spent handsomely. Alof built an aqueduct to give Valletta an adequate water supply at a personal cost of 30,000 scudi. He had fountains erected in the streets of the city, he constructed a number of coastal fortresses and had a *gran galeone* built in Amsterdam. In all, including the money he left on death, Wignacourt contributed nearly half a million scudi to the Order.

On top of private donations, all through the period of the Order's rule, knights were living at a high standard, in fine houses built from their own resources and staffed by Maltese servants. Lavish private spending of the type indulged in by members of the Order makes nonsense of attempts to estimate how much money the knights put into the Maltese economy. There is another point. By the end of the eighteenth century the spending of the Order did not look so vast in relation to the total annual turn over of the islands. However, this was not the case in the sixteenth century when the Order primed and refinanced the whole economy of the islands. Even at the end of the eighteenth century the Order remained the largest single unit in the economy of the islands and without the Religion's foreign investments Malta could not have balanced its overseas payments. Louis de Boisgelin in his *Ancient and Modern Malta*, published in 1805, could conclude with truth that 'Malta had become too populous to be supported by its commerce, unassisted by the riches of the Order.'

During the Order's rule the number and size of manufacturing concerns on the islands expanded enormously. The lack of the industries of war was a severe handicap to the Order during its first years in Malta and at an early stage certain manufacturing processes were introduced. The greatest expansion took place in the industries linked with the two spheres of military operations in which the Order was principally interested: the galley squadron and the development of defensive works around the Grand Harbour.

When the Order came to Malta, although there may well have been limited facilities for repairing vessels, the island did not possess a shipbuilding yard and it was not until 1540, at the earliest, that an arsenal was erected at Birgu. The delay in setting up this essential war industry was no doubt a reflection of the Order's ambivalent attitude towards Malta but once established the yard became increasingly important. Some galleys were built in the Malta yard and some were ordered from European suppliers. In the early years, when the Malta yard was small, much of the shipbuilding seems to have been put out to European yards and even some of the routine repair work was carried out at Messina. In time the shipbuilding facilities at Malta were expanded. The yard at Birgu was enlarged about 1600 and again in 1636. An auxiliary yard was also developed in the Grand Harbour outfall of the ditch fronting Valletta. Even with the combined production of the Valletta and Birgu yards the Order could not build all its own vessels during the seventeenth century. Work still had to be given to yards at Marseilles, Naples, Genoa, Pisa, Messina, Toulon, Barcelona, Civita Vecchia and Amsterdam. Normally only the hull was constructed abroad and then towed to Malta for fitting out. The need to get so much work done abroad was due partly to lack of capacity and partly to a group of problems affecting shipbuilding in Malta. There seems to have been some difficulty in obtaining suitable supplies of timber. Although the Order had plenty of wood on its European estates, not only was transport expensive but timber was regarded as a strategic commodity and permission to cut and export was not always forthcoming.

As in several other sectors of the armaments industry, the Order was unable to afford shipyards which not only supplied everyday needs but also had enough spare capacity to produce the additional war materials needed in a crisis. When a large-scale conflict threatened, the Order went cap in hand round the Western European powers in search of military supplies. This, of course, could be embarrassing and on occasions, when European nations were committed to their own wars, armaments were unobtainable.

Not only was the Birgu yard unable to produce and repair galleys quickly enough but it was for many years too small to build the largest type of galley which the Order used. It was not until the end of the seventeenth century that the Birgu yard was enlarged and this defect remedied. The Valletta yard was burnt down in 1685.

The number of galleys in service varied. From three in 1530 it rose to six in 1562 but in 1590 the number was down to four. Throughout the seventeenth and eighteenth centuries fluctuations in squadron size were brought about by the prospects of peace and war and the Order's financial position. In 1674 there were seven galleys, in 1686 eight, although this was later reduced again to seven due to the expense involved. During the latter part of the seventeenth century a galley was regarded as having an active life of seven years. A new vessel cost on average 7,400 scudi, allowing for the sale of the one taken out of service. Most of the money for new vessels came from the seven galley foundations.

At the beginning of the eighteenth century the Order revised its naval policy. Instead of a striking force consisting only of galleys (oar-propelled vessels with auxiliary sails) three round-bottomed sailing ships were introduced. The number of galleys was progressively reduced and by the middle of the century the navy consisted of four sailing vessels, four galleys and three frigates. From this point the size of the navy declined. By 1765 there was not enough work to keep the shipyard fully employed and it was ordered to be closed during periods of inactivity. However, during the reorganization undertaken by Grand Master de Rohan a new yard was started in 1776 and completed in 1783.

When the Order was expelled from Malta in 1798 the navy consisted of four galleys, one sailing vessel, three frigates and a number of smaller vessels. Such a force was technically and numerically insignificant in terms of the great European navies of the day.

In addition to the Order-controlled shipbuilding yards there was also an important private sector of the industry. During the course of the seventeenth and eighteenth centuries, with the increasing importance of trade and privateering, a strong demand for vessels developed from traders and corsairs. Many vessels were of course

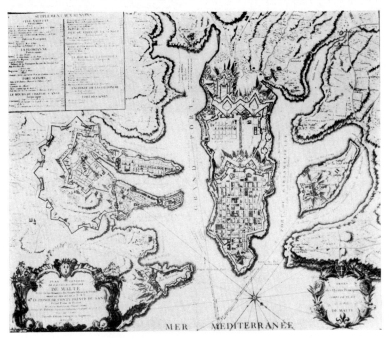

The Grand Harbour area in the mid-eighteenth century. By this time all the Order's major town and fortification building projects had been completed and only Fort Tigne, on Dragutt point, had yet to be built

The Grand Harbour area in the late eighteenth century

The village of Birkirkara from the air. Notice the
complex, entwined street plan of the older part
of the village which contrasts with the more
spacious layout of the later developments

A sixteenth century depiction of a phase in the
Siege of Malta

purchased outside the islands but significant numbers were built locally and ships of up to twenty-two guns were produced.

The Order's shipbuilding facilities were maintained until the end of its rule in Malta and in 1800 Captain Ball R.N. could describe the island as possessing 'a small but complete shipyard'. The existence of the yard proved to be extremely important for it gave the Royal Navy an initial repair base in Malta. Gradually the facilities were extended under British rule until, in the mid-twentieth century, over 12,000 people were employed in the yard.

The extensions to the urban areas and fortifications around the harbours were obviously a powerful stimulant to the building industry. The general increase in population led to the expansion of many rural settlements and here, too, the demand for housing was strong.

The numbers of men employed on the fortifications fluctuated with the likelihood of a Turkish attack but, overall, tended to expand.

The quarry industry remained largely in private hands and was split into numerous small production units. Around Naxxar and Luqa the Globigerina limestone was particularly suitable for use as a building stone and was widely employed over the whole island under the name of *franka*. The demand for harder stone, Coralline limestone or *zonqor*, was much less. Zonqor was used in the construction of poorer dwellings where franka was difficult or costly to obtain but it was in greatest demand for special purposes, for instance the production of millstones. Towards the end of the seventeenth century zonqor was discovered to be highly resistant to seaspray, in contrast to franka, and the rock began to be used extensively for facing fortifications which stood close to the sea.

The Order spent vast sums on the fortifications and public buildings. However, the effects of the spending were lessened, first, by the use of slave labour, and secondly, by the occasional pressing of the Maltese into working without payment for short periods. This last expedient was resorted to during the building of Valletta, and in 1644 and 1670. Sometimes all slaves in private employ were ordered onto the works. Although action of this type lessened employment opportunities the local economy still benefited as large numbers of craftsmen had to be employed on a permanent basis. Even when a fortification project had been completed stonemasons were required to service the works.

The amount of capital put into the fortifications was great: 70,000 scudi was put up initially to finance Margerita lines, whilst even in 1670, 30 years after they were started, 8,000 scudi a month was being spent on Floriana lines. Not all the money was found by the treasury of the Order. Some came as gifts from knights and infrequently special taxes were laid on the Maltese, as in 1574, 1644 and 1673. In the last of these years 100,000 scudi was raised for Cottonera lines. Normally the Maltese were unburdened by taxes except for import dues which were not excessive.

The Order occasionally created work on the fortifications to relieve unemployment. On Gozo, in 1742, after two bad harvests, work was deliberately started on some defences to mitigate hardship.

Not only did the building industry undergo considerable expansion during the rule of the Order but the range of its materials and techniques was enlarged. Prior to 1530 Maltese architecture was traditional with styles largely determined by the characteristics of the Globigerina limestone as a building stone. Some of the more ambitious buildings did exhibit the stylistic influence of Sicily. During the period of the Order, Renaissance, Mannerist and Baroque styles were introduced and the whole range of possibilities for the building industry was enlarged. Again in 1530 local quarries produced little but franka. However, by the end of the Order's rule several other types of rock were being produced and it is clear that there had been a growing sophistication in the use and exploitation of local stones. A small part of the island's stone production was exported and, of course, it was necessary to import a wide range of rocks for ornamental work.

In the country areas the manufacture of textiles became increasingly important during the Order's rule. The production of cotton had been undertaken in Malta during the Middle Ages, and although the industry had suffered decline in the fifteenth and sixteenth centuries it revived in the seventeenth century and attained a significant place in the economy in the eighteenth century.

Broadly the industry was organized on the following lines. Cotton was grown by small farmers and spun by their wives and offspring. A middleman then purchased the spun cotton and exported it, probably through other agents, or placed it with a different family which specialized in weaving. There was also some production of garments.

In country districts the processing of cotton meant the difference between poverty and a reasonable standard of life. The cotton industry depended to a very large extent on exports, and when these broke down the countryside quickly suffered hardship. This happened, for example, in 1743 when disease at Messina and in Reggio interrupted commerce and those 'who lived by working cotton and other merchandise were reduced to extreme poverty'.

In the eighteenth century cotton became so important, by virtue of the number of people employed in the industry and the foreign exchange earned, that it was necessary to regulate the activity carefully to protect the national interest. In 1733 attempts were made to control the quality of spun cotton after a complaint from Marseilles aroused fears that local cotton might be discredited. Regulations already existed but these were being circumvented and were tightened up. A little later, in 1735, regulations were promulgated on the way in which cotton was to be bound up for export. A few years later even more stringent quality control was introduced. Before export cotton was inspected by an official, it had to be packed in a standard bale, bales had to be made up of cotton of the same quality, wet or spoiled goods were confiscated, the quantity and quality of all cotton had to be declared and there were severe penalties for deception or error. These standards were enforced in official warehouses through which all cotton exports passed. It was only by such control that the problems of so many small manufacturers producing different quantities and qualities could be overcome.

On the other hand the industry was very carefully protected and local growers were frequently shielded by regulations controlling the import of cotton. The degree of protection varied; in some years all cotton imports were forbidden, but this occasionally created problems as local growers did not always produce enough to supply other sectors of the industry. Shortages led to speculation and the Order would then be forced to regulate prices. In the end efforts were made to ascertain how much local growers were producing each year in order to have the necessary information for the regulation of imports. Because it was the basis of the spinning and weaving industries the export of raw cotton was prohibited.

It is difficult in the absence of adequate figures to discern when and how quickly cotton production was expanding. The relative amounts of legislation probably indicate that the industry was considerably more important in the eighteenth century than in the seventeenth. The few surviving customs records show that the industry was still expanding in the late eighteenth century, although by this time it was becoming increasingly difficult to sell in certain European markets. In addition to spun cotton some cloth and articles of clothing were exported.

An early British administrator, Captain Ball, estimated the value of cotton exports, in the late eighteenth century, at half a million pounds sterling annually. Oranges were judged to be second in importance and worth £2,000 a year. Ball's estimate of the value of cotton exports is almost certainly too high but his figure does indicate the overwhelming importance of cotton in Malta's export trade.

The cotton industry was already in decline by the time the British gained control of the islands. In 1798 the French market was closed to Maltese cotton and in 1800 so was the Spanish. In 1801 the British declared Valletta a free port and this helped to introduce competition from American and Egyptian cotton. The arrival of English traders no doubt resulted in the introduction of cotton goods produced in Britain.

Apart from cotton several other textiles were produced and there were a number of ancillary trades. Certain dyes were made locally and there must have been a large number of craftsmen involved in the manufacture of spinning and weaving machinery.

The production of woollen yarns had been practised on the islands at least since the Middle Ages and it continued under the Order. The Maltese woollen industry never approached the size of the cotton industry, probably because the latter enjoyed superior locational advantages. In fact, up to 1696, there was not a good supply of locally produced woollen cloth and the galley crews were clothed with material imported from Sicily. The 1693 earthquake destroyed the plant of the Sicilian manufacturers and in 1696 two men approached the Order and suggested that they start production in Malta. The project appears to have been a success.

In the rule of Grand Master Pinto (1741–73) a scheme was suggested for the widespread introduction of silk production. Sicily had long been famous for its silk and there were hopes that the performance could be emulated in Malta. Mulberry trees were planted at various places in the islands and silk of reasonable quality was produced. However some unexplained problems arose and the industry died out within a few years.

Hemp and linen were also produced locally whilst sail making was a craft of some importance.

The manufacture of salt had been a royal monopoly within the Sicilian kingdom since Norman times and the right was inherited by the Order when it was granted Malta in fief.

Salt making was practised in medieval Malta and there seems to have been a large group of salt pans at Mellieha bay. These works were apparently disused by the time the knights arrived but a new group of pans was erected at Salina bay and enlarged several times during the Order's rule. The Salina works fell into disuse in 1798 but were repaired by the British administration and proved very profitable in the early nineteenth century. The Salina pans are still in operation today.

Besides the relatively large works at Salina smaller pans were constructed at various points around the coasts. A relatively large group of salines was constructed at Marsalforn, on Gozo, in the eighteenth century. The Order, whilst retaining a monopoly over salt making in the islands, leased parts of the salines which it owned and granted concessions for the development of new works. Part of the local production was exported but clearly the number of persons employed in salt making was small and the occupation was, in any case, seasonal for the evaporation pans could only be operated during the hot, rainless months of summer.

The Order also enjoyed a monopoly right to erect windmills. Occasionally a windmill belonging to the Order was sold or a citizen given the right to erect a mill but, by and large, the Order owned most of the windmills in the islands. A list compiled early in the nineteenth century shows that there were 26 government-owned windmills. Very few of these mills existed when the knights came to Malta and during their rule the *molino a vento* became one of the most characteristic sights in the local landscape.

In 1674 the *fondazione Cotoner* started work on windmills at Bormla, Zebbug, Floriana (two), Naxxar and Zurrieq. At a later date the same foundation built windmills in Lia, Zeitun, Gudia and a second one at Zebbug. In 1724 the *fondazione Manoel* built windmills at Rabat, Gharghur, Zurrieq, Birkirkara and one between

Ghaxaq and Zeitun. During the next couple of years another mill was completed on Malta and three on Gozo. The mills were normally let on short leases to Maltese millers.

Windmills were usually sited slightly away from the village they served, on open ground, to make the most efficient use of the wind. Not all milling on the islands was done by windmills. The bakeries of the Order in Valletta and the auberges used mills driven by donkeys.

There were many other small industries in the islands, usually dominated by one-man establishments. These included numerous goldsmiths, silversmiths, bakers, tailors, bootmakers, carpenters, smiths and similar craftsmen. It appears that each village had its own baker, miller and smith whilst in Valletta were found the more specialized craftsmen: gold and silver smiths and a large number of tailors.

Besides the craftsmen there were many traders involved in the economy as middlemen and in more dubious capacities. We have already mentioned the organizers of the cotton industry and there were similar men forming a marketing organization which served, and probably financed, Maltese agriculture.

The markets of Valletta were full of traders and pedlars. The latter were regarded as a nuisance and frequently efforts were made to rid the streets of them but without lasting success.

The fishing industry was of limited importance in the Order's time. Few villages were located close to the sea and the number of men engaged in the occupation was small.

In 1530 the external trade of the islands was inconsiderable, consisting of exports of cotton and cumin and the import of foodstuffs. The arrival of the Order quickly caused some increase in trade, for it was a relatively large organization, going through a phase of capital investment as Malta was developed to meet the military requirements of the time. A great deal of material was imported from Europe. Nor was it long before exports started to grow. As the Order's galleys began to take their toll batches of slaves were shipped out of the islands and there are references to Moslems being allowed to return home to collect their ransoms. Trade contacts with the North African coasts were developed, or renewed, and there are records of safe-conducts being issued to merchants, some of them Moslem, wishing to come from Barbary to Malta for purposes of trade. But the trade pattern of the islands was dominated by the great volume of imports which came from Western Europe. A wide variety of goods was shipped into Malta; often items of a very simple nature were imported which indicates how lacking in productive capacity the local economy was. For instance it seems to have been necessary to import nails and maca- roni. The greatest part of the imports appear to have come via Sicilian ports.

There were several disadvantages to Malta as a trading centre during the Order's rule. Possibly the greatest was the presence of corsairs, particularly from the Barbary coast, in the surrounding waters. At times their influence was so great that they were able to disrupt Malta's food supplies. For example, late in the seventeenth century, corsairs became such a menace in the channel between Malta and Sicily that special armed protection boats were employed to patrol the area. In 1695 a tartan and a brigantine were armed for the purpose and later in the same year another tartan was allo- cated to the task. Still the shipping losses mounted and food supplies became scarce. In 1696 the galley squadron had to be sent to Sicily to bring supplies and in the summer of the following year only five galleys went to join the Venetian navy on a campaign; the remaining two were retained for patrol purposes. This had the necessary effect and by the end of the summer the channel was clear. The episode was extreme but it illustrates a problem which was liable to afflict Maltese trade until the beginning of the nineteenth century when British naval power purged the area of its 'Oriental riff raff'.

Another disadvantage which traders based upon Malta suffered was the island's dependence upon Sicily for many essential supplies. This dependence was often exploited for political ends. A disruption of trade was threatened in the rule of Lascaris (1636–57) when France and Spain were at war and the latter feared that the French- dominated Order might give France help. In 1712 the ports of Sicily were closed to Maltese vessels for a while and in 1753 the ports and shores of the kingdom of the Two Sicilies were forbidden to all shipping flying the Maltese flag. The results of the latter action were soon felt, not only amongst the merchants, but also in the country districts which lost a large outlet for cotton exports. This disruption was not wholly a bad thing, for trading contacts were made with North Africa. Grain had already been obtained from Tunis in the previous century and there are, in general, rather more references to trade between Malta and Moslem states than would be anticipated considering the crusading nature of the Order. Malta and Tunis came close to political links as well, for in 1735 the Bey of Tunis, having tired of the harm done to commerce by corsairs using Sfax and Tunis, sought the Religion's help in exterminating them.

Another major problem was plague and whilst this was a disadvantage common to all ports, Malta, by its proximity to North Africa and the Near East, was well placed to pick up the *peste* regularly. An outbreak of plague at any port led to its closing. Thus an outbreak developing in Malta, or a Sicilian port, had disastrous effects on Maltese trade. In Malta disease was usually supported by famine as food supplies were cut off and this happened in the great plagues of 1591 and 1676. After the former outbreak trade was not freed until the beginning of 1594.

In the course of the seventeenth century, although the pattern of Malta's trade continued to be dominated by the import of foodstuffs and the export of cotton, a number of traders were beginning to use the island as a base. Nevertheless entrepôt trade was discouraged by the fact that goods could not be off-loaded from one ship to another, or stored ashore, without the intervention of the customs authorities and dues were high. In the eighteenth century the pattern changed. Malta began to develop as a convenient 'half-way house for Levantine trade' and many merchants bonded goods on the island or caused their ships to undergo quarantine there. In 1733 dues on transferred cargoes were reduced from 6⅓ per cent to 1 per cent and a similar rate was applied to bonded goods. There were even efforts to create a free port.

Apart from the entrepôt and transit trade Malta also exported her own products. Although the list of home-produced goods is extensive and includes cotton, lichen, oranges, lemons, pomegranates, seeds, stone and ashes of kalimagnum, the amounts involved, apart from cotton, were small.

In sum it is true to say that Malta's trade in the second half of the eighteenth century, although making a useful contribution to the local economy, was small compared with that which was to develop in the early years of the nineteenth century. Many of the vessels which called at the island did so simply because it was a convenient and relatively cheap port in which to undergo quarantine. Much of the entrepôt and transit trade was probably stimulated by the quarantine regulations. If vessels were stopping at Malta anyway, then the island was a sensible point at which to off-load goods from Europe or the Levant for bonding or to be placed on fresh vessels. Once the need for quarantine passed then so did the need to stop at Malta.

Malta-based shipping was involved in another rather peculiar form of *trading*. Piracy had long been associated with the islands but during the seventeenth century it became a highly organized and profitable activity. Many vessels were engaged not only in trade but, when the opportunity offered, in privateering as well.

In some respects crusading can be seen as a licence to pillage and the Order had not been in Malta long before knights, motivated by the desire for personal gain, began to fit out vessels at their own expense to go on cruises for booty amongst Moslem shipping. Grand Master Verdalle (1581–95) equipped his own galleys for this purpose and accumulated a sizeable fortune from the enterprise. Private individuals were soon emulating the lead of Malta's noble rulers and the industry grew at a fast pace. By the beginning of the seventeenth century quite a large number of vessels were using Malta as a base for corsair work and in 1608 the Order issued extensive regulations to control the activity.

Although modified from time to time the rules governing the *corso* were simple. Boats were licensed in Malta to attack Moslem shipping. This gave the vessels status in international law and prevented the crews being arraigned on charges of piracy. Additionally the Order provided basal facilities at Malta. In return all booty was supposed to be sold at Malta and the Order took 10 per cent of the resulting money.

Now, whilst this arrangement was well suited to the needs of the time when the Moslems were expansionist and feared, it was clearly not going to survive long once normal trading relations were established with Middle Eastern countries. When the great powers, and particularly France, became involved commercially with Turkey they brought pressure to bear on the Order to curtail privateering. The corso declined very quickly in the eighteenth century. However, during the seventeenth century piracy was an important industry to the islands. Three classes of people were involved as ship owners. Firstly members of the Order, secondly Maltese and thirdly foreigners using Malta as a convenient base for operations. The last group included Frenchmen, Corsicans, Tuscans and other nationalities. The majority of owners employed largely Maltese crews, although adventurers from many lands found their way onto the boats. Malta, although an important centre of privateering, was by no means the only port engaged in this form of seafaring. Apart from the well-known Moslem centres of the industry in North Africa, several Sicilian ports and particularly Messina were involved in the activity as were a number of other Italian ports like Naples and Leghorn. Privateers who were normally based on Italian ports would occasionally use Malta if conditions were favourable.

The autobiography of Alonso de Contreras, a pirate captain who operated from Malta, has come down to us and it throws an interesting light on the type of life corsairs enjoyed. Alonso was born at Madrid, in 1582, of impoverished but apparently noble parents. After an early life of fighting and brawling he reached Malta from Naples where he was wanted in connection with robbery and murder. He was, in fact, quite typical of a class of noble, impecunious opportunists who found their way into Malta and the Order. The painter Caravaggio made his hunted way to Malta via a series of brawls in Italy at about the same time. Although we have only his word for it, Alonso appears to have been a leader and warrior of some ability and he was soon making a name for himself as a pirate captain. Alonso records several action-packed voyages from Malta in search of loot and the retelling of the tale associated with one such journey will indicate the risks which corsairs underwent and the gains they stood to achieve. Having sailed from Malta, Alonso and his crew came upon a small island in the Levant where a Greek brigantine was sheltering. Suspecting that the vessel was carrying Turkish passengers Alonso tortured the entire crew, and after having prepared to kill the son of one Greek gained the admission that the vessel was transporting three Turks, who were now hidden ashore. The Turks proved to be a rich prize, for not only were they carrying valuable goods but one of them was a man of considerable means and therefore worthy of a high ransom. Negotiations on this last matter were quickly commenced and a price of 3,000 gold sequins was agreed. The money was to be collected close to Athens where the Turk lived. On reaching this area it was discovered that the Turk was a man of importance, for the local governor personally conducted arrangements for his release and even guaranteed Alonso a safe-conduct. While the ransom money was being raised, feasting and sports were organized on the shore, and when a local Moslem galley commander arrived with his powerful vessel he too joined in the festivities. All of which seems to indicate that ransoming was a quite normal affair, in which no particularly hard feelings were held and indeed business was conducted on both sides with a degree of panache. In the end the Turks paid up the agreed ransom money and gave Alonso a present as well, to which he responded.

The episode having been satisfactorily concluded, Alonso sailed next to an island inhabited by Christians but controlled by the Turks. Here a corsair out from Messina had come ashore, kidnapped the local priest and was demanding ransom money. Attacks of this type were not uncommon and Maltese corsairs occasionally raided Christian communities, particularly if they were isolated and poorly defended. Alonso quickly disposed of the Messina captain, returned the priest to his flock and after being suitably rewarded sailed off to his next adventure, which again involved removing Turks from a small Greek vessel.

After this, Alonso stopped at another island to share out the booty amongst his crew and was very nearly captured by two Moslem war vessels. It was only by a ruse that the privateer escaped although his ship suffered some damage. The expedition then returned to Malta where the rich spoils were dissipated on riotous living. Alonso spent most of his share on satisfying the demands of an avaricious wench whom he was keeping and for whom he was building a house.

During the greater part of the seventeenth century the Malta corso flourished and around the middle of the century there were something like thirty pirate vessels based upon the islands. But already restraints were beginning to be felt. In 1647 the Order was forced to forbid captains to go within 10 miles of the Palestinian coast and in 1697 the distance was increased to 50 miles.

In the early part of the eighteenth century the legal problems surrounding the corso became increasingly complex. French ships trading in the Levant were immune from attack, even if they were carrying Turkish goods. Soon Turks were acquiring French passports and gaining similar protection whilst Greeks, as Christians, exploited their position to the benefit of Turkish trade and themselves. By 1720 the *corso* was in rapid decline and although vessels based on Malta continued to work the North African coast their numbers were few.

Malta was for a long time one of the biggest slave markets in Europe. Both the *corso* and the galley squadron procured large numbers of captives in the course of their activities. The Order used slaves, together with convicts and *buonavoglia* (men who sold themselves as oarsmen), to row the galleys, to work on the fortifications and to act as servants. It has been estimated that there were about 2,000 slaves in Malta for most of the eighteenth century. To forestall rebellion all slaves, whether belonging to the Order or in private employ, were required to sleep in special prisons each evening. There were slave prisons in Valletta and the Three Cities.

Over and above their own needs for labourers the Order had slaves whom it was prepared to sell to other powers, and there were also a number of private-enterprise slave traders on the islands. Between 1662 and 1684 the English held Tangier and in 1672 they purchased from private traders a number of slaves at Malta for use on the galleys based at Tangier.

Agriculture

The urban population of Malta grew very rapidly during the Order's rule and a large number of new industries were introduced. However, although the islands became less dependent upon agriculture, farming remained Malta's principal industry in terms of numbers employed.

The origins of Maltese agriculture are obscure and it is not until the end of the thirteenth century that we begin to get a reasonable knowledge of the principal crops grown. By this time local agriculture had progressed far beyond subsistence level and was producing a number of products for export. The agricultural system depended principally on the production of three crops; grains, cotton and cumin. Now this crop structure is not typically Mediterranean and two staple crops of the region, vines and olives, were only of minor importance at the time. Yet we know that olives were once widely cultivated on the islands. Roman villas which have been excavated are normally equipped with olive presses and oil storage vats. A more important piece of evidence is provided by the island's place-names. Two of Malta's oldest villages, Zeitun and Zebbug, have names which literally mean olive and derivatives of these words turn up all over the islands. For example, at Birzebbuga (well of the olive), Ghajn Zejtuna (spring of the olive); and Gozo, too, has a village called Zebbug. Interesting though the information may be it is not of much use to us unless we can determine the date of origin of the place-names. It is reasonable to argue that the vast majority of Maltese place-names, in their present form, must date from some time after the Arab conquest because the Maltese language dates from that period. Some place-names, of course, would simply be translated from the pre-conquest form into Arabic but it seems highly unlikely that names of transitory phenomena, like crops, would be transliterated if the objects to which they referred did not still exist.

Assuming this argument to be true and accepting that there must have been a considerable number of olive trees in Malta, for at least part of the Arab period, the next question is: when did olive production decline? Here again it is impossible to give a precise answer but there are a few clues. It appears that the olive was not an important crop in Malta at the close of the thirteenth century. We know from an Italian trade manual, Pegolotti's *La Practica della Mercatura*, written in the first part of the fourteenth century, that southern Italy, Sicily and Malta formed an important cotton growing and exporting region at that time. Cotton was almost certainly grown in Malta during the Arab domination and although some may have been exported the quantity must have been very small, as the tempo of trade in the central Mediterranean was relatively low until the end of the eleventh century. With the rise of the Italian trading cities, during the eleventh and twelfth centuries, there was a quickening of mercantile activity. As demand rose it is possible that a change of land-use took place and a greater area was given over to cotton growing at the expense of the olive.

There is, of course, a great deal of supposition in the theory, although land-use changes of this type were to be expected on the islands. With a high density of population the Maltese needed to increase the intensity of land-use. The slow-maturing olive was a subsistence crop. Cotton not only gave work to farmers but required relatively complicated processing and valuable foreign exchange could be earned by exporting the fibre.

The decline of viticulture followed a slightly different course. Although subject to the same pressures as the olive, vines were still an important crop in Malta and Gozo in the first decades of the fifteenth century. During the large-scale raid from North Africa in 1429 much damage was done to farmland and many vineyards seem to have been ruined. Although the cultivation of vines never ceased completely the area given over to the crop was greatly curtailed. In the Order's time there was some replanting of vineyards but on a very limited scale and the islands lacked a wine-producing industry of any size until the nineteenth century.

The war which started in 1429 lasted for many years and did great damage to local agriculture. After the raid there were several years of almost total sterility and during the unsettled times that followed there was probably a tendency to abandon land in exposed and remote areas. In itself abandonment is not disastrous but in the Maltese setting, where so much land has been built-up by man, once fields are left untended they soon disintegrate. The retaining walls which hold the soil in place on hillsides require constant repair, for once they fall the soil is quickly washed away.

Damage to trees and shrubs, in 1429 and the succeeding years, tended to simplify the crop structure of the islands. Warlike conditions hampered trade with Sicily and it became increasingly difficult to export produce. As a result local agriculture probably tended to become more concerned with subsistence crops and less committed to production for export. Cotton suffered because it was a crop which depended to an important degree on overseas sales. There is no evidence to suggest that Maltese agriculture had fully recovered from the events of the fifteenth century by the time the Order of St. John of Jerusalem took possession of the islands in 1530.

In the years between the arrival of the knights and the Siege local agriculture was probably stimulated by the demands of the Order and its followers. However, any good that may have been done was quickly wiped out by the Turks during the summer of 1565. The Turkish army arrived in May, before much of the harvest had been gathered, and a great deal of produce was lost. Most of the islands' livestock was driven within the fortified positions to feed the defenders or was captured by the Turks. The Turkish army pillaged large areas of Malta and damage to buildings and equipment was heavy. There is no doubt that the life of the countryside was completely disrupted by the war and the loss of equipment, stock and seed prevented the land being properly worked for a number of years. Two years after the Siege 'the major part of the island remained uncultivated.' In 1569 a member of the Order wrote: 'this island of ours by its nature sterile has become more so after the coming of the Turkish armada.' The harvest for that year was very poor and the grain gathered in June had all been consumed by the beginning of September.

In the years immediately after the Siege the fortifications were repaired and expanded, and just as the Maltese formed the body of the defence force they constituted a large part of the labour force as well. Many peasants were required to work on the defences of Valletta rather than on the land. In the long term this probably helped the rehabilitation of agriculture by allowing peasants to earn enough money to re-equip their small farms. In the short term food production was curtailed.

Maltese agriculture reached a nadir in 1565. By this time large areas of land had been abandoned, or were under-utilized, and production was limited to the simplest crops, for which there was an immediate demand. Viticulture had suffered during the fifteenth century and what trees and shrubs remained had been torn up by the Turks to make gun platforms and fortifications. The land-use patterns on Malta were dominated by grains and stock. During the remainder of the Order's rule agriculture was rehabilitated and a number of new developments took place.

In the years after the Siege, as land was gradually brought back into cultivation, the size of the grain harvest increased. However, by the late fifteen-eighties, the process was complete although the population of the islands went on growing rapidly. One of Malta's great problems, throughout the rule of the Order, was getting sufficient grain to feed the inhabitants. Certainly since the thirteenth century, when documentary evidence first becomes available, the islands had not grown enough grain to satisfy local needs. The deficiency was largely made good by imports from Sicily, where Malta enjoyed the right to extract grain duty free. The right dates at least from the end of the thirteenth century and probably has its origins in the rule of Frederick II.

When the Order was granted the Maltese islands in 1530 the Sicilian authorities claimed that the islands were no longer part of the kingdom of Sicily and, therefore, not entitled to duty-free grain. The knights appealed to Charles V who ruled in their favour and subsequently, in 1532, increased the size of the grain rights to meet the needs of the Order. The scope and size of the duty-free food entitlements were gradually increased during the sixteenth century for both the Order and the Maltese. Convenient though the arrangements were they carried a number of disadvantages. By them Malta was made more dependent upon Sicily, the entitlements did not meet fully the islands' needs and Sicily, as a grain producer, became unreliable in the second half of the sixteenth century. In 1550 there was a famine in Malta and as it apparently proved impossible to get grain from Sicily many Maltese died. In 1562 there was a very bad harvest in Sicily and the Maltese islands again suffered scarcity. Poor harvests were experienced in Sicily in 1576 and 1577 and the irregular pattern of grain production continued for the remainder of the century. In all but the worst years the islands were provided with the greatest part of their needs. However, in 1591, there was a major crop failure in Sicily and many deaths from hunger in that island and Malta. During the remainder of the century grain shipments to Malta became irregular and the islands frequently failed to get their full duty-free allowance. In the seventeenth century Sicily often had to import grain and the cheap grain privileges, which the Maltese and the Order had so carefully negotiated, were worthless in many years, for there was simply no corn available for export.

Apart from Sicily the Maltese islands also acquired grain from other sources. Some came from Sicily through the normal, dutiable export channels. The European estates of the Order, at least in the the early years of the Religion's residence in Malta, supplied various foodstuffs including grain. Sardinia, Naples and other regions in southern Italy were sources which were occasionally exploited. At times grain was even imported from Tunis. The galleys of the Order spent a great deal of time hunting grain boats, not only along the coasts of North Africa, but also around the shores of Sicily. In the latter case payment was normally made.

By the end of the sixteenth century the Order and the Maltese were faced with a battery of economic problems: the population of the islands was growing rapidly, local food production was insufficient and the external sources of grain were unreliable. Consciously and unconsciously the Order and the Maltese adapted agriculture on the islands to alleviate the problems.

Agricultural development during the seventeenth and eighteenth centuries was not marked by the introduction of large numbers of new crops but rather by a steady modification of existing crop patterns brought about by economic, social and strategic pressures. From the beginning of the seventeenth century until the end of the Order's rule cotton became more and more important and there was a large increase in the acreage occupied by the crop. Cotton had to be grown on the better quality land and increased acreage was achieved principally at the expense of wheat. However, overall, the size of the grain harvest did not decrease although its quality altered. The production of barley and *mischiato*, a hardy mixed grain, was stepped up considerably on land of poorer quality. Barley and mischiato were consumed by the lower orders of society and were used as a feed for stock. In normal years the islands produced sufficient barley and mischiato for local needs but were chronically short of wheat. Much of the barley crop was pulled green and used to feed cattle.

The principal stock feed was cotton seed and thus the cotton plant occupied a central place in rural life. The crop was grown on a high proportion of the better quality land, the seed was fed to cattle, the fibre was spun by the peasantry and spun cotton was the principal export crop of the islands.

A number of other crops were significant. Malta had been famous for the production of cumin for many centuries prior to the coming of the Order and indeed the island of Comino takes its name from the plant. Cumin seed was used not only medicinally but also as a spice and considerable quantities were exported.

The Maltese islands enjoyed something of a reputation for the high quality of the citrus fruits grown there. The area occupied by the crop was small and made to appear more so by the fact that citrus groves were normally planted behind high walls to protect the trees from the wind. The distribution of the crop was highly localized for it is demanding in its requirements for irrigation water.

The growing of flax and hemp was of minor importance. Tobacco was introduced around the beginning of the eighteenth century. At first entry was opposed by the Order for it was feared that the plant would foul the air, but later cultivation was allowed. In the second half of the eighteenth century it was proposed to introduce a silk industry into the islands and, perforce, mulberry trees. A number of plantations were established but the industry subsequently failed.

The islands' most important source of meat was cattle, many of which were imported from Sicily for fattening. The principal source of milk was the large herds of goats which were maintained in most villages. Goats were grazed on small areas of uncultivated land and on fields which had been cropped. Flocks of sheep were kept on some of the waste land in northern Malta. The islands also supported large numbers of horses and pigs. There was very little good pasture land available as most areas were cultivated, and what grazing there was tended to be rough.

For centuries the Maltese have built-up fields on the barren limestone hillsides found in the islands. There is evidence of work of this type being undertaken in Roman and Arab times. During the seventeenth and eighteenth centuries attempts were made to construct new land in many parts of the islands. Fields built by man are normally vulnerable and when abandoned or neglected tend to disintegrate rapidly. Land on Marfa ridge, the northernmost area of Malta, was almost certainly cultivated during part of the Middle Ages but by the time the Order arrived the area was largely bare rock. In the seventeenth and eighteenth centuries efforts were made to rehabilitate such barren areas, in order to increase local food production. Private landowners, the Church, the Order, the Università of Mdina and the Università of Valletta and the Three Cities all encouraged the improvement of rocky land to enable it to be used for agriculture.

The Order was the prime mover and in this matter it was motivated by the desire not only to increase food production but also to provide a livelihood of some type for poorer peasants. Although the islands were generally prosperous during the rule of the Order, the population grew so quickly at times that it was not possible to provide work for all. In the first half of the seventeenth century, when population growth was most rapid, there were usually a significant number of unemployed on the fringe of a prosperous society. The Order owned large areas of rocky land and grants were made to peasants in the hope that they would eventually bring the land into cultivation. The Università of Mdina and the Università of Valletta and the Three Cities made similar grants from the land they held and on occasions also acted as development agents on land which the Order made available. Sometimes grants were outright but more normally the peasant got the land on a long-term, or perpetual, lease. Under a leasing system the land-owner could insist that the land was brought into cultivation or invoke forfeiture clauses in the event of the peasant failing to do so. A special long-term, emphyteutical, lease was employed. The lease gave security of tenure to the lessee at a nominal rental. The lessee was obliged to make the land cultivable and at the conclusion of the lease, usually 99 years or three generations, the land and all the improvements reverted to the owner. Tenure of land on a perpetual lease was only given up if the rent fell two or three years in arrears or if the development clauses were broken.

In the seventeenth and eighteenth centuries considerable areas of poor quality land were leased to peasants on this basis and brought into cultivation by a laborious process. The hard surface of the rock was chipped away and a bed of crushed limestone laid down to form the foundation of the projected field. Then soil was carefully collected from nooks and crannies in the surrounding rocks and spread over the chippings until a sufficient depth of earth for culti-vation had been accumulated. The field was enclosed by dry stone retaining walls. Many farmers, of course, found the task beyond them. Some lacked the capital to sustain their families during the development phase, others attempted to create farmland in areas underlain by the toughest limestones and found the difficulties too great. Others gave up the land when alternative opportunities for employment came along and there seems to have been a fairly constant migration from the countryside to the harbourside towns. The new land was at best marginal in quality and would normally produce little but barley and the poorer grains. In years of low rainfall the crops were especially liable to fail on marginal land and many farmers were ruined by such occurrences. Nevertheless, in spite of these problems, much new land was created and frequently the same poor, rocky area would be tackled by a succession of peasants until one eventually succeeded in bringing land into cultivation. At its height field building became something of an embarrassment to the Order for soil was being scraped up all over the islands by sedulous peasants and even the fortifications were being eroded by their efforts.

At the seaward end of most of the valleys finding an outlet on the east coast of Malta there were, at the beginning of the seventeenth century, small patches of marshland. The largest areas were found at Mellieha bay, St. Paul's bay, Salina bay and at the innermost recess of the Grand Harbour at Marsa. Attempts were made to drain and reclaim most of these areas for agriculture. The work was rarely entirely successful because the sea tended to flood the low-lying land during storms and sour the earth. The largest area of marshland was at Marsa and here an elaborate scheme was drawn up, in the middle of the seventeenth century, to build a sea wall across part of the Grand Harbour and reclaim all the land lying behind. The plan was never completed but some drainage canals were dug in the Marsa and part of the land was reclaimed and brought into cultivation. Small-scale draining schemes were attempted at Marsaxlokk, Mellieha, St. Paul's and Salina. Except for the first none were wholly successful, and to this day the land behind the foreshore at Mellieha bay floods in winter whilst at St. Paul's and Salina the earth is too sour to be cultivated.

When the Order of St. John was granted Malta it automatically acquired the crown lands within the islands. At the time of Frederick II these had been extensive but subsequent overlords had disposed of many of the constituent fiefs. In the later part of the sixteenth century the Order did buy a small amount of rural property but it was not until the first half of the seventeenth century that the knights began to organize their local land resources. In 1643 the Council of the Order heard that there were a number of fiefs in the islands, given to the Order in 1530, from which rents had never been collected. After a discussion it was decided to survey the lands and make efforts to develop them.

Many of the foundations set up by Grand Masters also had sizeable holdings of rural property and spent capital on developing the land. In fact many of the investments in agricultural land turned out to be non-profitmaking or low-yielding ventures and it was in the urban and harbour areas that the handsome returns were gathered. But the Order was always aware of the need to increase local food production and frequently invested capital in the rural economy, in an attempt to achieve this aim.

Not all parts of the islands were characterized by a similar type of agricultural system. The variations in geology, soil types and the settlement pattern made it highly likely that differing areas would be utilized in different ways and at varying intensities. Remote, underpopulated, northern Malta was unintensively utilized at the beginning of the seventeenth century. The intensity of land-use within the area increased considerably during the Order's rule but the limestone ridges, in spite of attempts to create fields on them, were principally used for rough grazing. By contrast the intervening, soil-filled depressions frequently possessed convenient sources of water where intensively worked irrigated gardens, or *gnien*, were developed. Land in central and southern Malta, around the old established villages, was usually intensively utilized and few areas were left idle.

Gozo was much less densely populated than Malta and throughout the rule of the Order Gozitans were able to export agricultural produce to the larger island. Even at the end of the eighteenth century, when the population of Gozo had increased considerably, five or six boatloads of provisions were shipped to Valletta each day by Gozitan farmers. The principal goods were fruit, vegetables and large quantities of sheep, goats, pigs, cattle and poultry.

7

The Order in Decline and Defeat

As we have seen, by the sixteenth century the Order had run into trouble as a result of nationalistic trends in Europe. The Religion no longer simply represented Christendom, it was now composed of members drawn from a congeries of nation states. The attitude of these states to the Order, to each other and to the Turks was to become a continual source of friction. On the one hand Spain, spurred by the threat to her possessions in southern Italy and North Africa, together with the *morisco* problem at home, was prepared to conduct a Holy War against the Turks. At the other extreme, Venice, when she could, sought an accommodation with the *porte* for commercial reasons, and France enjoyed alliances with Turkey in the hope of territorial gain. For the Order, challenging the Turk was no longer a simple business of fight and kill, win or die, for the struggle was continually overshadowed by diplomatic pressures and offended European interests.

By the end of the fifteenth century the Venetians were entering into commercial treaties with the Turks. In 1535 France 'concluded a valid and secure peace' and a trade treaty with the 'common enemy'. The agreement was renewed in 1581, 1597, 1604, 1673 and 1740. In 1553 the Englishman, Anthony Jenkinson, was granted trading privileges in the Ottoman Empire similar to those enjoyed by France and Venice. In 1580 the arrangement became a commercial treaty between England and the Turks. The French and the English were even prepared to form military alliances with the Ottomans against Spain. In the early fifteen-eighties, as the rivalry between England and Spain was coming to a head, English envoys were highly active in Constantinople. There was even a persistent rumour that the English intended to capture Malta.

Although, in the sixteenth and seventeenth centuries, some European powers were prepared to flirt with the Moslems for commercial gain, or to preserve their positions in relation to other western countries, the Turk was still feared and regarded as a potential enemy of Christendom in general. In this context the Order had a useful part to play. However, as time went by, the Ottoman empire became less and less able to challenge western powers. The role of a crusading organization was bound to become decreasingly important, particularly as the notion of a Holy War on ideological grounds came to have little attraction.

In 1565 the Turks were checked at Malta and in 1571 heavily defeated in the sea battle at Lepanto. During the seventeenth century, although the Ottomans attacked Malta once, besieged Crete in 1645 and took that island in 1669 they were not really a great sea force any longer. On land it was rather different and the Turkish armies continued to make gains in south-eastern Europe. But in 1683 the Turks were routed from their siege of Vienna and in the following years suffered a series of heavy defeats in the region. In 1699 the treaty of Karlowitz was signed and the Turks gave up their claims to many areas in south-eastern Europe.

Karlowitz was really the end of the Ottoman threat, as far as the larger Western European powers were concerned, even if the Order and the smaller Italian states were worried until the mid-point of the eighteenth century was passed. The Turks made an insignificant attack on Gozo in 1708, and appeared off the islands in 1722; and a large-scale raid was feared at about the middle of the eighteenth century. Activity of this type was not seen as a real threat by any but the smaller states. In fact the Turkish navy, employing the obsolescent galley, was involved in no big-scale fighting from 1718 to 1770 and in the latter year it was ruthlessly defeated by the Russians at Chesmé.

The Order did have a part to play in keeping the North African corsairs in check. But even the worth of this duty was declining for, in the second half of the seventeenth century, the Barbary pirates were forced to recognize British and French naval power and had to confine their attentions to the vessels of smaller states.

The Order's function gradually became less important in the eyes of Western European powers, until the knights were regarded as no more than a useful and exotic central Mediterranean police force. Additionally, as the Western European nations became increasingly developed, the military power of the Order became insignificant. In the late Middle Ages the Order had been a very useful ally but by the end of the eighteenth century its fleet, although similar in size to that maintained in the sixteenth century, was comparatively small and obsolete.

The Order's role gradually became outmoded and it was exceedingly difficult for the knights to develop new functions or to maintain their position in relation to other European powers. During the sixteenth, seventeenth and eighteenth centuries, as the more powerful European states emerged, the Order was placed at an increasing disadvantage by its lack of size. The Religion should have been associating itself with other powers but the statutes forbade the Order to enter into any alliance which might bring it into conflict with another Christian state. The statutes were not inviolable but, had the Order formed an alliance which was unfavourable to France, for instance, then in all probability the French commanderies would have been confiscated. Precluded from entering into larger political groupings another alternative was for the Order to develop an empire of its own. The knights did attempt to pursue this course of action but here there were problems generated by lack of resources. In 1653 the Order acquired a number of small West Indian islands for an estimated £5,000. However, the distances between colony and overlord were too great and development was never seriously undertaken. In 1665 the investment was sold for about four times the original outlay.

In the first half of the eighteenth century there was talk of the Order stationing a naval squadron on the Red Sea, to clear the area of slave traders and to establish a foothold in the spice and precious materials trade. Once again the Religion was frightened to face the problems of communication and heavy capital outlay. The scheme came to naught.

In 1763 the Order attempted to acquire Corsica but, when the negotiations had reached an advanced stage, the French stepped in and eventually took the island for themselves. The Order could not argue with France.[1]

Another solution to the Order's problems would have been to

[1] Napoleon, who terminated the Order's rule in Malta, was born in Corsica in 1769, just 15 months after Genoa ceded the island to France.

transfer capital from the territory of European nations and reinvest the money within its own domain. This course of action was excluded by the geography of Malta. Physically the islands were too small to sustain development on a sufficient scale and the local economy could not undergo the required expansion. There was no convenient territory around to which the Order could lay claim. The knights had lost their foothold in North Africa in 1551 and even if Tripoli had been retained it is doubtful if the economy of the town and surrounding area could have been greatly developed.

When all was added up the Religion and the islands were highly dependent upon outside agencies. The Order had to worry about the reaction of the Vatican to its actions, France was a protector which had to be sweetened and respected, Spain, by its control of Sicily and therefore the islands' foodstuffs, could not be flaunted. This last difficulty was increased when, in the first half of the eighteenth century, the kingdom of the Two Sicilies ceased to be administered directly from Spain and acquired a monarch of its own. In 1735 Bourbon Charles VIII acceded to the throne and attempted to meddle in the affairs of Malta. After the Grand Master had refused to allow this, the ports within the kingdom of the Two Sicilies were closed to Maltese shipping for a time.

The Order's fleet enjoyed considerable success at the beginning of the eighteenth century. In 1704 round-bottomed sailing vessels were introduced into service and produced impressive results in a number of sea battles. The Order's navy gave useful service in the Turkish-Venetian war which lasted from 1715 to 1718. Under the command of Jacques de Chambrai a whole string of exciting naval battles were fought against the North African corsairs and the majority of the encounters brought victory to the Order. But these battles were really engagements between small pirate states and were far removed from the mainstreams of European history. Attacks on shipping in the Levant, both by the Order's navy and the corsairs based upon Malta, were cut down by diplomatic pressure and, by the middle of the eighteenth century, the cost of maintaining the squadron. Between 1722 and 1741 the Order's navy took approximately 20 Turkish and Barbary vessels, and some 1,500 slaves. These results were excellent in the league in which the Order was fighting but they were of little account in European affairs. The spoils, in fact, would not pay for the Order's naval expenses. In the second half of the eighteenth century many fewer prizes were taken.

The Order's fate depended principally upon France. Any other power could display hostility to the Religion and fail to do terrible damage, but if the French turned against the knights then the Order was likely to fail. However the French, throughout the greater part of the eighteenth century, were prepared to take a tolerant attitude, in spite of the cost. The monies transmitted out of France to Malta each year by the commanderies cannot have been totally approved of in a merchantilist nation. But the Order did keep Malta out of the grasp of rival powers and did help to check the Barbary corsairs. Besides, the Order had many friends and great influence within France. Nevertheless, French politicians cannot have been anything but alarmed by certain events which took place in the second half of the eighteenth century. To begin with, the Russians began to show an interest in Malta again; there had been a brief hint of this by Peter the Great late in the seventeenth century, which could be seen as developing into something far from casual. The Bourbons were not prepared to let anyone forget that they had a claim on the island and even the Maltese were becoming restive. The rule of Grand Master Pinto (1741-73), although marked by periods of considerable prosperity, had suffered economic setbacks as well. The Grand Master had ruled despotically and a great deal of resentment had been generated amongst the local population. Trouble had not come in Pinto's time but the next Grand Master, Francisco Ximenes (1773-75), ran into a complex situation which was not entirely of his own making. Certain sections of Maltese society were becoming tired of the Order's absolutist ideas and arrogant assumption of superiority. If the knights of St. John had trod the islands like heroes in the sixteenth and seventeenth centuries there were many Maltese who now saw them as philandering lay-abouts who were unfitted to rule.

Nowhere was there greater friction than between the Order and the other clerics on Malta. This situation was of long standing. During the rule of La Cassière an inquisitor had been appointed to the islands and he reported directly to the Pope without prior reference to the Order. The Bishops of Malta, too, claimed to be outside the jurisdiction of the Grand Master in many matters, frequently appealed directly to Rome and generally tried to make administration difficult for the Order. If the Order's control was never seriously disputed it is still true to say that there were three separate authorities on the islands. The appeals and reports of the Bishop and the Inquisitor frequently gave the Vatican access to local affairs. The Pope was the ultimate earthly head of the Order but few Grand Masters were prepared to have the Vatican dabbling in the affairs of Malta and listening to the petitions of the islanders over their heads. Matters frequently got extremely heated and there had been a number of affrays, from the sixteenth century onwards, between the Order's followers and supporters of the Bishop or Inquisitor.

Grand Master Ximenes triggered off another incident with the promulgation of a quite trivial regulation on hunting, which he insisted the clergy should respect. How exacerbated relations were between the Order and the local church can be judged by the fact that this minor dispute was taken to Rome for settlement.

A number of discontented priests had been plotting for some time against the Order and the troubles generated by this latest situation presented an opportunity for them to launch an insurrection. On September 9th, 1775, whilst the Order's navy was away attacking Algiers, fort St. Elmo was surprised and taken. There is no doubt that a Russian agent was partially involved in plotting the revolt but the whole affair had been badly planned and the rebellion was quickly squashed. The conspirators had probably anticipated a popular uprising, but this failed to materialize and several of the ringleaders were executed or given long terms of imprisonment.

Calm was soon restored to the islands and later in the same year, upon the death of Ximenes, a very able Frenchman, de Rohan, succeeded to the Mastership of the Order. During Pinto's reign, it appears, the finances had not been well managed and de Rohan was faced with a large deficit. Reorganization, allied with careful administration, soon created a situation of greater financial rectitude but the wider political situation, which was controlled by factors largely outside the Grand Master's influence, was less susceptible to reform. In France a considerable debate developed as to whether or not the services which the Order performed were worth the price the country had to pay. And as the Revolution progressed an aristocratic and religious body like the Order got a less and less sympathetic hearing. The knights made one compromise after another, often providing considerable sums of money in the process. But concessions did not prove to be of much value for in 1792 the Order's possessions in France were confiscated. The knights of St. John were no longer an economically viable organization.

From this point it was only a matter of time before the Order collapsed. Freed of the French hold over them the knights did begin to cast around for alliances and Russia showed increasing interests in the islands.[1] However, diplomatic activity of this type, unless it was quick and decisive, was likely to hasten the end, for once the other great powers decided that the Order was about to ally itself with Russia, they were liable to try and snatch Malta for themselves. The French, having kicked the Religion to its knees, had no option, if they wished to retain their hold on Malta, but to kill off the weakened organization before another force did. As the Order was seen to be failing France became alive with rumours: the kingdom of the Two Sicilies wanted Malta, Austria and England also had designs on the islands, whilst the Russian interest was well known. In 1797 the Directory discussed the Malta situation and agreed with Talleyrand that it would be 'advisable to anticipate the action of Austria, England and Russia on this point'.

The French had long been cultivating subversive elements in the islands and in 1797 the campaign was stepped up. The Order's treasurer, the commander of the fortifications and many French knights were in league with France when on June 9th, 1798, Napoleon, on his way to Egypt, stopped at Malta and demanded to be let into the Grand Harbour, to enable his ships to take on water. The request was refused. The following day French troops were put ashore; the fortifications were not properly manned, resistance was further weakened by the pro-French factions and the the vacillating Grand Master, Hompesch. A Maltese deputation made it clear to the Order that there was no popular desire for a battle against the French.

As resistance crumbled the Grand Master asked for an armistice on June 11th and then sent representatives out to Napoleon on board the *Orient* to discuss the capitulation of the Order. The terms offered by Napoleon were harsh. The Order would give up the islands and all its property therein, the Grand Master was given

[1] In 1794 an alliance was proposed between the Order and the United States.

the promise of a pension, the French knights would receive pensions and be allowed to remain in Malta or return to France. Members of the Order were to retain their private property in the islands; and the Maltese were given the usual promises about the maintenance of their religion and privileges.

Within a few days the Grand Master and his followers had been bundled out of the islands. The party was allowed to take few of the Order's moveable possessions and even the archives were left behind. The Order found temporary shelter under the Czar of Russia and although he undertook intensive diplomatic activity on the Religion's behalf, in an attempt to get the knights reinstated at Malta, the organization quickly ceased to be a factor in European diplomacy. The Order, although greatly altered in form and functions, exists to this day, maintaining a headquarters in Rome, together with hospitals and representatives in many parts of the world.

The departure of the Order was heartily welcomed in Malta for the islanders had come to dislike the Religion intensely. Nevertheless, the knights had left an almost indelible stamp upon the islands. During the Order's rule the population had increased approximately fivefold, new towns and villages had grown up, the older settlements had developed in size and prosperity. A whole range of new industries had been introduced. Yet the period cannot be seen simply in terms of numbers, prosperity and material relics; the whole quality of life in the islands was altered. Remote Malta, just 'a rock in the middle of the sea far from help and comfort', became the home of a rich, noble, cosmopolitan Order, which drew its members and its style of living from European society.

In 1530 Malta had been a predominantly agricultural country, the majority of its islanders living in villages which were cut off from the outside world. Perhaps the inhabitants of Mdina, through the nobility and the Università, had some contact with Sicily. The population of Birgu was subject to outside influence but the greatest number of Maltese consisted of villagers who lived in isolation. The two and a half centuries of the Order's rule altered this pattern of life. By 1798 the majority of the inhabitants of Malta lived, not in remote villages, but in the group of settlements which the Order had laid out or developed close to the harbours. Here the Maltese were in close contact with the knights and many other persons from

Western Europe. The Grand Harbour became a centre of trade and in general the Maltese were subjected to a large number of contacts with European communities.

Not only did the knights create prosperity during their stay but they have, in a peculiar way, been responsible for Malta's continued economic health since 1800. As a military base Malta has several disadvantages. Certainly the island is well placed strategically and possesses some fine harbours, but any base requires a large amount of capital to be spent on development before its potential is realized. In Malta's case this expense is made greater by the lack of local resources. The Order spent vast sums on developing and securing the harbours of Malta and it was this high state of development which attracted Britain and France as the Religion's power waned. Neither could allow the other to possess such strength. By attracting British naval power the Order's investments insured the prosperity of the island for another century and a half.

8

Malta and Britain

Having disposed of the ailing Order, Napoleon attempted to reorganize the life of the Maltese, in accordance with revolutionary principles. The local nobility was abolished, escutcheons were defaced, and something like £250,000 worth of precious objects and materials were removed from the establishments of the Order. The French then began to restrict the influence of the Church in Malta in a manner which amounted to a direct assault upon the position of the Roman Catholic Church in Maltese society. Foreign clerics were told to leave, the religious orders were restricted to one convent each and the superflous establishments were to be closed down. No one was to be allowed to take holy vows before the age of 30 and no new clerics were to be created until all existing priests had been found employment. These measures, together with a number of other anticlerical ordinances, were politically foolish for the Church was the only influential organization which could stir up country-wide trouble against the French.

But this was not all. The French administration lacked a sound financial basis, indeed it was founded upon the principle of looting a conquered land. As a great deal of the Order's wealth had been removed to sustain French armies elsewhere, the Malta administration was soon short of funds and resorted to expedients which were bound to kindle further unrest. The French refused to meet the debts of the Order in the islands and suppliers were left unpaid for the goods they had provided. The Order had always been relatively generous on the question of pensions to loyal servants but the French ceased to honour these commitments. Interest rates were put up at the official pawnshop, new taxes were introduced and the terms of leases on government land were altered in the administration's favour. In a country which had suffered damage, disruption of trade and employment, due to the French invasion, the new measures could only cause increased hardship. Add poverty to the humiliations already served on the Church and nobility and an explosive situation existed.

Napoleon only remained in Malta for six days and then pressed on with his expeditionary force for Egypt. Approximately 4,000 troops were left behind to garrison the islands, under the command of General Vaubois. At first all went well but, as the implications of the French measures began to be comprehended, opinion hardened against the new rulers. On August 24th, 1798, the Maltese learnt that the French fleet had been splintered at Aboukir Bay by the Royal Navy and that the position of the Malta garrison had become tenuous. Had the Frenchmen remaining in Malta concentrated upon producing a sound administration and a contented population they might have survived the military set-back. But the depredation of local churches continued and on Sunday, September 2nd, as an effort was being made to strip ecclesiastical establishments in Mdina, the Maltese decided to put an end to these indignities. The small garrison in the town was massacred and within a matter of hours the whole island had risen up against the French. There is evidence to suggest that the Maltese had been planning a rebellion for some time before September 2nd. A military organization emerged very quickly indeed and the French were convinced that the uprising was not wholly spontaneous.

General Vaubois soon gave up all attempts to regain control of the countryside. He kept a tight hold upon the fortified places around the Grand Harbour, confident that a poorly armed, irregular force would be unable to dislodge him.

The Maltese formed a National Assembly and immediately sent out messengers to seek help from Sicily and the British fleet which was harbouring there. The British vessels were still undergoing repair after the Aboukir battle but Nelson was able to despatch a Portuguese squadron to the islands. Within a short time Captain Ball R.N., together with a small detachment of British vessels, arrived, and in October Nelson came from Sicily to discuss the conduct of operations. It was decided to subject the islands to a total blockade in the hope of preventing the French receiving supplies and reinforcements. Ball was appointed to the command of the blockading squadron but he was soon drawn into the conduct of land operations as well. After the Mdina uprising the Maltese rebellion had been commanded by three men: a notary, Emmanuele Vitale, Canon Caruana and Vincenzo Borg. Able and courageous though these men proved to be, they were all proud and found it difficult to co-operate, particularly when it meant taking orders from each other. Ball, who was certainly a skilled diplomat, was able to smooth over many of the troubles which developed between the three commanders. Eventually Ball became recognized as the spokesman of the Maltese cause.

It quickly became apparent that, although the French lacked the forces to regain control of the countryside, the local insurgents were equally incapable of expelling the troops holding the fortified towns. The Maltese were poorly armed, muskets were in short supply and there was no heavy artillery available to enable breaches to be made in the fortifications. After several brave, but unsuccessful, assaults the Maltese settled down to starve the French out. However, it was debatable who would die of hunger first, the besiegers or the besieged. The islanders soon became desperately short of funds as economic life had been disrupted. Local food production was insufficient to sustain the population and with money in short supply it was not always possible to purchase sufficient quantities of grain from Sicily. The kingdom of the Two Sicilies did support the uprising but that part of southern Italy had its problems as well. The kingdom was no longer wealthy. French forces were gaining victories in Italy and France could well come to control the entire peninsula and Sicily. In these circumstances it might not be wise to give wholehearted support to the enemies of the Republic. Aid from the kingdom was spasmodic, although Nelson estimated it amounted to £40,000 during the two years in which the French were at Malta.

Starving the French out would probably have been accomplished more quickly than it was but, in May 1799, the blockading ships had to be withdrawn to help deal with the Brest fleet, which had succeeded in getting into the Mediterranean. It was over a month before the blockade could be resumed and the French took advantage of the respite to run additional supplies into the Grand Harbour. After this set-back to the Maltese cause the pressure on the French was gradually built-up. In December 1799 a detachment of British troops was posted to Malta. Two months later over 1,000 troops from the kingdom of the Two Sicilies were brought in and a desperate French attempt to run the blockade with supplies and fresh troops was foiled.

Meanwhile, poverty, disease and hunger were beginning to take a large toll of Maltese lives. At times food became desperately short and British naval vessels had to be sent to Sicily to seize grain boats. However, the plight of the French was worse and during the long hot summer months of the year 1800 they slowly consumed what remained of their supplies, together with the dogs, cats and rats of Valletta. By August the French commanders recognized that their position was nearly hopeless. They hung on for another month, hoping for an improvement in the military fortunes of France, but early in September Vaubois indicated to Pigot, the commander of the British land forces, that he was prepared to surrender.

On September 5th Vaubois affixed his name to the capitulation under which the French were to give up the fortified places which they held in Malta and return to France. It was agreed that none of the Frenchmen were to fight against Britain again until a like number of English prisoners of war had been surrendered by France. Within a few days the greater part of the French force was on its way to Marseilles. There has been some criticism of the surrender terms given to the French but it should be remembered that the British wanted unhampered possession of Malta as quickly as possible. The French were denying the use of the Grand Harbour to shipping and apart from the inconvenience which this was causing to the Royal Navy it added greatly to the problem of food supply. Another factor which helped to make the British conditions relatively easy was the shortage of food supplies within the islands. There was only enough food in Malta for a few days and the British commander did not want the added burden of having to feed several thousand French prisoners of war.

Having acquired Malta almost by accident, for British involvement had been an opportunist reaction precipitated by the Maltese uprising, the new masters of the islands were not quite certain what to do with their possession. Undoubtedly the British were determined that the French should not regain a hold on Malta but the political situation was highly complex. First, the Maltese were making it quite clear that they wanted some part in deciding the future of the islands. Secondly, the kingdom of the Two Sicilies, which had provided men, money and materials during the siege of Valletta, had a claim on the archipelago based upon the former attachment of Malta to Sicily. The claim had been at least partially recognized by the British. Thirdly, the Order of St. John, with the backing of the Czar of Russia, felt it had a right to the islands and this pretension had also gained a degree of recognition from the British. The claims of the Order and the Two Sicilies were not irreconcilable as they both sprang from the previous situation whereby the knights held Malta in fief.

The British, if they wished to press a claim, had a much simpler case than any other party. Their commanders had received the capitulation of the French forces who in turn held the islands by right of conquest from the Order of St. John. Britain was the *de facto* ruler of Malta.

The British were undecided as to the value of the island and whether or not it was worth retaining once the French had been expelled. As an interim measure it was decided late in 1800 to make the islands a British Protectorate and see how international affairs developed.

Captain Ball soon produced a number of documents outlining the state of affairs in Malta and the advantages of retaining the islands. He suggested that the Grand Harbour might become an important entrepôt centre for British Mediterranean trade. Commerce with Barbary had grown quickly once the Order had left and this was doubly important for it meant that the islands had another source of food supply apart from Sicily. Ball pointed out that the harbours at Malta would provide a secure base for naval operations as, unlike Port Mahon at Minorca, they were not vulnerable to attack from the land. What was more, the Grand Harbour also possessed a small but complete shipyard. Ball felt that because of the limited area of Malta it would be difficult to blockade, particularly in view of the size of the force which would be necessary to exclude the British navy. The revenue produced by import dues and the Order's property would be sufficient to pay for the administration of the islands and they would not be a liability to the British treasury.

Administrators in London, viewing the matter in its wider

international context, would not give Ball a definite reply, although he was allowed to get on with the running of the islands. To the British Government Malta was a possession which might well have to be given up or bargained away in peace negotiations. There were also fears that the costs of garrisoning the islands might be excessive and there was generally no great awareness in London of Malta's strategic value. Nelson expressed a very unfavourable view of the island's location as a British naval base. In fact, almost unwittingly, the British had stumbled into a French sphere of influence which was commercially and militarily regarded as being of immense importance in France. Napoleon made the point when he told a British ambassador he would rather see the English in a Parisian suburb than in Malta.

The Maltese, or rather the politically active section of the population, soon made their views clear on what should happen to the islands. The population had tasted and evicted French administration, the Order was heartily despised, the kingdom of the Two Sicilies was partially distrusted and partially recognized as being too weak to afford adequate protection to the islands. From the available evidence the Maltese could see that the British were certainly a great sea power who were restoring prosperity by using the islands as a naval base and as a trading centre. The British and the Maltese had fought as allies and Captain Ball was regarded by the local population as being a man of considerable stature, who was always ready to listen to the Maltese point of view. However, it must also have been clear, even at this first stage, that the British would not regard the Maltese as equal partners in the running of the islands. The Maltese had been excluded from the negotiations leading to the capitulation of the French, and although Ball was sympathetic there were many men above him who were not prepared to give much weight to Maltese opinion. Whether or not politically minded Maltese realized the true state of affairs is doubtful; in any case they had limited room for manoeuvre. One fact was certain: Malta would not be left to the Maltese for all the interested powers feared that the others would try to occupy the islands. Early in 1802 a deputation from Malta reached London and requested that the islands be placed under the permanent protection of His Britannic Majesty. By this time the British Government was far advanced in peace negotiations with France and one of the conditions for the cessation of hostilities was that Malta be relinquished by Britain. When the treaty of Amiens was signed on March 25th, 1802, article 10 defined a new status for Malta. The islands were to be restored to the Order of St. John but the constitution of the Religion was to be altered. The English and French langues were to be suppressed whilst a Maltese langue was to be formed. Efforts were to be made to create peaceful relations between the Order and Barbary. The independence of the islands was to be guaranteed by Britain, France, Austria, Russia, Spain and Prussia. The ports of Malta were to be open to ships of all nations at moderate dues. The treaty also made provision for the Maltese to have a large share in the administration of the islands and at least half the civil posts were to be allotted to them.

On paper this was not a bad agreement for all parties, not least the Maltese, but its implementation relied upon the Order of St. John which was now impoverished and scattered. Resuscitation would not be easy even given goodwill, and Napoleon soon embarrassed the noble Order further by ensuring that a great deal more of its European property was confiscated. It was quickly recognized that article 10 was unworkable.

Whether or not the Maltese ever clearly understood what was to happen to them under the treaty of Amiens is doubtful. To the islanders the Order was returning and this was intolerable. Public meetings were organized and Ball reported to London not only that he felt disturbances would accompany the return of the Order but that virtually 'all the English Merchants have left the Island. So little confidence do they place in the Government of the Order.'

On June 15th, 1802, a group of prominent Maltese again made their views felt in a declaration of rights. Item one held that 'the King of the United Kingdom of Great Britain and Ireland is our Sovereign Lord, and his lawful successors shall, in all times to come, be acknowledged as our lawful Sovereigns.' The document also reserved certain rights to the Maltese. The islanders were to have their own assembly, the *consiglio popolare*, which was to have the power to legislate and to tax, with the consent of His Majesty's representatives.

Maltese fears regarding the reappearance of the Order quickly receded as the treaty of Amiens was soon being heartily violated by the British and the French. In October 1802 orders were sent from London to the effect that the preparations for the British departure from Malta were to cease and in May of the following year hostilities recommenced.

By this time the British Government was beginning to perceive just how important Malta could be in Mediterranean affairs. The Order's small shipyard provided a useful repair base for the Royal Navy and French interests in the Levant could be squeezed from Malta. Nelson modified his earlier view of the islands as a naval station and in June 1803 he wrote: 'I now declare that I consider Malta as a most important outwork to India, that it will give us great influence in the Levant and indeed all the southern parts of Italy. In this view I hope we shall never give it up.' And early in 1805 when Admiral Keith was asked for his opinion on the utility of the different naval stations in the Mediterranean he replied unequivocally: 'Malta has this advantage over all the other ports that I have mentioned (Mahon, Elba, Sardinia), that the whole harbour is covered by its wonderful fortifications, and that in the hands of Great Britain no enemy would presume to land upon it, because the number of men required to besiege it could not be maintained by the island, and on the appearance of a superior fleet, that besieging army would find itself obliged to surrender . . . or starve. At Malta all the arsenals, hospitals, storehouses etc. are on a great scale. The harbour has more room than Mahon and the entrance is considerably wider.'

Commercially, too, the islands were becoming an increasingly important asset to Britain. Prior to the Napoleonic Wars British merchants had been established in Leghorn, Palermo and Trieste, particularly the former, but hostilities had either dislodged them or rendered their businesses highly vulnerable. Malta offered a convenient alternative which was made more attractive by the presence of the Royal Navy. At the beginning of the nineteenth century British commerce was becoming increasingly interested in the Mediterranean—an area which formerly had experienced relatively little commercial penetration by English merchants. Malta was seen as a base from which commercial intercourse might be prosecuted. In 1804 John Jackson Esq. published his authoritative *Reflections on the Commerce of the Mediterranean*. The work notes Malta's advantages as a trading base and suggests that the island would develop into the great centre of British entrepôt trade in the Mediterranean. Similarly, when Boisgelin's *Ancient and Modern Malta* (1805) was reviewed in a fashionable London magazine, the reviewer laid emphasis on Malta's future importance to British trade. There was no lack of commercial interest in Malta and this was a very strong factor in early British concern with the islands. At this time Malta was far from being simply a Royal Navy base; the islands were becoming increasingly a storehouse for goods which were eventually to be distributed into Italy, the Morea and the Levant. Malta was a convenient and secure quarantine port besides being a useful collecting point for return cargoes. However, the real commercial boom was to come. In 1806 Napoleon issued the Berlin Decree which closed European ports to British shipping and declared the United Kingdom to be under blockade. This measure, together with the Milan Decree of the following year, set off a trade boom in Malta and a few other centres which were well placed to serve as bases for vessels trading with Europe by circuitous routes.

The British replied to the French actions with a blockade of their own but it was a selective blockade. Trade was still permitted with the continent provided merchants were dealing largely in British goods. Malta, together with Gibraltar, Heligoland, seized in 1807, and Sicily, where British troops were stationed from 1806, and later the Ionian Islands, several of which were occupied in 1809, were soon doing a roaring trade as shipping points for British goods into Europe. Malta was particularly favoured as it was one of the centres from which licences were issued to vessels and it was virtually obligatory to call at the islands to obtain clearance from the Royal Navy.

The number of vessels entering the harbours increased rapidly and the American Embargo Act of 1808 accentuated prosperity for it drove up the demand in Britain for produce from the Levant and Sicily. Vessels coming out to Malta with goods were now likely to obtain a profitable return cargo. The warehouses around the Harbour were filled with goods in transit and numerous Maltese, British, Italian and Greek export-import firms built up profitable businesses in the islands.

Although Malta was undoubtedly a convenient base from which traders could work the Levant, Sicily, Barbary and the Morea, the great bulk of the early nineteenth-century trade passing through the islands was stimulated by the war in Europe; once hostilities ceased trade was bound to follow more normal and convenient routes. In fact the boom did not outlast the war. In 1813 the islands were struck by a virulent outbreak of plague; not only was it estimated that over 4,000 persons died but the harbours were obliged to close and all trade ceased. The goods which had formerly flowed through Malta's warehouses were now forced to seek other routes and many competing ports exaggerated the process by not lifting quarantine regulations on vessels coming from Malta until 1826—many years after all trace of the epidemic had disappeared.

The administration of the Maltese islands presented the British with several problems. First, they were taking over a country which had been organized in a manner strikingly different to prevailing British practice. Secondly, in the early years, the British were unsure as to how long they were going to remain in the islands and thus uncertain as to the basis on which an administration should be founded. Thirdly, as Malta developed into an important military station there was a growing conflict between the civil and military authorities. Under these heads there were many fruitful sources of disagreement and the relationship between civil and military affairs was never solved until the islands became independent in 1964.

Once the French were expelled in 1800 the position of Captain Ball was quickly clarified. He was placed in charge of the civil administration but the ultimate authority on the islands was the garrison commander, General Pigot.

In February 1801, Ball returned to active duty with the Royal Navy and was rewarded for his efforts, after a little delay, with a large cash bounty and a baronetcy. Ball was replaced by Charles Cameron whose terms of appointment to the post of civil commissioner clearly set out the British attitude towards Malta at the time. 'For the present . . . no alterations should be made in the modes, laws and regulations according to which the civil affairs and the revenue of the island have been heretofore managed, unless the same shall appear to the officer commanding His Majesty's forces to be required for the safety and defence of the island, or to be so evidently beneficial and desirable as to leave no doubt of its expediency.' However, Cameron was not to allow any malpractices in the courts, his budget should balance and any surplus revenue be applied to the repair of buildings and fortifications. Clearly this is little more than an administrative holding operation until Britain decided what to do with the islands. In the meantime Cameron was to look after the local inhabitants and 'to use every endeavour, consistent with your public duty, to meet their wishes, to show yourself indulgent even to their prejudices, and to omit no fair opportunity of conciliating their affection and ensuring their fidelity to the Government under which they are now placed'.

Cameron was hardly installed before negotiations for a peace were set in train and Britain agreed to give up Malta. In June 1802, consequent upon the treaty of Amiens, Sir Alexander Ball was appointed His Majesty's Plenipotentiary to the Order of St. John and posted to Malta to help arrange the hand-over of the islands to the Religion. Ball soon took over the administration of civil affairs from Cameron and when fighting started again with France he began the difficult task of reorganizing the local administration after years of interim arrangements. Ball was not a particularly efficient administrator but he remained popular with the Maltese. He died in office on October 25th, 1809.

Although in the first decade of the nineteenth century the islands enjoyed rapidly increasing prosperity there was a body of opinion in Malta which became disillusioned with certain aspects of British rule and hankered after the formation of a Maltese parliament. In July 1811 a petition was sent to George III requesting that the ancient rights of the Maltese, which had been suppressed by the Order of St. John, should be restored. The list of demands included the restitution of the consiglio popolare, a free press and trial by jury with the right of appeal to the consiglio.

In 1812 a Commission of Inquiry was sent out from Britain. The instructions to the commissioners pointed out that Malta had become increasingly prosperous and although 'valued formerly only for its military importance has now a further claim on the attention of His Majesty's Government as one of the most flourishing of our commercial positions'. The commissioners were instructed to examine everything apart from military matters. They were to make recommendations as to the manner in which the civil government of the island was to be run, and to give the Maltese 'as large a share of civil liberty as is consistent with the military circumstances of the island'.

The commissioners took evidence with great care and their report is an important document. It is an early nineteenth-century stock-taking, detailing the state of the islands when they were acquired by the British, outlining the changes which had taken place in the first decade of the century, precisely describing many facets of local life and opinion in 1812. Finally the document contains recommendations, many of which were implemented, as to the course of future actions. Little escaped the sedulous commissioners; the operation of the legal system, the Church, the state of agriculture, commerce and industry, the views of local politicians: they examined them all, recorded and concluded.

To the commission 'it was a matter of gratification to find, that in opposition to some representations made by a small disaffected party in the island, the great mass and body of the people were happy and contented; warm in their professions of attachment to Great Britain, and thriving in wealth and population to a degree almost unprecedented. The commercial part of the community we found daily increasing in prosperity and opulence, fully sensible of the peculiar advantages derived from the protection of Great Britain.' Any discontent, it was concluded, was springing from the higher orders of society which were not finding life so profitable as the merchant classes.

There were, of course, matters in the running of local affairs which needed alteration but the commissioners advised caution as 'it will always be expedient to bear in mind that it is our object to provide for the happiness and tranquillity of a people, whose habits, customs, religion, and education, are in direct opposition to our own.' For this reason although many local laws were thought to be in need of alteration the commissioners suggested as few changes as possible. Maltese law was based upon the code drawn up under Grand Master de Rohan, which in turn was a revision of Vilhena's code. De Rohan's code reflected current European practice and would conflict with much standard English usage. The commissioners suggested few alterations and rejected the proposed introduction of trial by jury. They did, however, recommend that judges should be salaried and not paid by fees as had previously been the case. This practice had given the judiciary a vested interest in prolonging cases to inflate the size of the fee.

The local Church, with its ecclesiastical courts and special privileges, was even more difficult ground for the commissioners and they immediately saw that any suggestions for the alterations of practices here would undoubtedly 'draw down the indignation of an angry priesthood'. With this observation the commission hurried on to a consideration of political matters. Any hopes that the consiglio popolare would be revived were quickly drowned. The commissioners were not impressed by the validity of a case which had to go back several centuries to discover precedents and then attributed to the consiglio powers which it had never enjoyed· However, the commissioners were not really concerned with historical validity but rather with the function of the consiglio in the contemporary scene. Most nineteenth-century British administrators connected with Malta were convinced that the more active and critical local politicians were unstable rabble-rousers who only reflected extreme opinions. It was deeply felt that the majority of the Maltese were not very interested in politics and simply wanted a sound administration, prosperity and peace. Now, although this was a convenient point of view, it did contain a deal of truth as quite clearly local politicians only represented sections of opinion amongst the nobility and certain professions. The commissioners were converted to the same view, not least by the turbulent politicians who harangued them. The commission eventually concluded that any consiglio would be composed of illiterates and fanatics who might well manipulate the gathering to stir up the population against Britain. However, the commissioners did decide that the prevailing division of Malta's government into civil and military compartments was unsatisfactory; in future the two spheres should ultimately be the responsibility of one man; a governor and commander-in-chief of the island of Malta and its dependencies. The governor was to be advised, if he so wished, by a committee of local citizens.

The commission then proceeded to report on the economic affairs of the island. The population of Malta was found to have increased very rapidly since the arrival of the British. The commission commented that the Maltese 'all marry early, are extremely prolific and from the temperate habits of their lives generally attain to a mature old age'. As a result the population was increasing alarmingly. The number of people in Malta alone was estimated to be 120,000 and, although this is almost certainly too high a figure, the commissioners were justified in regarding overpopulation as one of the islands' major problems.

The finances were found to be in a progressive state of improvement. However, if Malta was to be developed economically it would be necessary to find new sources of revenue. Here there was a considerable difficulty. Previously the Maltese had rarely been subject to income or property taxes and although urged that the former should be introduced the commissioners rejected the idea on the grounds that it might be resented by the population. This was a decision that lacked both courage and wisdom. The commission recommended a 1 per cent duty on all imports, together with taxes on foreigners and wine houses, whose profits 'arise principally from the vices of our countrymen'. The last measure was clearly sound but the first placed a tax burden upon the one really important sector of the local economy and this imposition proved to be a disincentive to growth. Here local persons of influence had won a battle which helped to keep direct taxation out of Malta for nearly another century and a half and placed upon the humbler inhabitants a not inconsiderable burden. A large part of Malta's food requirements was imported and bore import dues. The lower classes could, therefore, not avoid contributing relatively heavily to this source of revenue whilst most of them would not have qualified for income-tax payments.

The commissioners thought that there was little hope of increasing agricultural production on the land which was already cultivated but did feel that in a few exposed areas, which were relatively empty due to the fear of corsairs, it might be possible to bring more land into cultivation.

So worried were the commissioners about the need to increase Malta's food supplies that they considered the possibility of developing the islands of Pantelleria, Lampedusa and Linosa as food-producing areas for Malta. The last two islands had been virtually emptied of people as a result of the activities of corsairs and Pantelleria was only sparsely populated. The idea was abandoned; the conclusion reached was that the scheme would only delay matters, as in the end if population growth went on unchecked it would outrun the new sources of supply. A private-enterprise colonization of Lampedusa was undertaken in 1800 by a small group of Maltese who remained on the island until the eighteen- forties.

The economic activity which engaged most of the commissioners' attention was of course the islands' buoyant trade. Here there was nothing but general satisfaction to be recorded at the manner in which commerce was daily making an increasing contribution to the economic welfare of the islands.

Overall it is true to say that the commissioners made a better job of recording the state of the islands in 1812 than they did in recommending future courses of action. Their approach to the question of taxation was limited by the fear they held of upsetting certain sections of the local community. Reform of legal affairs was hampered by similar considerations.

Maltese politicians were bitterly disappointed that the commission did not recommend that the consiglio popolare should become one of the islands' established institutions. Yet their hopes for a part in the conduct of affairs were based on emotions and the Maltese could not logically have expected an allocation of real political power. Malta had become an important base of the Royal Navy and the British would certainly not allow the utility of the station to be diminished by local political pressures. The protection of a great power, particularly when it involves the development of extensive basal facilities, can be a huge advantage economically. But economic gain is counterbalanced by political retardation and any Maltese who thought they could enjoy His Britannic Majesty's protection and also have a hand in taking decisions, that might influence events in a great maritime empire, was deluding himself.

The report of the commission was speedily digested in London and a man was sought to take on the new position of Governor and Commander-in-Chief of Malta. The man chosen was Sir Thomas Maitland, who had made a fine reputation as an administrator in Ceylon. Maitland arrived to take up his new position in the midst of the epidemic of 1813. His characteristically determined measures helped to contain the outbreak and in 1814 it was possible to remove restrictions on movement around the islands.

Maitland then set about the task of reorganizing the administrative machine of the islands. There is no doubt that he had exceptional abilities as an organizer but his methods soon earned him many critics. The old Università, which still ran the corn import trade of the islands, was found to be operating inefficiently and abolished. The courts also received some much-needed reforms, the scope of the ecclesiastical courts was restricted and it was decreed that all property left to the Church had to be sold within one year. Notaries and advocates were henceforth to have written and verbal facility in the English language before they could qualify. All petitions and government contracts were to be presented in English, which was to become the language of government rather than Italian. The proposed council of citizens, suggested by the 1812 commission, never materialized and Maitland made his decisions unaided. Although the great majority of these measures were undoubtedly necessary they were bound to give offence to certain sections of Maltese society. Maitland's autocratic manner only made matters worse and soon earned him the name of 'King Tom'. However, there is no disputing Maitland's efficient management of affairs during a period of economic difficulty. He made efforts to recapture some of Malta's former trade, lowering dues, quarantine and transit charges. Attempts were made to stimulate the declining cotton industry by the setting up of factories, although these establishments turned out to be loss makers.

The British possession of Malta was recognized by the other European powers in the Treaty of Paris signed in 1814. After the declaration of peace military expenditure in the island naturally declined and this added to the economic problems. During the next 25 years British defence spending was on a limited scale, except when danger threatened. Economically the islands were normally in a weak position. The Navarino incident, when combined naval forces from Britain, France and Russia defeated a Turco-Egyptian fleet in 1827, gave a brief boost to the economy. The French seizure of Algiers in 1830 had a similar effect, as the British judged that the strategic situation in the Mediterranean had altered unfavourably from their point of view. The French now had potential control of the western basin of the Mediterranean and there were fears that they might attempt to oust the British from Malta. Calm was restored within a short time but when the French started to court Mehemet Ali, the ruler of Egypt, and induced him to adopt policies which were embarrassing to Britain, the extent of French ambitions was recognized and the British became thoroughly alarmed. Egypt lay astride the most convenient land route to India—Britain's prime imperial possession. A hostile government in Cairo could certainly cause difficulties and when in 1837 Mehemet Ali sent his forces careering off into Arabia with the object of securing a position on the Persian Gulf and taking Baghdad, which stood on the alternative land route to India, Britain reacted purposefully. Aden was seized in 1839 and preparations were made to attack Egypt's Mediterranean coastline, if strong measures should prove necessary.

The French became increasingly hostile to Britain and as a result of the general raising of tension alterations were made to the defence structure of the Maltese islands. New armaments were provided, the garrison was increased in numbers, the fortifications were repaired and modernized. A new water supply system was installed for Valletta and the Three Cities, grain fosses were excavated in Floriana, a large bakery was built to supply the needs of the Royal Navy and in 1848 the British admiralty's first dry dock was opened at Malta. All this activity led to a return of prosperity. During the Crimean War (1853–56) Malta became a forward supply and refit station for the British forces being used in support of the Turks against the Russians.

By the end of the eighteen-forties British military spending in Malta was running at about £200,000 p.a., in 1854 it reached well over £400,000 and in 1856 exceeded £800,000. Although spending on this scale was not maintained year after year, and indeed military expenditure fluctuated widely, Malta was now established as a major base of the Royal Navy. In 1869 the opening of the Suez Canal placed the islands upon the major British imperial seaway; the Mediterranean route to India.

Nor did the development of other British bases lessen the value of Malta. Aden was acquired in 1839, Cyprus leased from the Turks in 1878, Egypt occupied in 1882; but these new possessions were to become links in a great chain of imperial stations which stretched from the United Kingdom, to Gibraltar, through the Mediterranean and the Red Sea, down to India, the Strait Settlements and Singapore. Eventually the chain of command and communication served the stations on the China coast to say nothing of the important colonies of Australia and New Zealand. The islands were one of the hinge points in this imperial system. Malta was the headquarters of the Mediterranean fleet and secured a seaway which was considered vital to British interests.

These new strategic developments, largely consequent upon the cutting of the Suez Canal, were reflected in the military installations erected at Malta in the second half of the nineteenth century. The naval dockyard underwent a major development programme, the harbours were improved, new static defences were constructed, barracks and military hospitals were erected.

During most of the first half of the nineteenth century the British had been content to adapt the military installations of the Order of St. John to their needs but from about 1840 the islands were redeveloped, militarily, on a vast scale as Malta became a key position in an extensive maritime empire. Under the Order Malta had been valued for its strategic position at the heart of the Mediterranean, under the British it came to hold a place on a seaway which served a great part of the world and became a base from which ships of war sailed into many spheres of influence. These strategic changes found expression in the quality of life the Maltese lived and in the local economy. When the Order of St. John was forced out of the islands in 1798 the population numbered about 100,000 persons. The succeeding two years, marked as they were by fighting, hunger and disease, did not provide the conditions in which populations prosper and undoubtedly there was a decline in numbers. Once life returned to normal matters changed, and by the end of the first decade of the nineteenth century the population was once again growing rapidly in response to prosperous times. The outbreak of plague in 1813, which killed over 4,000 Maltese, marked not only the end of a period of prosperity but also the end of a decade of population growth. From this point the economy stagnated for many years and population increase slowed down. In 1830 an outbreak of smallpox killed 756 of the islanders and in 1837 a cholera epidemic despatched a further 4,253. Additionally the Maltese had begun to emigrate to escape the low wage levels which were persisting in the islands. When the first census was taken in 1842 the total population of the islands was found to number 113,864. This figure is not a great increase on the more reliable early nineteenth-century estimates of population numbers and probably indicates that there had been a relatively slow rate of increase in the years between 1813 and 1842—slow, that is, for Malta. From 1842 onwards population growth speeded up. In 1851 there were found to be 123,494 persons living in the islands, by 1871 the population exceeded 140,000, soon after the turn of the century it topped 200,000 and years before the Second World War the quarter million mark was passed. The census of 1948 revealed that the islands contained 304,991 persons and that of 1957 a total population of 319,620. From this last point population numbers have tended to decline due to a fall in the birth rate and the large number of Maltese who have chosen to migrate.

The rate of population increase which was experienced under British rule was higher than that recorded in the Order's time and the size of the islands' economic problems multiplied with the number of inhabitants. In 1842 there had been, on average, 935 Maltese to every square mile of the islands; by 1956 there were 2,511. The towns and villages had swelled in size and consumed considerable areas of land, but no large new sources of civil employment had developed, with the result that more and more people had become dependent upon the one important local employer: the British services.

Nineteenth-century administrators were very concerned with the problems generated by a high rate of population growth but their room for manoeuvre was limited.

Given that the population was apparently to continue increasing in numbers then one possible palliative was to persuade some of the surplus inhabitants to leave and settle elsewhere. Although the Maltese are strongly attached to their island home they have long tended to have something of a tradition for moving into neighbouring areas in search of economic advancement. Sicily and Naples, for instance, apparently became the homes of many Maltese in the latter part of the sixteenth century and during the course of the Order's rule small communities became established at a number of ports in the western Mediterranean. During the years of high prosperity at the beginning of the nineteenth century there had been little incentive to migrate but by 1820 individual Maltese were moving out of the islands to seek opportunities elsewhere. The British administrators, urged on by various private persons, seriously considered instituting officially sponsored migration. From this point of view South Africa, Australasia, the West Indies and Greece were all commended to official attention. In the end it was decided that public funds could not be expended on emigration although the local administration did help to organize a number of schemes, none of which were particularly successful. Public money was, however, used in bringing distressed Maltese back to the islands if they failed to establish themselves abroad and fell upon hard times. The provision of such a safety net was obviously an encouragement to the potential migrant.

The Maltese who emigrated went principally to North Africa; exploiting the existing trade links and travelling very cheaply on the small vessels which plied the central Mediterranean and the coast of North Africa. By the end of the nineteenth century there were well over 50,000 Maltese scattered around the shores of the Mediterranean. Algeria, Tunis, Tripoli and Egypt contained the most important colonies but there were also significant communities in Smyrna, Constantinople, Gibraltar, Sicily and the Ionian islands. Attempts to settle groups of Maltese in the West Indies had failed and only a few of the islanders had reached North America and Australia.

After the First World War the pattern of migration altered, the Mediterranean littoral became less popular and the Maltese moved increasingly into Britain, America and Australia. The last-named country has accepted many thousands of Maltese migrants since the conclusion of the Second World War.

The great increase in the numbers of persons living in the islands, which took place under British rule, was reflected in changes in the number, size and form of towns and villages. When the British took control in 1800 the settlement pattern consisted of two basic structures: namely the large, compact villages of the Maltese countryside and the group of towns which the Order had founded, or developed, around the Grand Harbour. The coasts and remoter areas contained few dwellings. During the British period settlements developed in the outlying areas and a string of suburbs grew up around the existing harbourside towns.

At the beginning of the nineteenth century the population of Valletta numbered about 20,000 persons, by 1861 the figure was 25,000, but this marked a high point in the development of the city. From 1861 onwards people started to move out of Valletta and sought dwelling places in the suburban areas. The other harbourside towns had a similar history to that of the capital. The number of people living in Floriana increased very rapidly in the first half of the nineteenth century but in 1871 a peak was reached and since then numbers have declined markedly. After the mid-point of the nineteenth century the populations of Vittoriosa, Cospicua and Senglea grew very slowly in numbers.

The majority of the old established villages fared rather better than the harbourside towns and most of them grew steadily, if unspectacularly, in size.

The settlements which have displayed very rapid growth in the nineteenth and twentieth centuries have been the suburbs. In 1833 Sliema was described as being a little village consisting 'principally of the summer residences of the inhabitants of Valetta'. By the end of the century it had become the nucleus of a small town and similar settlements were beginning to grow up at Msida and St. Julians. In 1861 there were 324 people living in Sliema, by 1957 there were over 23,000. At St. Julians there were 600 inhabitants in 1871; at the conclusion of the Second World War the figure was 9,122. Today the suburbs of Sliema, St. Julians, Msida, Pieta and Gzira form a continuous urban area occupying the north shore of the Marsamxett.

The suburbs which developed in the Sliema area were inhabited predominantly by the professional and commercial classes but the working-class suburbs at Hamrun, Paola and Marsa underwent even more explosive growth. In 1871 there were 3,200 people living in the Hamrun, Marsa, Santa Venera area; by 1948 there were ten times as many. Paola had 488 inhabitants in 1861 but 14,793 in 1948. Some of the older villages such as Zabbar, Quormi and Bir-kirkara, which were well placed to develop as suburbs to the harbour area, also increased their population numbers rapidly.

In the outlying coastal districts settlements grew up at St. Paul's bay, Marsaxlokk, Birzebbugia and Marsascala. All these villages were originally small fishing settlements but in this century they have developed as holiday resorts.

In north-western Malta settlements have grown up at Mellieha, Mgarr, Manikata and Zebbieh in association with the agricultural colonization of the area in the nineteenth and twentieth centuries.

During this century there has been a marked alteration in building styles and in the form of Maltese villages. Traditional building methods have been replaced by more modern techniques and the villages, which were formerly very compact settlements, have spread out in ribbons of development along the access roads. The great increase in the number and size of Maltese settlements has given rise to some complex town-planning problems.

The islands' internal communications underwent development during the course of British rule. Some roads were improved for military purposes, others were constructed to serve new settlements, but by and large the system of tracks, which the islands had acquired over the centuries, was adapted to the needs of the modern world. The majority of the islands' roads were not metalled before 1920 and it was not until the conclusion of the Second World War that significant mileages of relatively modern road were laid down.

Malta's connection with the railway age was comparatively brief and unsuccessful. In 1880 the Malta Railway Company was founded and in 1883 opened a line between Valletta and Mdina. The venture was not a success and in 1890, under the terms of the company's concession, the Government took over the line as the railway was judged to have become a danger to the public. The line underwent a thorough overhaul; in 1892 it was reopened and quickly started to make money for the local treasury. There was talk of extending the service to Mosta, Zebbug and Sliema. In fact, the only extension brought into operation was at Mdina, where a tunnel was driven through the hill on which the town stood and a line laid to serve the barracks and military hospital at Mtarfa. The cost of the extension was about £20,000 and it is highly doubtful if the added receipts ever justified the expenditure. Overall, however, the line continued to do well financially but in 1903 the administration allowed a company to start building electric tramways in Malta. Services were run on three lines which connected Valletta with Birkirkara, Cospicua and Zebbug. The Valletta-Birkirkara line operated in direct competition with the railway and soon led to a decline in railway receipts.

Eventually the losses made by the railway could be borne no longer and on April 1st, 1931, it was closed down. The extension of motor-bus services in the end killed off the tramways and the railway.

Under British rule Maltese agriculture underwent a number of profound changes and hopes were continually expressed by the administration that the productivity of local farming could be raised. Increased productivity would have made the islands less susceptible to a blockade and provided more jobs on the land for the Maltese. The administration got itself involved in a variety of schemes to improve local agriculture but none of them proved wholly successful. One of Ball's first actions was to introduce the potato into the islands and although the crop took some time to get established with local farmers it did eventually become one of Malta's principal exports. Ball also invested in a botanical garden and small horticultural establishments in the villages. His hope was that, by example, the standards of local agriculture would be improved but the return on the investment does not appear to have been commensurate with the capital involved.

The British, like the Order before them, became interested in the possibility of establishing a local silk industry. In 1826 the British Silk Company set up in Malta and was given a large area of land, which the civil administration owned, rent free. Thousands of mulberry trees were planted and it was the intention that the company should provide home workers with silkworm eggs and a regular supply of mulberry leaves. The Maltese would be responsible for rearing the grubs, letting them pupate and then winding the silk thread which the company would buy. For a time all went well, the mulberry trees flourished, the Maltese took to the scheme and in 1831 some 400 lbs. of silk was produced. Due to various unexplained factors production did not increase to the expected totals. Then, in 1836, the grubs were struck by a disease and the industry ceased to function.

This was not the only attempt to develop new agricultural industries. In 1824 an effort was made to introduce the mango tree and certain Jamaican plants. In 1827 the cochineal insect was brought into the islands but without any lasting success. Another attempt was made about 1870 and this failed as well. During the Governorship of Sir William Reid (1851–58) the idea of restarting the silk industry was taken up, using Assam silkworms, but the project came to naught.

An idea which occupied the minds of British administrators for long periods was the possibility of establishing farmers on some of the vacant lands found in the islands. Ball was interested in the idea, the 1812 commission commented on the matter and Governor Ponsonby (1827–36) attempted to press the scheme during his term of office. It was not until the eighteen-forties that a wholesale attempt was made to start an agricultural colonization of some of the vacant lands in north-west Malta, which were the property of the civil administration.

In fact most of these vacant 'lands' had been owned by the Order and it had attempted to raise agricultural productivity in the area but, by and large, had only succeeded in making unprofitable investments. A great part of the area was composed of limestone which had, at best, only a thin soil cover. In the valleys good quality land existed but much of this was already being farmed. Nevertheless, it was argued that the Maltese had had centuries of experience in bringing poor quality, stony land into cultivation. Although there was a deal of truth in this contention, it tended to be overlooked that previously much of the new land had been created by established farmers seeking to extend their cultivated holding. A large-scale colonization of extensive barren areas by under-capitalized, previously landless, peasants was another matter. However, between about 1840 and the end of the century, large areas of government land in north-west Malta were divided up into geometrical blocks and given to farmers on long-term, low-cost leases which stipulated that the holding had to be developed and brought into cultivation. The colonization was carefully planned; access roads were laid out and new villages established at Mgarr and Mellieha to house the farmers moving into the north-west. In spite of a large number of failures new fields were built-up and a great deal of marginal land was brought into cultivation, much of which has since been abandoned.

After the colonization had been in progress for some years it was discovered that potential sources of irrigation water lay at not too great a depth beneath the surface in several parts of the north-west. Wells were dug to tap these sources of supply and several rich irrigation farming areas were brought into existence.

Towards the end of the nineteenth century strenuous efforts were made to increase vine cultivation in the islands; the crop had previously been relatively unimportant. Planting proceeded fairly rapidly but early in the twentieth century a bad outbreak of Phylloxera developed and caused a serious set-back. The problem was overcome by distributing the disease-resistant American vine to growers. The acreage under vineyards then grew quickly and the wine industry started to expand until today the islands even manage to export a small quantity of wine.

There were a number of other changes in farming practice which took place in the British period. With rising living standards the growing of the hardy grain *mischiato* declined very rapidly, particularly in the second half of the nineteenth century. As the cotton industry declined so did the demand for raw cotton and the acreage given to the crop decreased. There was a brief revival during the American Civil War but when more normal market conditions returned the downward trend resumed. Between the two world wars the crop ceased to be grown in Malta. Associated with the decline of cotton was the increased acreage given to potatoes, wheat and sulla. The last-named crop, a member of the clover family, was cultivated to provide a feed for animals; cotton seed having previously been extensively used for this purpose.

Rising living standards, coupled with the growth in size of the English community, helped to increase the demand for fresh fruit and vegetables. As a result a large number of irrigated horticultural establishments developed in various parts of the islands.

At a very early stage the British introduced milch cattle to supply the demand for fresh milk. Sir William Reid imported Angus cattle but until recently large herds of goats were the islands' principal source of milk. Since the Second World War a subsidy has been successfully used to bring about an increase in the number of milch cattle at the expense of goats.

In general, industries which were not in some way associated with the British services did not flourish. During the period many of the local craft industries declined when faced with competition from imported goods. The activity most severely hit was the cotton industry which in the latter part of the eighteenth century had been an important exporter of spun cotton and cotton goods. By the time the British gained control of the islands the industry was already in difficulties and it continued to decline throughout the nineteenth century. The industry's demise was slow for the home market continued to absorb its products and it was possible to keep prices down by the depression of wage rates. In 1839, for instance, it was calculated that a woman received less than one penny for spinning cotton for 17 hours a day. In 1842, 25 per cent of the gainfully employed population claimed to be operatives in the industry, although it is certain that the majority of these persons were in work only fitfully. The industry had virtually disappeared by the beginning of the First World War.

The British inherited the Order's small shipyard and at a very early stage the Royal Navy laid plans to expand these facilities. However, it was not until 1844 that the foundation stone was laid for the first dry dock, which was built at the head of Galley Creek. (The British renamed this part of the Grand Harbour Dockyard Creek.) The dry dock was opened in 1848 and shortly plans were drawn up to build similar works to cope with the increased volume of naval repairs. A great debate started as to whether the French Creek or the Marsa would be the best site. The choice of the latter site would have involved the movement of the entire naval dockyard but in compensation a large area of flat land would be available to allow all foreseeable expansions to develop unhindered. The French Creek site was hampered by lack of space. Against this the inner area of the Grand Harbour was shallow and would require considerable dredging. In the end the debate was resolved in favour of the French Creek and a start was made on the, then, huge Somerset Dock, which was opened in 1871. For a time this dock was larger than any available to the Royal Navy at Portsmouth. In 1892 the Hamilton Dock was completed and in 1899 a start was made on two more dry docks. Development went on until the naval dockyard consisted of one dock in Galley Creek and four in French Creek. The docks were supported by extensive harbourside workshops and refit facilities. Naval repair establishments were developed in the Marsamxett as well; a small boat yard was erected on Manoel island and provision was also made to enable work to be undertaken on submarines and destroyers. During the First World War the naval dockyard employed 10,000 men.

The commercial facilities built in the Grand Harbour by the Order also underwent huge extensions. With the introduction of steam-propelled vessels large coal-bunkering installations had to be provided, not only for ships of the Royal Navy but also for private vessels calling at the island to refuel. With increasing traffic it became necessary to improve the harbour facilities available to this last class of vessel. About 1840 the inner part of the Grand Harbour was extended and in 1859 extensive new commercial port facilities were started in the area.

In 1873 the Anglo-Maltese Hydraulic Dock Company opened a commercial repair yard in the Marsamxett which flourished for many years.

During the first half of the nineteenth century the external trade of the islands experienced widely fluctuating fortunes. The prosperity of the early years of the century had been cut short by the plague of 1813 and a decade of difficulty had followed. It was not until 1825 that trade began to pick up once more. However, the general health of the economy remained fragile; large numbers of Maltese continued to endure low living standards and the reports of the 1836–8 Royal Commission indicate a considerable degree of poverty in the islands. In the eighteen-forties prosperity returned and during the Crimean War (1853–56) boom conditions were enjoyed. Prosperity was not solely due to the increased military spending but also to the general increase in Mediterranean trade which took place around this time. The Peninsular and Orient Line was carrying increasing amounts of traffic through the Mediterranean and in 1858 the company opened a railway which linked Alexandria to Suez, thus facilitating the transport of goods and passengers across the neck of land which separated the Mediterranean from the Red Sea. The next step was, of course, to cut a canal, allow the direct passage of vessels and dispense with the expensive unloading and loading of goods, which the railway link involved. A canal had long been thought of but it was not until the eighteen-fifties that, in spite of British opposition, the project was undertaken.

Governor Sir William Reid (1851–58) perceived that the cutting of the Suez Canal would turn the Mediterranean into a major seaway and laid plans to cope with the new situation. Reid's schemes were pressed by his successor, Sir John Gaspard Le Marchant (1858–1863), and when the canal was opened in 1869 Malta was ready to take advantage of the new patterns of trade which were to develop. From 1859 onwards, at the innermost part of the Grand Harbour, new facilities for commercial vessels were constructed. After the opening of the canal the number of vessels calling at the islands rapidly increased and within a short time Malta was enjoying a trade boom. By 1880 the Grand Harbour was firmly established as the chief coaling station for vessels plying between Britain, India and the East, entrepôt trade was flourishing, and over 3,000 steamers called at the island in the course of the year, not to mention nearly 2,000 sailing vessels. Hundreds of thousands of tons of coal were heaved in and out of the bunkers around the harbour and the port labour was almost incessantly employed.

Government revenue was very largely drawn from dues levied

on port activity and income rose rapidly. The building of the railway between Valletta and Mdina, high spending by the Admiralty and the Royal Engineers, all contributed towards the maintenance of full employment and good rates of pay. Yet the structural weaknesses in the local economy were apparent to all who studied the matter and were constantly being debated in the Council of Government. By 1890 it was clear that Malta could not rely indefinitely upon the trade boom. The islands had got a flying start in the competition to capture the new trade passing through the Mediterranean but other ports were not content to allow Malta to retain an unchallenged lead. Algiers, Gibraltar, Port Said spent heavily on harbour works and their facilities became not only better than those offered at Malta but coal at these ports tended to be cheaper.

The chief Secretary of the Malta administration, Sir Gerald (later Lord) Strickland (1889–1896), started to make some spirited pleas in the Council of Government for the harbour facilities to be improved and for the encouragement of new industries, trade and agriculture in general. There was even talk of creating a free port and starting a tourist trade. Unfortunately this was a bad time at which to urge such matters. In 1887 the elected majority on the Council had been given the power to control financial affairs. Now most of the elected members were uninformed on matters relating to capital investment projects and intransigently selfish on questions of taxation. Many councillors simply failed to grasp the essential fact that if Malta was to have new services and attractions these would have to be paid for by raising new capital. The more the Chief Secretary urged this point of view the less positive response he got, one elected member expressing his position in the phrase—'No loans, no new taxes, no increase in the existing ones.' Strickland got little support when he attempted to get funds voted for the introduction or improvement of essential services. The idea of free education was not received enthusiastically and even the cost of introducing electric lighting had to be smuggled through the Council. Eventually, in 1901, an Order in Council had to be passed by the British Government to override the Malta Council of Government and sanction spending on services like schools, drainage, waterworks, hospitals and roads. However, in the same year the Chief Secretary, Francesco Vella, failed in an attempt to get some financial assistance for the Hydraulic Dock Company. The firm wanted to invest in new capital equipment to cope with the increasing size of vessels calling at Malta. Vella proposed that the Malta Government should guarantee the interest, under certain conditions, on the new capital which would be required. This was not a revolutionary proposal as interest guarantees had long been given by governments attempting to encourage new enterprises. The Council would have none of it and the proposal had to be withdrawn; the company failed to raise the capital it needed and in due course it was closed down.

Competition from other ports and the inability of Malta to make the right investment decisions were not the only reasons for the island's decline as a coaling station and entrepôt centre. The size of ships was increasing rapidly and this fact, together with the introduction of the triple expansion engine, meant that vessels could travel longer distances without refuelling. As a result intermediate coaling stations, like Malta, were bound to be used by fewer and fewer vessels.

Malta entered the twentieth century with the trade boom already showing considerable signs of tarnish, government revenue falling and unemployment rising. The underlying problems were to be masked by new short-term factors. Early in the century the Admiralty started to construct a large breakwater system at the entrance to the Grand Harbour. The mouth of the harbour had been difficult to negotiate when the *grigal*, or north-east wind, was blowing and conditions even within the harbour could be made difficult. The new breakwater was designed to alleviate some of these problems. The project involved relatively huge numbers of workmen and the demand for labour was such that men had to be brought in from Spain and Italy. With labour becoming so scarce wage rates doubled in the course of a few years. In 1905 there were over 9,000 Maltese employed in naval establishments but much of the work was of a temporary nature and once the projects were completed men were laid off very quickly indeed. In 1911 the number of Maltese employed by the Admiralty had dropped to about 5,000 and wage rates had fallen as well. At about the same time, due to the German naval building programme, Britain strengthened the Home Fleet at the expense of Malta and the departure of units from the Grand Harbour added to the islands' difficulties. Hardship was soon widespread and in 1911 a Royal Commission was sent out to look into the affairs of Malta.

The commission quickly perceived the extent of the local problems; the decline in trade and the reduction of British defence spending were the primary causes of trouble but other factors had also to be taken into account. Many of the older craft industries had declined in competition with more efficient foreign enterprises, lack of security induced local capitalists to invest abroad rather than in productive concerns in Malta and the revenue system was in need of much improvement.

The commissioners were anxious to see basic foodstuffs freed of duty as this imposition fell most heavily upon the lower classes. The commission proposed the introduction of a new taxation system which would raise more revenue from the property-owning classes. On this point the report echoes the financial review of a few years previously which stated that the islands were not subject to income tax, estate duty, legacy duty, property tax or rates; in short landed property 'does not contribute one farthing to the revenue'.

The British services were not left untouched by the commission's comments upon revenue. To start with, the local treasury put up £5,000 each year to help meet the costs of garrisoning the island, the services paid no customs dues on their imports and they had the free use of the lands and buildings which they occupied in the islands —that is, lands and buildings which were the property of the civil administration. The commission did not mention the fact but the situation had been worse in the first half of the nineteenth century when the local exchequer paid a higher direct contribution to the costs of the garrison and also, for a short period, gave up any annual surplus that accrued for the same purpose.

The counter argument, which the military advanced against the commission's viewpoint, was that the services spent such large sums of money in Malta that they virtually supported the local economy, and to ask them to pay customs dues and rent on buildings was unreasonable.

The commissioners then moved on to positive recommendations as to how the local economy might be improved. It was suggested that the emigration rate should be stepped up, agriculture might be developed by encouraging the growth of small irrigation schemes, there might be a case for starting some new industries and they thought tourism might well be developed. Much of this is reminiscent of recent talk about prospects for economic development in Malta and might indicate that the commission was exceptionally forward-looking in its views. However, the recommendations are little more than a restatement of the ideas and plans which the administrators on the spot had been trying to implement for over 20 years. For instance, in 1902, in an effort to improve tourist facilities a block of Valletta had been offered for development as a hotel on a 99 year lease. Initially a syndicate from London showed a great deal of interest but in the end the scheme came to nothing. The problems associated with stepping up the migration rate and with starting new industries had been talked about for decades but under the latter head the commission brought to light one important fact: namely that there was no shortage of private capital in the islands, but rather that a lack of opportunity and security prevented its being invested profitably. As a result a very large part of Maltese savings was invested abroad.

Efforts were made to implement parts of the commission's findings. The £5,000 contribution which the local treasury paid each year to the costs of garrisoning the island was abolished, and an attempt made to introduce new sources of revenue. But this last measure ran into all the difficulties that had been generated previously when reform was mooted. Local pressure groups were able to stir up resentment to the idea of direct taxes and the proposals made little headway. In any case the economy began to improve, by 1914 the islands were no longer on the verge of insolvency and with the outbreak of the First World War full employment returned. Malta was used increasingly not only by the Royal Navy but also by the warships of allied navies, particularly the French. The dockyard was working at full capacity repairing damage and refitting vessels. Malta became a hospitalization centre for casualties from the Dardanelles and Salonika campaigns and tens of thousands of wounded men were treated in the islands.

However, the First World War was not an unmixed economic blessing. The disruption of trade reduced government revenue, and food prices tended to rise in response to shortages and higher freight rates, with the result that the cost of living was soon rising rapidly and the price of several basic commodities became inflated. The incomes of all sections of the community did not increase proportionately and in 1917 the dockyard workers came out on a token strike after being granted a 10 per cent wage increase, which was generally conceded to be inadequate. The wage rate was readjusted in the dockyard workers' favour but this did nothing to cure the underlying inflationary tendencies; and indeed the forces bringing about inflation were largely outside the power of the Malta authorities. The cessation of hostilities in 1918 did not ease matters for the cost of living continued at a high level while service spending and employment opportunities declined rapidly.

The high cost of living gave rise to increased dissatisfaction among many groups of persons who were suffering hardship. Dissatisfaction became unrest and in June, 1919 there were riots in Valletta. In August the Governor, Lord Plumer (1919–1924), reviewed the financial position of the islands and made strenuous efforts to relieve hardship. A bread subsidy was introduced, a programme of public works started and the salaries of many government employees were raised to provide them with a living wage. Yet the financial problems underlying the islands' situation were formidable. Due to wartime inflation the value of the fixed interest stocks which the Malta government held had fallen by nearly two-thirds, expenditure was exceeding income by a handsome margin and new sources of revenue would be difficult to find. Raising a loan to provide for the relief of hardship was not felt to be sound economics, and although the government had considerable properties the selling of these would only provide short-term relief and increase the long-term problems.

The British Government helped out with a grant of £250,000 later in the year but this was soon spent. By January 1920 the administration was spending over £4,000 per week on the bread subsidy alone.

Fortunately the economy did begin to pick up again. The number of ships calling at the islands slowly increased, the cost of foodstuffs did improve in Malta's favour and migration began to relieve some of the population pressure.

With the immediate financial pressures lifted the whole question of diversifying the economy was again examined in detail. There were hopes that one of the larger British shipbuilding and repairing companies could be persuaded to commence operations at Malta. Efforts were made to encourage small industries and agriculture, whilst in 1924 a tourist bureau was started and the possibility of the government's building hotels was examined. Little came of much of this discussion largely because the world economic situation was unfavourable. Nevertheless, the years between 1923 and 1926 were reasonably prosperous and some economic progress was made. However, 1927 saw adverse world economic forces once more starting to impinge upon life in the islands. As government revenue fell so did public works expenditure and unemployment mounted. The deepening depression made labour plentiful throughout the world and it was difficult to find outlets for Maltese migrants. It was not until 1934–35 that the island started to revive economically under the stimulus of the general increase in world trade and due to British rearmament to face the threat from the Axis powers. In 1935 Italy invaded Abyssinia. World opinion was very much against this act and, although in the end no effective action was undertaken, Britain did build up her military strength in the Mediterranean to the benefit of the Maltese economy. From this time onwards the British spent increasing sums improving the military facilities on the islands in preparation for the coming battle with Italy and Germany.

Throughout the period of British rule described so far, the economy of the islands had been liable to considerable fluctuations. As a military base Malta was clearly vulnerable to variations in defence spending but this problem was accentuated by the fact that the islands lacked diversity in their economic structure. The only other considerable source of income was gained from commercial vessels calling at the Grand Harbour. Yet this activity was also cyclical and suffered variation not only as a result of alterations in the volume of world trade but also from the changing patterns of trade within the Mediterranean. Technological changes relating to the size and range of vessels also had an adverse effect. Malta did not always react quickly enough in a fluid situation and as a result lost trade on occasions to competing ports. Similarly many small local industries were unable to cope with competition from imported products and went into decline. Efforts to create new industries were made but a high proportion of these attempts were failures due to adverse local conditions. It is significant to note that although some Maltese could command considerable amounts of capital, during the second half of the nineteenth century, very few of them invested money in new productive enterprises. Clearly the economics of producing many goods locally were not sound. The greatest part of Maltese money found its way into savings abroad or was invested in service industries which existed upon the spending of British military personnel. In sum, it is fair to conclude that, although the islands increased considerably in wealth, prosperity and population under British rule, they were always liable to suffer alarming economic fluctuations which could cause great hardship.

Constitutionally the islands also suffered fluctuation. In 1813 Malta became a Crown Colony and was ruled by a Governor whose power was unfettered by any consultative or legislative body in Malta. The Governor was, of course, subject to control and instruction by the British Government. In 1835 a revised constitution was introduced which laid down that the Governor should be advised by a council consisting of seven members and the Lieutenant Governor. The Council, on which the Maltese were represented by at least three members, was only an advisory body and the Governor retained overall responsibility.

The form of the Council was altered slightly as the years went by and in 1849 considerably enlarged. The 1849 constitution provided for a council of eighteen members: the Governor, nine official members and eight elected members. Although the Council had a built-in official majority the Maltese were at least being allowed to take part in the debates leading to the formulation of policy. The constitution did enable the Governor to act over the Council's head if he thought it necessary.

The new constitution did not work particularly well, as the Maltese members felt that they should have a measure of real control over internal affairs and should not have to operate within the constitutional strait-jacket provided by the official majority.

The British administrators were divided in their viewpoint by this time. Sir William Reid felt that the Maltese should have a greater share of responsibility whilst others felt that the majority of Maltese politicians were unfit to hold public office. As one described it, 'the small legislative council was palpably factious and unreasonable' and in it the 'few agitators who strutted on this miniature political stage represented very imperfectly the views and true interests of the mass of the population'. The 1849 constitution virtually ceased to function as intended under Sir Gaspard le Marchant (1858–1864) who employed the cruelly effective method of ringing the division bell every time one of the 'strutters' got up to oppose a measure introduced by the Governor. This brought the debate to a close and the official majority did the rest.

In 1864 Sir Henry Storkes replaced le Marchant and it became policy not to press matters relating to expenditure against the wishes of the elected members.

In 1887 a new constitution was introduced which gave the elected members of the Council a majority. The Council had the power to legislate on most matters relating to the islands' internal affairs and it controlled financial matters. The British Crown retained the right of intervention but these powers were only to be used in exceptional circumstances.

At this period there was a development of two bodies of opinion amongst the Maltese members of the council. A reform group tended to be pro-English while the anti-reform group was pro-Italian, at least in a cultural sense. The latter group was opposed to the teaching of English in Maltese schools at the expense of Italian and it made strenuous efforts to block the voting of money for the development of an educational system of which it disapproved. The group was also against proposed reforms to the civil service and system of taxation. In general the anti-reformers disapproved of increased public expenditure and were uncooperative in expediting the business of government. In 1903, largely as a result of this unsatisfactory situation, the 1887 constitution was replaced by another which returned to the principle of an official majority.

The 1903 constitution prevailed until the conclusion of the First World War. After the war a body of politicians founded the Maltese National Assembly which made demands for a higher degree of autonomy. At the same time not only were the islands enduring very difficult economic circumstances but students started to demonstrate against a proposed modification of the rather extravagant titles which were given to degrees awarded by the University. Tension built-up until on June 17th, 1919, rioting broke out in Valletta and a considerable amount of damage was done to property. Troops were called into the city, and when the rioters attacked them three Maltese were shot dead on the spot and another died later of his wounds.

There is a controversy as to the cause of the riots, some claiming they were motivated by anti-British feelings, others that they were a reaction against the high price of bread. If the choice of targets attacked by the mob is anything to go by several factors were involved. The University suffered much damage, the pro-British *Malta Daily Chronicle* was ransacked, the homes of several politicians with similar sympathies were wrecked and some flour mills were broken up.

A new Governor, Lord Plumer, arrived to take up his appointment in the midst of the chaotic political and economic situation. Plumer's actions were at one and the same time firm and conciliatory. Some local politicans had been making statements which could be interpreted as incitements to violence and these men were told categorically that if they did not moderate their behaviour the Governor would act severely against them. At the same time, working upon instructions from London, he made it clear that the Maltese were to get a larger share in the running of the internal affairs of the islands.

In December 1919 Malta was granted full self-government 'in all matters of purely local concern'. The despatch from Downing Street declared that 'there will in fact have to be two concurrent systems of government in the Island: a government of matters of Imperial concern which must take orders from the Imperial Government and a government for local affairs which will be controlled by the wishes of the inhabitants of the Island expressed through popular institutions.' The two forms of government were to be united in the person of the Governor. On paper this system of diarchy, as it was termed, went a long way towards satisfying the interests of all parties but the key problem was one of definition: where did Imperial interests end? Although this matter was worked out in the detailed wording of the constitution in practice the system did not function well. The new constitution became effective in 1921, the same year in which the British introduced diarchy into India.

At first all progressed well and the new Maltese Government got on with the business of developing the economy and the social services. However, after a few years, considerable trouble developed as a result of conflicts not only between the Church and the internal Government but also between the upper and lower houses of the

Maltese parliament. In 1930 the British Government suspended the constitution and although this was restored in 1932 it was suspended again in the following year. Malta was not to return to internal self-government until 1947.

One of the problems which dominated the internal political scene in Malta until the outbreak of the Second World War was the language question. When the British came to the islands they found a population in which the majority of persons spoke Maltese. The middle and upper classes used Italian not only for business and professional purposes but also in everyday speech. The Order had conducted the administration of the islands in Italian and the British continued to use this language for official purposes. As we have seen, Sir Thomas Maitland laid it down that English had to be used for administrative business but this measure does not appear to have been fully enforced.

As British rule developed the great body of the islanders went on speaking Maltese, whilst the middle classes and above continued to use Italian. Many Maltese, of course, cultivated a knowledge of the English language if it were necessary for business purposes but Italian remained the language of education and the language of the law-courts.

Now clearly, as more and more Maltese became dependent upon Britain and the British services for a livelihood, it would be to their advantage to learn English. To a lesser degree Italian was an important language, for the islands had many links with Italy. In the normal course of events it would be expected that the educational system would adjust itself to the needs of the islanders. In fact the introduction of the teaching of the English language, on a basis equal to that enjoyed by Italian, was fiercely resisted by certain sections of Maltese society and the language question developed into a burning issue which dominated local politics for decades.

The first shots in the battle were fired in the late eighteen-seventies when a report on the civil establishments in Malta recommended that all the business of government should be conducted in English and promotion should not be given unless the candidate displayed a thorough knowledge of that language. Within a short time another report was published recommending the reform of the education system. The report proposed that both Maltese and

English should occupy a more important place in the syllabuses of the islands' schools. These suggestions raised violent feelings amongst the anti-reformers and many bitter debating contests developed in the Council of Government. But slowly and inevitably reform came, for it was patently ridiculous to attempt to maintain the supremacy of Italian in a country where the vast majority of the population did not use that language.

Gradually the teaching of English and Maltese came to occupy a more important place in local curricula and eventually the local population got the right to be tried in their native language. In 1899 it became permissible to use the English language in the law-courts in certain circumstances but it was not until 1934 that Maltese was made the principal language of the courts, in preference to Italian. The 1921 constitution declared that Italian and English were the official languages of Malta. In 1934 Maltese was added to the list and in 1936 the position was simplified by making English the language of administration and Maltese the language of the courts. All subsequent constitutions have maintained this position.

The language question has comic opera qualities but it is a mistake to take the controversy entirely at its face value. The problem was but one facet of a struggle in which a relatively privileged group in Maltese society attempted to maintain its position. The language question also represented a cultural clash as Maltese middle and upper classes tried to retain certain cultural traits which they felt the English influence was eroding. Italian language and culture became a rallying point for these groups.

Inevitably the language question was exploited by the Italian fascists during the nineteen-thirties in their efforts to give substance to spurious claims for possession of the Maltese islands. The Maltese who admired Italian culture had always maintained their loyalty to the British Crown. Unfortunately in the thirties a number of pro-Italian politicians in Malta were thought by the British to be displaying irredentist tendencies. When the Second World War broke out some of these men were deported to East Africa while others were held in custody. Needless to say, what sympathy there was in the islands for Italy did not last long once the bombing of Malta started.

A review of the political scene in the islands during British rule leaves the impression that the islanders and the British were continually in conflict. In fact this impression in quite untrue. To begin with only a limited number of Maltese were involved in political matters during the nineteenth century. At the turn of the century, out of a population approaching 200,000, only about 10,000 persons had the vote and less than half of these ever bothered to use it.

By and large the British and the Maltese enjoyed cordial social relations. To British officers Malta became a relatively popular station with its swimming, sailing, reasonably good sports facilities and opportunities for social occasions. There were, of course, the usual problems associated with English aloofness and the ill manners of British forces stationed overseas but as time went by these difficulties became less troublesome. The Maltese soon picked up the English language, by the end of the nineteenth century they held most of the jobs in the civil administration, a group of influential Anglo-Maltese families came into being and sections of Maltese society started to imitate certain English habits. Sons were sent off to English public schools, one such institution was even founded on the island, Maltese officers received training at British military establishments and, perhaps above all, in the growing town of Sliema and the adjoining suburbs, English and Maltese families lived side by side. Imported patterns of life were imitated by the local inhabitants, particularly in this century, and the ability to speak good English came to be regarded as increasingly important. Maltese living in the Sliema area, or *Ta'Sliema* as they are termed, became recognized, by the remainder of the islanders, as being culturally distinct.

The British, like the Order of St. John before them, modified the whole economic, social and political structure of the island. The modifications took place in a society which was highly individual and the new social patterns which emerged were distinctive and Maltese; the islands retained their character and personality.

9

The Second World War

During the Second World War Malta underwent another siege which was every bit as heroic as the battle of 1565 and probably more important to the Western World. There are a number of similarities between the two sieges for both were fights against very high odds, in both battles the Maltese played an outstanding part and in each case the defending commanders had not prepared the islands adequately. There is even a similarity in the way the respective chroniclers describe events. All Moslems are bad and all Christians good in 1565. In the early nineteen-forties Germans are efficient, ruthless and evil, whilst the Commonwealth heroes are brilliant, daring and fearless—even when they are putting the final torpedo into an already stricken troopship or shelling an enemy submarine as it tries to surrender. And, of course, the Italians are frequently described as cowardly, although this reputation is certainly not altogether true with regard to the fighting around Malta.

Since the conclusion of the First World War military technology had undergone very rapid development and it was not until the nineteen-thirties were well advanced that Britain started to modernize its fighting services and re-arm. Malta, as a major base of the Mediterranean fleet, also required considerable development if it was to be effective in a war in which air power was going to play an important part. Unfortunately the Royal Air Force became convinced that, however thorough the preparations made to resist air attacks on Malta, Italian aircraft could not be prevented from breaking through to bomb the naval dockyard and the airfields. The Royal Air Force pointed out that Sicily was only 30 minutes flying time away, that there was no possibility of air defence in depth or of adequate dispersal of aircraft and above all there was the problem of supplying the island.

The viewpoint of the Royal Navy was very different. Malta was the Mediterranean fleet's most important base and many of the repair facilities available on the island could not be easily moved elsewhere. If Italy came into a war and threatened Suez and the Mediterranean sea-routes, then the Royal Navy saw amongst its principal tasks that of severing sea communications between Italy and her North African colonies, together with ensuring the free passage of British shipping through the waist of the Mediterranean. In these tasks Malta was obviously a key position. Additionally combined operations with the French navy could be more readily worked from Malta rather than Alexandria.

The British army came to similar conclusions about the defensibility of Malta as the Royal Air Force, with the result that only limited preparations were made for the defence of the island before the beginning of the war. No one seems to have taken the indefensibility argument through to its conclusion—if Malta was not going to be properly defended then the British forces were virtually giving up the challenge for supremacy in the central Mediterranean and its sea-routes. Further, if Malta was not defensible, then there was no point in leaving the meagre garrison and its equipment on the island to be overrun at a later date.

The story is reminiscent of the attitude of the knights to the island in their early years on Malta. Several factions were unable to decide among themselves whether Malta was a good base or not and, by diligent argument, achieved nothing until they were forced to fight for the island from an inadequately prepared position.

The Royal Navy was to be proved right in this matter. Malta could be and was used as a successful offensive base, provided adequate air defence was available. The Royal Air Force was unduly pessimistic about the island's prospects. Technically the air officers may have been right in their arguments but there is a world of difference between what is correct in Staff College war games and what resourceful commanders may achieve in the field. If Malta was only 30 minutes flying time away from Sicily then the reverse was also true and, although the Malta targets suffered the disadvantage of excessive concentration, a reasonable degree of aircraft dispersal was eventually achieved and it was found that

The Second World War

bombed runways could be more quickly serviced than had been anticipated.

It is fair to say, in defence of the Royal Air Force viewpoint, that the strategic situation looked very different in the late nineteen-thirties when France had potential control of a large part of the western Mediterranean. The Royal Air Force was hoping to build-up a bomber force at Tunis for operations in the central Mediterranean. Against this it is possible to argue that Italy would only be seen in the war if France were crushed, in which case Malta would become a vital position.

The general uncertainty surrounding the island led to the situation in the summer of 1939 when 'the broad general policy for Malta was still undecided.' War was declared in September of the same year. The island's anti-aircraft defences were still inadequate, fighter cover was completely lacking, there were no air raid shelters and aircraft servicing facilities were limited. There was a lack of reconnaissance aircraft and bombers. It was extremely doubtful if the coastal defences were strong enough to resist a seaborne assault and stocks of food and other supplies were miserable. In these conditions there could be no thought of using Malta as an offensive base and the British Mediterranean fleet was forced to withdraw to Alexandria. Only the submarines were left behind.

When war was declared Italy, being under-prepared and short of various strategic resources, announced a policy of non-belligerence but with the fall of France Mussolini's advisers could restrain him no longer. Declaring that 'to participate in the peace one must participate in the war' the Duce brought Italy into the fighting on June 11th, 1940. On the same day Malta suffered its first air attack when Italian aircraft bombed the naval dockyard and one of the airfields. At this time the islands possessed the following anti-aircraft defences: 34 heavy anti-aircraft guns, 8 light anti-aircraft guns, 24 searchlights, 1 radar station and a few Sea Gladiator fighters. Airfields were available at Ta'Qali, Luqa (finished May 1940) and Hal Far together with a flying boat base at Kalafrana on Marsaxlokk.

Late in 1939 it had been decided, by the Committee of Imperial Defence, to provide Malta with an effective air defence system and the island was allocated four fighter squadrons and 172 anti-aircraft guns. Of course, as the war in Western Europe had warmed up,

200

very little of this material had been delivered and Malta's Air Officer Commanding had been forced to look around elsewhere for help. It was discovered that the Royal Navy held a number of unassembled Gloster Sea Gladiators. Permission was obtained for the Royal Air Force to use four of the aircraft and they were taken out of store and assembled in April 1940. Volunteers came forward to fly them and seven pilots were selected. All the volunteers had considerable flying experience but none were fighter pilots at the time and some came from chair-borne jobs.

The Gloster Gladiator had come into service with the Royal Air Force in 1937 and the modified Sea Gladiator had been delivered to the Fleet Air Arm in 1939. Although a biplane of obsolete design the Gladiator was highly manoeuvrable, reliable and airworthy. Its maximum speed was only 250 m.p.h. at 15,500 feet but it had a relatively good rate of climb to that height and its operational ceiling (32,500 feet) was about equal to that of the Italian fighters against which it was pitted. The Gladiator's great advantage was that it proved exceptionally difficult to shoot down over Malta— due to the plane's sturdy structure and manoeuvrability. The biggest disadvantage was that it was hardly fast enough to catch the Italian bombers used against Malta in June 1940. The Savoia Marchetti 79, which was extensively operational over the island, had a top speed of 255 m.p.h. at 13,000 feet and it was only by modifying the Gladiator engine that the aircraft was given enough speed to make contact in running fights. The modifications, however, wore out the engines fairly quickly.

On the first day of the Italian campaign against Malta the Gladiators brought down an enemy aircraft, and although one of the four was quickly damaged beyond repair the remaining three continued to make a considerable nuisance of themselves and were soon nicknamed Faith, Hope and Charity. Of course, three aircraft could not take on the 200 the Italians had in Sicily with any hope of winning but Faith, Hope and Charity did force the Italians to bomb from a greater height and thus lose accuracy. For a while the *Regia Aeronautica* even resorted to night attacks and the Italians were obliged to send large fighter escorts along with the bombers. Some measure of the Gladiators' effectiveness is given by the fact that Italian airmen operational over Malta estimated the strength of the defending fighter force at 25! How many aircraft Faith, Hope and Charity accounted for is in doubt as in the hectic battle conditions it was rarely possible to confirm a kill. One Gladiator pilot was credited with six victories in about a month and awarded the Distinguished Flying Cross early in July 1940. The most important aspect of the Faith, Hope and Charity campaign was not the number of kills the few aeroplanes and pilots obtained, although these were not negligible, but the fact that they represented a means by which Malta, the garrison and the people could feel they were fighting back and defiant. Nothing is worse for the morale of a garrison under siege than to feel that it is merely a sitting target with no hope of victory or retaliation.

The three Gladiators, or less, for rarely were they all serviceable, fought alone for about three weeks until at the end of June 1940 four Hurricanes, the fighter which replaced the Gladiator in the service of the Royal Air Force, were detained at Malta as they stopped to refuel on a flight to the Middle East. About a month later a dozen Hurricanes were flown into the island from an aircraft carrier which had sailed part way from Gibraltar to Malta. From this point the Gladiators became less important although they continued to be used as combat aircraft for many more months until eventually all were destroyed or worn out.

By the end of June 1940 it had been realized that aircraft could be operated from Malta effectively and a slow build-up of forces developed. Apart from the Hurricanes mentioned above torpedo-carrying Swordfish were brought in to start operations against Italian shipping. Some Sunderland flying boats were moved to Malta from Alexandria and soon started to harry Italian submarines. In September 1940 Marylands were brought in to undertake much-needed aerial reconnaissance work and more Sunderlands arrived from Alexandria. Shortly afterwards Wellington bombers were stationed on the island and began making effective raids on Italian seaports and shipping.

At the same time as the Malta-based aircraft were becoming an effective power the Allied land forces in North Africa began to enjoy success. Initially the Italians had advanced into Egypt but on December 7th, 1940, the Eighth Army attacked Sidi Barrani. By December 15th, Egypt had been cleared of Italian troops and when the advance halted, at El Agheida, on February 1st, 1941, the British had taken about 130,000 prisoners and a great deal of equipment for the loss of 2,000 men, including the wounded.

But the very success of these efforts attracted attention and helped to convince the German High Command that the Italian forces were incapable of nullifying the British in the Mediterranean. In December 1940 *Fliegerkorps X* was moved into southern Italy and Sicily. This air force had been hardened by its experiences in the Norwegian campaign and was by this time highly skilled. By early January 1940 Fliegerkorps X had in Sicily 61 dive-bombers, 77 long-range bombers, 12 reconnaissance aircraft and a force of fighters. With the Italian aircraft there were about 250 available for attacks on Malta, which possessed about 60 aircraft in all.

The German air force was soon producing impressive results. In its first action Fliegerkorps X badly damaged the British aircraft carrier *Illustrious* and forced it out of the Mediterranean for repairs. Air attacks on Malta were intensified and soon the Royal Air Force began to wilt under the pressure developed by the superior Axis forces. As a result sinkings of vessels plying between Italy and North Africa, with supplies for the Italian armies, started to fall off. And when in February, 1941, the Italians transported the German *Afrika Korps* to Libya the losses were negligible. At the end of March, Rommel was able to launch a new Axis offensive in North Africa and by mid-April he had overrun Cyrenaica and gained the Egyptian border. From an Allied viewpoint the loss of Cyrenaica was particularly important for it made the running of convoys from Alexandria to Malta a hazardous business. Aircraft based in the bulge of Cyrenaica could attack allied convoys far from Malta.

Rommel's successful attack in North Africa was not the only reverse that the British suffered in the spring of 1941. Early in April the Germans attacked Greece and by the end of the month the British forces fighting there had to be evacuated. Following upon this success the Germans attacked Crete at the end of May and, although the cost was high, the island was taken. Crete gave the Germans additional airfields from which to squeeze the Malta-Alexandria supply line.

The pressure on British forces in the Middle East was now extremely high and Malta had become a very insecure position. Fortunately for the British cause, the Germans attacked Russia on June 22nd, 1941, and forces had to be withdrawn from the Mediterranean to support the new campaign. From Malta's viewpoint, the redeployment of a large part of Fliegerkorps X was particularly welcome.

By this time the strategic importance of Malta had been fully appreciated by the British and belated efforts were being made to build-up the island's striking power. In May 1941 Air Marshal Sir Hugh Lloyd was posted to Malta as Air Officer Commanding and expressly instructed to concentrate upon the sinking of Axis supply vessels serving North Africa. This tardy recognition of Malta's importance could not immediately overcome the neglect of the pre-war years. When Lloyd arrived he was appalled by the inadequate base from which the island's air force operated. There was little dispersal of aircraft; stores, including petrol, were piled in the open; and equipment for servicing aircraft was desperately short. There were not enough radar stations to give all-round coverage of the island's sky approaches. Nor were there sufficient personnel to ground-staff the aircraft which the island possessed. The years of neglect and muddled thinking in the period leading up to the Second World War had produced a hazardous situation. There is no doubt, for instance, that losses of stores and aircraft, on the ground, could have been greatly reduced had preparations been made before the war started. Had more spares and personnel been available aircraft could have been operated more efficiently. Had more air raid shelters been dug losses of civilians and servicemen would have been lower. Now Malta was under blockade and the cost of getting spanners, radar sets and personnel into the island was brutally high. The building of air raid shelters and dispersal areas was slow because there was simply not enough labour on the island to undertake all the tasks that had to be completed.

Nevertheless initiative and ingenuity, backed by a greater availability of aircraft, brought a coherence to air operations which had previously been lacking. A huge network of taxiways and dispersal points was constructed around the most important airfields, making it much more difficult to destroy aircraft on the ground. The island lacked night fighters but an ingenious technique was developed whereby Hurricanes flew behind searchlight beams and attempted to shoot down any Axis aircraft which was illuminated. The intelligent use of photo-reconnaissance techniques enabled the aeroplanes striking at Axis shipping to operate with a relatively high degree of efficiency.

Under Lloyd's command three principal types of aircraft were used for attacks on Axis shipping and ports: torpedo-carrying Swordfish, Blenheims and Wellington bombers. Conventional bombing raids on shipping had been shown to be largely ineffective. The targets were not large enough and even where a high degree of accuracy was obtained a large proportion of the bombs normally fell into the sea around the ship. To counteract this the Blenheim squadrons had developed a method of low-level combat. The bomber was brought to the attack at deck level. At the last moment the aircraft was pulled up and over the target, and the bomb released. The weapon normally pierced the side or deck of the ship and was armed with an 11 second fuse to allow the aircraft to clear the blast zone. Attacks developed in this manner were highly successful and for a time the Malta Blenheims prospered. However, in August 1941 Axis vessels were armed with anti-aircraft guns and casualty rates started to increase very rapidly. Soon the chances of a Blenheim crew's surviving for long in Malta became very limited indeed. But the attacks went on. Quite simply if three Blenheims struck at an Italian ship and sank it together with its supplies for North Africa this was a good victory for the Allies, even if one or two Blenheims failed to return from the mission. The aircrews appreciated that the Axis forces in North Africa were being made desperately short of war materials by their efforts and went on undertaking sorties on supply convoys even when the missions became almost suicidal. A knight of the Order of St. John had about an even chance of surviving the four months of the Siege fighting in 1565. Blenheim airmen in late 1941 had a much poorer chance of surviving even for one month.

Blenheims were also used for attacks on Italian ports but here the most widely employed weapon was the Wellington bomber. Tripoli was pounded until the efficiency of the port was greatly reduced and Naples, too, suffered heavy bombing. Hurricanes and Beaufighters were used for ground attack work on targets in Sicily, North Africa and Sardinia.

Target information for the units striking at Axis shipping was provided by Maryland photo-reconnaissance aircraft which had been purchased from the United States. For a large part of the year the Mediterranean offers relatively good conditions for aerial photography and the Marylands provided regular cover of the Italian ports used by vessels loading for the North Africa run. With this information it was possible to build up the pattern of Axis shipping operations and take appropriate measures. Regular surveillance of Naples provided information as to when convoys were about to sail and the vessels were later picked up en route and attacked.

Airborne attacks were not the only hazard which Axis shipping had to avoid, for the Malta submarines were insatiably voracious during the summer of 1941. At the beginning of the war in the Mediterranean British submarine operations had been unhappy. There were four submarines stationed at Malta in June 1940 and three of these were lost during their first patrol. The vessels employed were of the wrong type and showed up too easily in the clear Mediterranean waters. Early in 1941 a flotilla of U. class submarines was stationed in Marsamxett harbour and began to produce impressive results. Amongst the newcomers was *H.M.S. Upholder*, commanded by Lieutenant-Commander M. D. Wanklyn, who eventually won a Victoria Cross and two Distinguished Service Orders for his Malta exploits. Before being killed in April 1942 Wanklyn undertook 24 patrols in *Upholder*, sinking 94,900 tons of Axis supply shipping plus two destroyers and two submarines. *Upholder* also severely damaged a cruiser. Wanklyn's exploits were exceptional, he was certainly the most successful British submarine commander of the Second World War, but several other Malta-based submarines sank large tonnages of Axis shipping.

German and Italian submarines were active against convoys bringing supplies into Malta. The Italians had a very large submarine fleet but the force never achieved results commensurate with its size. The Italians did, however, develop a number of successful special naval vessels for strikes at ships in anchorages.

In July, 1941, the Italians made a bold attack upon the Grand Harbour. A few months previously the Italian navy had launched explosive motor boats at British shipping in Suda Bay (Crete). The attack had been highly successful and amongst other vessels a British cruiser had been put out of action. The explosive boats were fast hydroplanes which were piloted to within a short distance of the target before the helmsman went over the side. The missile careered on, rammed its target, sank, and then exploded under water. In suitable conditions explosive boats were a fearsome and effective weapon but against well-organized defences, as those around the Grand Harbour were, losses were bound to be high and the chances of success low.

Just before midnight on July 25th, 1941, an Italian sloop put down a gaggle of explosive motor boats, some 20 miles to the north of the Grand Harbour. These craft set off escorted by larger motor vessels but by this time the sloop had been picked up on the Malta radar and the coastal defences were alerted. As the little flotilla approached the Grand Harbour the noise of the boat engines was heard by the shore batteries. It had been intended to bomb Malta during the course of the operation and obscure the noise of the seaborne attack. The air raid did not materialize and the Italian air force had also failed to carry out an intended photo-reconnaissance on the previous day. As a result even if the explosive boats had got into the harbour they would have lacked target information. However, in spite of these failures, the men of the motor-boat flotilla refused to be discouraged and pressed their attack.

The long breakwater at the entrance to the Grand Harbour had a narrow boat passage in it, close to the shore and just below the guns of St. Elmo. The passage was blocked by steel netting but the Italians proposed to breach this using a small torpedo piloted by two men. The weapon would be attached to the netting and then timed to blow up when the crew had cleared the blast zone. Unfortunately the torpedo arrived late at the objective but in order to maintain the synchronization of the operation the crew apparently zeroed the weapon's time fuse and blew themselves up with the charge.[1] Cruelly, the netting failed to be dislodged. Realizing this one of the explosive motor boats attempted to force an entry. As the target was small the helmsman stayed aboard his boat until it struck the net. He, too, was killed and although he had succeeded in breaking through the original obstruction he had created another which was impassable. Over the boat passage, between the shore and the breakwater, was an iron bridge and the explosion brought part of it down into the channel. Brave men had died uselessly and the operation had to be abandoned. However, by this time, the searchlights had picked up the remaining vessels lying off

[1] Accounts of the raid differ as to whether or not the submarine was detonated. In any case the crew did not survive the operation.

the entrance to the harbour and the shore batteries, manned by the Royal Malta Artillery, started to blow them out of the water. There was nothing to do but turn and flee for Sicily. But dawn was not far away and at first light the Hurricanes were scrambled. Part way to Sicily they caught the remaining boats and sunk or crippled them all. It was a harsh ending to a boldly conceived and courageously conducted operation. The balance was to be re-dressed at a later date by Italian midget submarines in the harbours at Gibraltar and Alexandria.

The results of the Allied air and naval activity in the summer of 1941 were startling. In September 28 per cent of the war materials despatched from Italy to North Africa failed to arrive. In October the figure was 21 per cent and in the following month over 60 per cent. Not only were the Axis forces in North Africa being seriously under-supplied but no nation could afford to sustain shipping losses on this scale.

As a result of the destruction of supplies on their way from Italy to Libya, the Axis advance in North Africa came to a halt and the Allied Armies were able to prepare for an offensive. In November operation 'Crusader' was launched by the Eighth Army and very quickly the Axis forces were in rapid retreat. A quick allied victory in North Africa appeared certain.

In December 1941, the Germans had to withdraw squadrons from other theatres of war to strengthen the Axis air forces in Sicily and North Africa.

The Malta striking forces continued to sink Axis shipping in spite of increased bombing raids on the islands but supplies started to get through to North Africa at a slightly higher rate. These supplies enabled Rommel to develop an attack on the Allies at El Agheila on January 21st, 1942. The result was one of the most brilliant victories of the Second World War. With sufficient supplies of petrol for only a few days the Axis forces achieved not only a victory, but a rout in which vast quantities of military stores and fuel were captured. The Axis supply problem was eased, the heroic achieve-ments of the Malta aircraft and submarines over the past few months had all been set aside as the result of a brilliant, piratical thrust. But this was not all, for in the course of the next few months the British Eighth Army gave ground in North Africa all the way to El Alamein. The loss of the Royal Air Force fields in Cyrenaica made it much more difficult to supply Malta by convoy from Alexandria, as Axis air attacks were now substituted for British air support. The opening up of other ports in North Africa to Axis shipping made the targets for the Malta aircraft less concentrated and widened the area of sea over which supply convoys could be run. From the threshold of victory the Eighth Army had come to the brink of defeat. The position of Malta had been grossly weakened.

Throughout the early months of 1942 the island was raided almost incessantly. In February over 1,000 tons of bombs were unloaded onto the island, in March the figure exceeded 2,000 tons and in April the total reached the astonishing figure of 6,700 tons. This was a considerable feat of organization on the part of the Axis air forces. The effects of the bombing were quickly apparent. Air operations on the island were greatly hampered, after a time little attempt was made to operate the bomber striking forces and all efforts were concentrated on keeping the remaining fighters flying. The Wellingtons were withdrawn to Egypt and eventually even the submarines were forced to move to Alexandria. The British, however, were not prepared to concede the island easily and in March, April and May significant forces of Spitfires were flown in from aircraft carriers. The carriers penetrated into the western basin of the Mediterranean to a position south of Sardinia at which point the Spitfires took off for Malta. The planes were quickly consumed in the fighting but they were able to inflict some heavy defeats on the Axis air forces. Gradually the number of fighter squadrons in Malta was increased. By July 1st, 1942, there were over 200 aircraft operating from Malta and over 100 of these were Spitfires. The Hurricanes had been outfought by the latest Messerschmitt 109's and the Spitfire gave the Royal Air Force weapon superiority again. Additionally the Spitfire, with its more rapid rate of climb, was able to make interceptions sooner and thus attack formations of bombers before they had unloaded at Malta.

Yet the midsummer resurgence of British air power in Malta took place principally because the Axis commanders repeated their mistake of the previous year. In May 1942 part of the bomber force which was pounding Malta was withdrawn from Sicily and moved to other fronts. However, at the same time, it is fair to say, the Axis powers were planning the capture of the islands. A striking force was prepared for the operation and a date in June was tentatively fixed for the attack. Various reasons are given as to why the invasion did not take place, including the over-enthusiastic Rommel demanding additional forces to sustain his advance into Egypt, but in fact few of the German and Italian Commanders wanted to undertake the operation. The paratroopers and seaborne troops, who were to spearhead the attack, would certainly have suffered exceptionally heavy losses before they even landed on the island. The ground defences had been very carefully organized, the coasts were covered with thickets of barbed wire and three lines of intervisible, concrete, strong points had been built inland.

Losses to an attacking force would be high and none of the Axis commanders wished their troops to suffer, for it was very doubtful if the island would be taken in the end. The successes in North Africa appeared to make the Malta operation unnecessary and there was general relief when it was postponed and eventually cancelled.

By the time the Axis advance was checked at El Alamein in July 1942, the Malta air force was beginning not only to dominate the sky over the island but to make effective strikes again at enemy shipping. In July, also, submarines were moved back into Malta. To counter the island's resurgence Axis bombing attacks were developed with increasing intensity but now that Malta possessed a strong fighter force a higher proportion of the bombers was shot down. In August and September the bombing raids continued but so did the losses of Axis aircraft. At the same time sinkings of supply vessels by the Malta striking forces attained high levels once more. In October 1942 the Axis air forces conceded defeat over Malta; the sea-routes to North Africa were once more under constant Allied surveillance and threat.

When on October 23rd, 1942, the British Eighth Army was launched into the battle of El Alamein, the Axis forces were low on ammunition and the armoured units were critically short of vital petrol. The British victory at El Alamein proved to be decisive. In November 1942 Allied troops, largely American, were landed in western North Africa and by May 1943 all North Africa was in Allied hands.

In the battle for North Africa Malta had played a crucial part. The fight had revolved essentially around logistic problems and Malta lay close to the arteries of the Axis armies. When Malta dominated the seaways of the central Mediterranean the Allied campaigns in North Africa almost invariably prospered. The costs of operating from Malta were not low and the island's inherent geographical disadvantages were the cause of this. The limited extent of the island concentrated targets, local food production was hopelessly inadequate, there was a dearth of industrial capacity which involved the defenders in importing vast quantities of materials. The question of supply was as critical to Malta as it was to the Axis forces in North Africa. The battle for North Africa and the central Mediterranean was a battle for supplies and just as the Malta striking forces squeezed Axis supply lines German submarines, together with aircraft of the Regia Aeronautica and the Luftwaffe, attacked ships bringing stores to Malta. Allied shipping losses were huge and on a number of occasions the convoys to Malta were wiped out or forced back to their ports of departure. During the first half of 1942 the island came very close to starvation and supplies of aviation fuel reached dangerously low levels.

The failure of the Axis powers to take Malta in the siege of 1941–42 can be ascribed to a lack of consistent planning on the part of their commanders. It was never certain whether the commanders intended to subdue the island by aerial bombardment, by direct assault or by starving the population and garrison into submission. Too frequently policy was changed and Malta's defences were given time to recover when air striking power was moved away to other fronts. In the long run possibly the cheapest way to subdue the islands might have been by direct assault. The initial losses would have been horrifying but a landing on Gozo and the northern part of Malta, where the defences were relatively soft, at one of the periods when the Axis powers enjoyed air superiority, might well have proved successful. Of course, the Italians missed the opportunity of taking the islands cheaply in 1940 before the coastal defences had been properly prepared.

After the close of 1942 Malta moved quickly out of the theatre of hostilities. During the Allied assault upon Sicily in 1943 Malta was the operational headquarters in the early part of the campaign. The island was too small to hold the entire invasion force but it was used as a fighter base to give air cover to the main body of the attack. Here again Malta was not quite large enough for the purpose and, although every fighter possible was crammed onto the island, 30 squadrons in all, including three on a specially built strip in Gozo, there was some doubt as to whether this would be enough to achieve air superiority. In the event all proved well and air dominance was maintained until Sicilian airfields were captured. Once Sicily was in allied hands the strategic value of Malta declined, for the Axis powers could no longer contest the passage of Allied shipping through the central Mediterranean narrows.

Thus far we have concentrated upon Malta as a military base and the part the island played in the battle for the Mediterranean. There is another side to the story.

Just as the military organization of the islands had been neglected in the pre-war period so had the provision of an efficient civil defence system. The compact, congested towns, which lay around Marsamxett and the Grand Harbour, were bound to be heavily damaged by air attacks. This proved to be the case and the problem was exacerbated by the lack of air raid shelters. At first the severity of the aerial attack was limited. At the end of November 1940, after nearly six months of war, only about 200 dwellings had been destroyed or damaged by bombing. In the meantime the construction of air-raid shelters was pressed. Fortunately it was possible to construct highly effective shelters in Malta and hundreds of tunnels and chambers were made in the soft Globigerina limestone. The task was of course vast—as the Lieutenant Governor described it, 'the most extensive constructional project that has been undertaken in Malta since the time of the knights'—and the amount of manpower that the works absorbed was huge. At this time labour was scarce, there were not enough experienced miners and, of course, essential equipment for the work, automatic and pneumatic drills, was lacking. The problem was made worse by the fact that individuals were employing the miners to dig private shelters. In the end the practice had to be forbidden by law for the miners were so tired by their private-enterprise efforts that they were unable to work hard on the public shelters. By May 1941 minimum shelter space, two square feet, had been provided for 165,900 people and there was an efficient, if uncomfortable, shelter service in the harbour area where about 18,000 persons slept regularly in the shelters of Valletta, Floriana and the Three Cities. Many of the dockyard workshops were also moved into caverns excavated in the rock.

Life in large areas of Malta was disrupted. Maltese houses, built principally of stone blocks, collapsed when bombed and soon many streets were blocked with rubble. If in November 1940 only 200 dwellings had been destroyed or severely damaged, a year later the figure had reached 2,552. And in April 1942, alone, 11,450 buildings were destroyed or damaged. Fortunately the numbers killed did not rise in proportion and up to November 1941 only 344 civilians were killed as a result of bombing raids. The low casualty figure had been achieved partly by the construction of shelters and partly by evacuating the population into areas of relative safety. In May 1941 55,000 people were living away from their regular homes. A large number of people had moved out of the harbour areas to the country districts and the population of Mdina, a traditional refuge, had nearly doubled since the beginning of the war. Evacuation resulted in overcrowding in many homes whilst numerous evacuees were forced to live in wooden huts.

Large sections of the island's commercial life were disrupted but there was no unemployment. Indeed such a scarcity of workers developed that direction of labour became necessary. National service regulations were also introduced and men between the age of 18 and 41 became liable for service with the armed forces in Malta. The total number of Maltese enlisted, including volunteers, was 14,650.

One section of the commercial community which had a peculiar war was the bankers. At the outbreak of hostilities a French bank and the *Banco di Roma* in effect failed—the latter to the tune of £400,000, which was a powerful disincentive to pro-Italian sentiment. These events led to a general loss of confidence in banks, hoarding started and regulations had to be introduced to prevent a run on banking institutions. After a time English banknotes were withdrawn from circulation and special notes issued for the islands. The reasons for this were twofold. First, if the islands fell into Axis hands the conquerors would not acquire considerable sums of sterling and, secondly, there were not enough of the old notes to go round. Once full employment returned to Malta, wages started to rise rapidly and it became necessary to provide increasing quantities of paper money in order to pay wage bills. The administration was repeatedly printing money and in the end notes took the place of much silver coinage as well. Naturally the wartime currency was redeemed at the cessation of hostilities.

The islands accumulated a relatively large amount of capital during the Second World War. Imports were drastically cut and as the service departments were paying out increasingly large sums in wages savings were, perforce, high. The wealth, however, tended to concentrate in the hands of those with goods to sell, particularly farmers, many of whom made considerable sums during the war. There were powerful regulations to prevent the development of a black market but one certainly existed and in the period of excessive scarcity eggs were bringing two shillings and sixpence each.

During most of 1942 the greatest part of Malta's population, both civil and military, was slowly starving. A soldier on active service was supposed to be fed 4,000 calories a day—in Malta he got 2,000. An adult Maltese male worker got 1,690 calories and an adult woman 1,500. By May 1942 there was such an acute shortage of so many essentials, including fuel for cooking, that Victory kitchens had to be set up to provide a communal feeding service for the civilian population. Thistles and weeds were being collected from waste ground to heat bakeries and wood was being salvaged from bombed buildings to fire the Victory kitchens. In June 1942 the island was existing very largely on its own fat. The large herds of goats, which had been a characteristic of the islands, were rapidly being killed off. Goat stew became the staple dish at the Victory kitchens and large quantities of horse-flesh were also consumed as the local equines were slaughtered. In spite of these expedients the population continued to waste away. In August 1942 the military commanders were becoming alarmed at the speed at which their men were losing weight. The shortages continued long after the air victories in the late summer of 1942. Convoys were put through but the ships brought only enough food and supplies to keep the population and fighting machine going. It was not until the beginning of 1943 that food supplies really became adequate and it was possible to increase rations.

With the Sicilian landings in June 1943 Malta was virtually out of the Second World War. The island's war had been short but fiery. Malta suffered some of the heaviest bombing of the war and the damage to parts of the island had been huge. Fortunately, because Maltese houses are built principally of stone, incendiary bombs had proved ineffective and there was no burning out of large sections of towns, as happened in northern Europe. Civilian war deaths, 1,490 not including Maltese serving with the British forces, had not been particularly high but the islanders had been subjected to the tension of bombing raids for long periods, the discomfort of evacuation and acute food shortage. The morale of the civilian population, as a whole, had never cracked although 'in the more exposed places, such as on the airfields and in the dockyard, the local labour was not always dependable.' One important result of the war was to bring the Maltese and the British much closer together. On April 15th, 1942, a simple message came from Buckingham Palace to the Governor of Malta:

> *'To Honour her brave People I award the*
> *George Cross to the Island Fortress of*
> *Malta to bear witness to a Heroism and*
> *Devotion that will long be famous in*
> *History.'*
>
> *George R. I.*

In the following year President Roosevelt called at the island on his way from the Teheran conference and gave Malta a 'Presidential Citation.' During the course of the same year the return to internal self-government was announced and by mid-September the captured Italian fleet lay at anchor in the great harbours.

Damage to the island, particularly in the dockyard and harbour towns, was on a very large scale; 35,000 homes had been destroyed or damaged together with a number of important historical monuments in Valletta and the Three Cities. Before the war nearly 8,000 people had lived in Senglea, yet in 1948, five years after bombing had ceased, the town contained less than 3,000 inhabitants. The settlement lay in the heart of the naval dockyard and large areas of the town were flattened during attacks on the yard. The population of Vittoriosa was reduced in similar manner and at Cospicua, where the pre-war population had exceeded 12,000, there were only 5,000 inhabitants in 1948. The islands entered the post-war era with an acute housing shortage.

Malta was given £30 million by the British Government to finance reconstruction and this was of immense benefit to the islands. Just as the reconstruction and development spending of the Order of St. John, after the Great Siege, refinanced the Maltese economy and raised its earning capacity so the war damage fund kept the economy of the islands running at a high level and generally helped to increase wealth.

In the short term the Second World War had been economically advantageous to Malta, but the long-term problems remained, for the islands were still almost wholly dependent upon British military spending, in one form or another. The problem of constitutional development also required attention.

Post-War Malta

O n Wednesday, July 7th, 1943, the Governor of Malta
announced that it was the intention of the British Government to restore internal self-government to the Maltese
after the war. 'All matters appertaining to the position of Malta as
an Imperial Fortress' were, however, to be reserved as they had
been in the pre-war constitutions.

The Maltese set up a National Assembly for the purpose of making
recommendations as to the form of the new constitution and a
constitutional commission was sent out from the United Kingdom.
On September 5th, 1947, the islands once more attained internal
self-government. At first a Labour Party administration held office
with Dr. (later Sir) Paul Boffa as its head. But in 1949 the Prime
Minister and Don Mintoff, the Minister of Public Works and
Reconstruction, disagreed about the handling of negotiations with
Britain over the dismissal of redundant workers at the naval dockyard. Subsequently the Labour Party supported Mr. Mintoff, and
the Prime Minister resigned and formed an Independent Labour
Party. At the 1950 elections the Nationalist Party obtained the
most votes although it failed to attain a majority. Dr. Enrico Mizzi,
however, formed a Nationalist administration but he was to enjoy
office for just a few months before he died and Dr. Giorgio Borg
Olivier became Prime Minister. The minority government only
survived for a short term and fresh elections were held in 1951.
Once more no party gained an overall majority but the Nationalists
formed a government with the help of Sir Paul Boffa's supporters.
Another election was held in 1953 with a similar result. In the
elections of 1955 the Malta Labour Party, led by Don Mintoff,
obtained a clear majority. Mintoff started to develop an ambitious

programme. The expansion of the social and educational services was accelerated and the new administration began to tackle the long-term economic problems. The possibility of integrating Malta with the United Kingdom was discussed with the British Government. In the end agreement could not be reached on two major issues. First, the British Government was unwilling to allow the Maltese to become full beneficiaries of the United Kingdom social services without a substantial contribution to costs from Malta. Secondly, there was the complex problem of religion. Malta, an intensely Roman Catholic country, would become part of a Protestant entity. The Catholic Church in Malta has enjoyed an especially privileged position and it feared that some of the privileges would no longer be guaranteed if integration took place. A referendum was held on the integration issue but only 45 per cent of the Maltese voted in its favour and the British Government felt that the proposal did not command majority approval.

After the failure of the integration proposal relations between the governments of Malta and the United Kingdom rapidly became strained. In April 1958 the Mintoff administration resigned and after a series of demonstrations the then Governor, Sir Robert Laycock, assumed powers to ensure the maintenance of law and order. The constitution was suspended in 1959 and the islands were once more placed under a colonial administration.

The Government of the United Kingdom, however, was not anxious that this situation should remain in being for long. In July 1960 a constitutional commission was set up under Sir Hillary Blood and recommendations, which were to be the basis of a new constitution, were published in February of the following year. The Blood commission recommended that there should no longer be reserved matters. The Maltese Government would be able to legislate on all questions but in certain areas it would have to consult with the United Kingdom and, if it became necessary, Britain could overrule. The Blood report was accepted and Malta once more attained a degree of self-government. In February 1962 a general election was held and the Nationalist Party, led by Dr. Giorgio Borg Olivier, won. In August of the same year the new Prime Minister informed the British Secretary of State for the Colonies that the Maltese wished to be granted full independence. About a year later an independence conference was held in London under the chairmanship of Mr. Duncan Sandys, the man who had guided the re-appraisal of British defence commitments in the late nineteen-fifties and drastically altered Malta's status in the military world. At the opening of the conference Mr. Sandys stated his government's point of view: 'We, in Britain, have no desire to hustle Malta into independence or to lay down our responsibilities so long as you need us. On the other hand, once you are ready and willing to take over full management of your own affairs, we have no wish to hold you back.' This new British viewpoint had been born of the defence rethinking referred to earlier and Mr. Sandys added: 'With regard to defence, we no longer have an absolute need for a military base in the central Mediterranean. Nevertheless we would like to retain facilities for our forces, if this is acceptable to you.'

The two major parties, the Nationalist Party and the Malta Labour Party, were both in favour of independence but the smaller parties represented at the conference—the Christian Workers Party (a break-away from the Malta Labour Party), the Democratic Nationalist Party and the Progressive Constitutional Party—were against the proposal, at least for the time being. Eventually, however, the Secretary of State for the Colonies accepted the argument that, since the two major parties had polled 76 per cent of the votes at the last election and both had included independence in their election manifestoes, then independence should be granted in accordance with their wishes. The conference concluded by announcing that Malta would become independent in the following year and on September 21st, 1964, the Maltese assumed full responsibility for their own affairs.

Political independence was, of course, useless unless adequate provision could be made for the economic well being of the islands and the United Kingdom did undertake to provide large-scale economic aid. However, an effort had been made since the conclusion of the Second World War to make Malta less dependent upon British military spending. During the early post-war years people of vision were beginning to foresee that Malta's usefulness as a military base was likely to decline. The advent of strategic bombing forces, armed with nuclear weapons, made the concentrated military base look particularly vulnerable. Clearly the British Empire was to decline in importance and Imperial defence spending would decrease. There was also the growth of the supranational organizations which led to a considerable degree of rationalization in the defence structure of the Western nations. Eventually Italy and the United Kingdom became part of the same defence pact, N.A.T.O., which lessened the strategic importance of the Malta base. However, these long-term factors did not have an immediate economic impact. The cold war kept military spending at a high level. The British services continued to employ large numbers of Maltese and considerable sums were spent not only on repairing the damage caused to military installations during hostilities but also on rectifying some of the previous deficiencies. The airfields at Luqa, Ta'Qali and Hal Far underwent development, new, longer-range radar was installed, the food storage capacity of the islands was increased and improved fuel bunkering systems were provided for the Royal Navy and the Royal Air Force. Although Britain's wider defence interests were merging with those of her Western allies there was also judged to be a need for independent bases which might be used in support of purely British interests. Throughout the long series of small, post-war, colonial troubles and Middle Eastern tensions Malta played an important role and in 1956 the main weight of the attack on Suez was launched from Malta as Cyprus lacked a deep-water harbour. But 1957 was the year of the radical British defence review, conducted by Duncan Sandys, in which it was decided that some of the overseas bases, including Malta, were to be less heavily manned and equipped than had previously been the case. From this time forces stationed in Malta were progressively run down and Malta is now classed as an auxiliary base in the British defence structure. The airfields at Ta'Qali and Hal Far are no longer operational and the Royal Air Force operates from, and maintains, the civil airfield at Luqa. The Royal Navy has of late stationed at Malta no more than one escort squadron, a few minesweepers and auxiliary vessels.

The service run-down involved a considerable loss of jobs for large numbers of Maltese were employed in the military establishments and many made their livings from the spending of British servicemen and their families. To tide the islands over this period of transition the British Government made large sums of money available to help diversify the economic structure of Malta. When the islands became independent they entered into an agreement on mutual defence and assistance with the United Kingdom. Under this agreement the British Government, in return for the use of military facilities, undertook to provide Malta with £50 million over a period of ten years. In the first five years of the agreement, during which just over half the total funds would be made available, 75 per cent of the money would come by way of gift and 25 per cent on loan at the current lending rates of the United Kingdom exchequer. In the second half of the agreement the division between loans and gifts was left open for discussion. In addition the United Kingdom is to advance £1 million for the restoration of historic buildings which had been occupied by British forces.

Within the space of the last few years the structure of the island's economy has, perforce, been greatly altered. These changes were not unexpected and indeed since the end of the Second World War efforts had been made to diversify the local economy. Towards the close of the war the British Government started to despatch a series of experts to Malta to advise upon post-war developments. Amongst other things a comprehensive plan was drawn up for the rebuilding of Valletta, the Three Cities and the surrounding areas. Parts of the plan were implemented but as a comprehensive development it never came into existence. In 1945 Sir Wilfred Woods came to Malta to advise on the island's finances and future economic development. Sir Wilfred suggested that there were four lines of development which the islands might follow. Small industries should be encouraged, agriculture should be improved, the fishing industry could be made more productive by the introduction of trawlers and tourism might be developed. Overall, Woods did not feel that local production could be greatly increased.

In any event little was done to develop these ideas for in 1947 internal self-government brought a change in the administration and a different point of view on the way the island's affairs should be conducted. Additionally with the economy running well and the islands enjoying prosperity it was difficult to allocate resources for new activities. There was, of course, the perennial problem of population increase but the migration policy was reintroduced to relieve pressure here. In the Second World War, with the disruption of families, deaths caused by enemy action and later marriage due to the housing shortage, population growth had slowed. But in 1946 the trend was reversed and the population increased by about 9,000, as it did in the following year. In 1947 the Maltese Government started to pay 75 per cent of approved migrants' costs and this helped to slow the rate of population growth. In 1949 a passage assistance agreement was signed with Australia and in the same year 3,500 Maltese migrated to that country. In 1950, 5,000 Maltese went to Australia and population growth was halted. Then followed a couple of years during which the Australian economy suffered a recession and the country was unable to maintain the high rate of migrant acceptance. Once more the population of the islands started to increase rapidly but within a few years the Australian economy was again expanding and able to absorb Maltese workers. In 1954 more than 11,000 people left and the population declined by over four and a half thousand. 1955 was another *good* year and over 9,000 migrated but in 1956 hopes of integration with the United Kingdom, together with relatively prosperous economic conditions in the islands, encouraged large numbers of Maltese to return from Australia. 1956 marked the end of a period of rapid migration. The emigration policy had a serious drawback. Countries like Australia were only too willing to accept skilled Maltese and large numbers of trained men left the islands. As a result in the mid nineteen-fifties a shortage of skilled labour developed in Malta and it was realized that a policy of wholesale migration was not completely in the best interests of the islands.

During the first half of the nineteen-fifties the effort to achieve economic diversification was stepped up. In 1955 Britain made a declaration assuming responsibility for attaining diversification of the Maltese economy. Numerous British Colonial Office experts visited the islands to appraise local resources. Agriculture, forestry and dairying all received careful study and a number of reports were also prepared on the general state of the economy. The Department of Geography, in the University of Durham, formed a team of research workers to undertake a land-use survey, study rural society, climate, population trends and some aspects of economic development. The Colonial Office supplied a soil survey officer and as a result of an abortive search for oil new geological maps were produced. Using aerial survey techniques new topographical maps of the islands were published. The Royal University of Malta and the F.A.O. also produced a number of reports. Government departments were expanded so as to be able to produce the background information required for the formulation of economic policy.

Although not always soundly based on the survey work outlined above, the elements of a development plan emerged. Basically industry, tourism and agriculture were to be encouraged with the help of government grants. By the time the programme had been properly formulated internal self-government had been suspended once more and the first five-year plan was published by the colonial administration in 1959. The plan envisaged the expenditure of £32,250,000 between 1959 and 1964. £22 million was to be provided by the United Kingdom in the form of loans and grants.

Subsequently, in 1961, the plan had to be revised as the planned spending of the first years had not been completed, principally because the local economy could not expand rapidly enough to absorb the increased investment.

The greatest part of the development funds was to be expended upon encouraging the establishment of new industries. Malta has many disadvantages as an industrial base and it was necessary to offer inducements to industrialists in the hope that these would help to overcome the initial problems of setting up factories in the islands. An industrial estate was laid out at Marsa, firms were offered tax-free holidays, factories at extremely low rentals, tariff protection, generous grants and loans were made available. The factories on the Marsa industrial estate, and others which were built elsewhere, were quickly taken up. The results were mixed. A great problem associated with offering generous inducements is the tendency to attract marginal firms. A number of manufacturing concerns came to Malta to take advantage of the grants etc. without making proper assessments of local factors and the real economic feasibility of their planned enterprises. An outstanding example of a company failing to obtain reliable data on potential markets was the project to assemble Rambler motor cars under licence in Malta for sale in the Middle East. Within a short time the firm undertaking this work was in financial difficulties and production ceased. As a result the largest factory on the Marsa industrial estate was left unused for several years. On the other hand, where companies were prepared to examine Maltese conditions carefully and tailor operations accordingly, success has normally been obtained. The Dowty Group set up a branch factory in Malta to manufacture products which were able to take advantage of the low labour costs in Malta yet at the same time were light enough not to incur heavy transport costs on export. This venture has been a great success and production capacity was rapidly increased.

After the early disappointments the Malta Aids to Industries Board became much more selective in choosing firms to receive aid. As a result the pace at which new concerns are coming to the islands has slowed down.

During the period of the first five-year plan it was intended to convert the Royal Naval Malta dockyard to commercial use, in order to avoid the large number of redundancies which would otherwise result from the closing of the establishment. There was a series of problems associated with this project in addition to the difficulties which would be experienced in changing from military to civil work. Not having been primarily concerned with costs the yard was uneconomically run and overmanned. Men were under-employed in the establishment in order to keep unemployment down. Under-employment was, and still is, common in certain sectors of the economy of the islands. The shipping industry as a whole started to run into the problems of over capacity in the late nineteen-fifties and this gave rise to a great deal of uncertainty as to whether or not additional repair capacity was required. The Malta yard was established but it had no established customers apart from the Royal Navy. Work would have to be won from other Mediterranean yards and it was doubtful if Malta could compete. It was certain that the yard would have to be thoroughly reorganized if it were to be a commercial success. Clearly in the unstable political conditions then existing in the islands, and with the probable need to retain every possible job, a drastic course of action might well not be possible. Apparently some of the larger concerns in the British shipbuilding and repairing industry weighed these problems against the attractions of Malta: the existing physical assets of the yard on a 99-year lease, large development grants, a pool of skilled labour and a position on a major tanker route. The general opinion seems to have been that the proposition was risky. None of the larger firms approached was prepared to come. A relatively small firm from South Wales, C. H. Bailey & Co. Ltd., was interested and eventually took over the running of the yard. By British shipbuilding and repairing standards Bailey's was a very modest firm indeed. The largest dry dock operated by the company had a capacity of only about 20,000 tons and in South Wales the ports were declining and the long-term prospects did not look good. The board was dominated by the Bailey family and in coming to Malta the management would have to tackle numerous problems on a scale which it had never previously attempted.

In 1959 C. H. Bailey & Co. Ltd. formed a company in Malta in which it was the controlling shareholder. The new firm was known as Bailey (Malta) Ltd., and in the same year it took a 99-year lease on the dockyard from the British Admiralty. (The ownership of the yard was transferred to the Government of Malta at independence.) C. H. Bailey & Co. subscribed £750,000 and was issued with a controlling equity shareholding whilst the British Colonial Office undertook to provide £6 million (subsequently increased to £7¼ million) in the form of loans to be used principally on converting the yard to civil use.

Bailey's and the Colonial Office could not agree on certain financial matters and after a lengthy series of arguments the dockyard was taken over in 1963 by a Council of Administration and Bailey's ceased to operate the undertaking.

The Council of Administration very quickly started talks with a number of British shipbuilding companies with a view to appointing one of them as managing agents of the Malta Drydocks. At first it appeared that Smith's Dock Co. Ltd., a firm based on north-eastern England, would take over but they eventually dropped out and Swan, Hunter and Wigham Richardson & Co. Ltd.[1] undertook to manage the yard. This company has brought the yard close to profitability and although the Malta Drydocks still get nearly half their work from the Royal Navy there is a good chance that the enterprise will prove to be a commercial success. Under the management of Swan, Hunter, conversion, modernization and diversification schemes at the yard have progressed well.

The islands were not left unmarked by these events. Apart from the delay in bringing about the dockyard conversion there was a great deal of bad publicity. The dockyard troubles, the poor results of the Bailey (Malta) subsidiaries (the company had set up a series of small firms in Malta including a light engineering works, a hotel, a bacon factory and a fishing company), the Rambler fiasco and

[1] Smith's Dock Co. Ltd. and Swan, Hunter have since merged.

the demise of one or two lesser concerns all helped to create a picture of difficulty in the islands for new industries although, in truth, the difficulties were very largely the creation of the failed companies. These problems did not help the islands to attract new concerns but the bad publicity was probably not a crucial factor. New industries certainly have a place in a diversified Maltese economy but it is now recognized that their range is relatively limited. Certain small import substitution industries will do well; the modest car assembly plant, which uses components imported from Britain, is a good example of this type of enterprise. A number of other industries which can take advantage of Malta's low labour costs also have a place if they are exporting to the United Kingdom, some Commonwealth countries, and parts of Europe. But to think of Malta as a manufacturing centre exporting extensively to North Africa, southern Europe and Middle Eastern markets is a mistake. Many of these markets are hedged by high tariff barriers and frequently local labour costs match, or undercut, those obtaining in Malta. Additionally there is the problem of export costs and although Malta holds a central position in the Mediterranean it is not in fact well served by communications links with other countries.

Agriculture and tourism have not attracted as much attention as the attempts to establish new industries nor were they allocated funds on as large a scale in the first five-year plan. However, both have advanced steadily and are making worthwhile contributions to economic development. Malta has some interesting agricultural resources. The long growing season, high light intensity and warm climate make the islands well suited to the production of horticultural crops. The well-developed air link with London offers the chance to export high-quality goods to one of the world's largest fruit, vegetable and flower markets. On the debit side the islands' water shortage may place a limit on development, and although there are a number of schemes in hand to provide more water they are bound to be expensive and this will be reflected in local production costs. Another problem arises from the potential lack of export capacity by air. A number of firms, not only horticultural concerns, export by air from Malta to the United Kingdom but freight carried in the opposite direction is limited and extra aeroplanes flying empty 'legs' will again add to costs.

Possibly the largest obstacle to horticultural development is the structure of Maltese agriculture. Essentially the Maltese countryside is farmed in small units using methods which are largely traditional. Farmers are not used to producing relatively high-quality products for sophisticated markets. Even if new crops are introduced a host of problems will arise when numerous growers start producing small quantities of varying quality. To overcome these difficulties it is necessary to re-educate rural society, offer extensive advisory and marketing services and encourage the growth of larger production units, possibly in the form of co-operatives. A great deal is being done, particularly in the provision of advisory services, but changes are bound to come slowly for what is involved is the alteration of traditional rural society until it accepts ideas on cost-account farming, quality production and rapid response to market conditions, all of which are at present largely foreign to its nature. Maltese farming will in any case have to change quite rapidly for as it stands large sections of it are, or are quickly becoming, uneconomic. There is a movement away from the land and many areas of marginal land are being abandoned. A good sign is that productivity is rising on the land remaining in cultivation.

In spite of the problems a number of advances have been made. A large English horticultural firm propagates chrysanthemum cuttings close to the old Ta'Qali airfield. The equable climate cuts heating costs to low levels and the high summer temperatures and long sunshine hours throughout the year enable propagation to proceed rapidly. The entire production of cuttings is exported, polythene-wrapped, by air to the United Kingdom.

The Maltese Government is subsidizing farmers who erect greenhouses. Tomatoes are the major crop and although, theoretically, large-scale production of the plant should be profitable in Malta, the effect of the present policy is to encourage the development of a large number of small producers who may well run into problems later.

At the time of writing potatoes remain the largest single agricultural export from the islands. Potato production is not particularly profitable and growers have had to be subsidized. What is more, the land and water used to grow the potatoes could be used for the production of higher-value crops.

It is fair to conclude that agricultural development has an

important part to play in economic diversification of the islands. This sector of the economy probably warrants more attention than it has been receiving. Demand for horticultural products could rise rapidly if tourism develops well.

It is true to say that in the nineteen-fifties the major hope of economic development in Malta was the establishment of new manufacturing industries. However, it is now the tourist industry which appears to be the largest potential growth area in the economy of the islands. The new trend is partially the result of purely Maltese efforts but it is equally due to external agencies. For instance, many real-estate companies have discovered Malta and there is now something of a boom in the buying and selling of land and the building of holiday flats and houses. This is an important development for previously there was a considerable amount of building and letting of flats to British service personnel. The activity now has a new outlet.

It has been evident for some time that a tourist flight to the south is in progress and Malta, along with North Africa, Sicily and southern Spain, has become increasingly popular. The islands do enjoy some advantages as a tourist resort, apart from the fine climate and good swimming facilities. The most important asset is the English connection. Britain is by far the largest source of tourists coming to the islands. English is widely spoken (it is the language used principally in Maltese schools), and the currency is the same except that the Maltese issue their own banknotes. The islands are part of the sterling area and this makes them an attractive place for Englishmen wishing to buy holiday homes as there are few currency restrictions. Air fares are relatively cheap although large-scale charter work, which will reduce costs even further, has not yet started. The islands are packed with historic remains and there is a wealth of good things to see.

On the debit side, apart from the disadvantages associated with any resort area in an early phase of development, all the black marks are really caused by the Maltese failing to understand the necessity for very careful land-use planning on a group of islands which total just over 120 square miles and hold well over 300,000 people. Post-war building has been very largely a free-for-all. Long stretches of ribbon development now blight the outskirts of many towns and villages. Poor-quality building has been allowed close to some of the best bays and industry has developed in a number of areas which formerly enjoyed considerable charm. Little effort has been made to preserve Valletta and a number of unsuitable developments have taken place.

The Order of St. John did enforce town-planning regulations even if they were relatively limited. By contrast the British had a *laissez faire* attitude to planning and made very little effort to guide development in Malta. Planning legislation was limited in Britain until relatively recently so that Malta was hardly likely to do very well. Besides there were, and still are, powerful local interests that have been completely opposed to restrictions being placed upon property development. Most people in Malta with savings have some of their money invested in property and thus efficient land-use planning would be seen as a measure which, in the short term, was potentially liable to make certain investments less profitable. This group of people has always been politically significant. In the long term, of course, unless development within the islands is carefully planned Malta will lose its charm and thus its attractiveness to tourists. Then everyone in the islands will be poorer.

Over the last few years the number of tourists coming to Malta has rapidly increased and in 1966 the total was 72,791. Several new hotels have opened whilst many existing establishments have expanded.[1]

1964 marked the end of the first five-year plan and afforded an opportunity for assessing the results of the first plan and of drafting a programme for the next quinquennium.

The first plan did not achieve all its planned aims by a long way. Not all the projected capital spending was undertaken and the number of new jobs created fell short of the original hopes. On the credit side some new industries had been started, the situation at the dockyard could at last be described as hopeful, tourism was beginning to catch on and the islands' industrial infra-structure had been greatly strengthened; a deep-water quay had been constructed on the shore of the Grand Harbour (it did not work efficiently for a long time due to labour troubles), more roads had been built and many areas with tourist potential had been opened up, work had been started on a new electricity generating station and

---

[1] Of the 72,791 tourists 21,647 were short-stay visitors from cruise boats calling at the island.

water distillation plant. Many lessons had been learned during the course of the first five years and the experience was incorporated within the second plan which was to run from 1964 to 1969. Manufacturing industry, whilst remaining the largest single sector of development in the second plan, lost ground to tourism and agriculture. The allocations of development finance were greatly increased in these last two sectors. It was proposed to become more selective as to which companies were to be the recipients of grants and loans from the Aids to Industries Board to 'ensure that only the more efficient enterprises are attracted'. It was decided to set up a development corporation into which Maltese investors could put their money with security and the funds could then be lent, by the corporation, to concerns requiring capital for development. One of Malta's problems is that, although the Maltese have very substantial saving—for a start there is over £60 million in giltedged securities in London—the economy lacks mechanisms to allow the money to be invested in local enterprises. A development corporation provides one such mechanism. It was also proposed to establish a central bank to help guide monetary policy and there were hopes that an export credit agency and a stock market could be founded.

One of the most controversial proposals contained in the new plan was 'the establishment of a limited free port area' which 'should ensure that Malta will regain its former position as a centre for entrepôt trade'. This proposal is undoubtedly speculative; we have noted the island's relatively poor communications links and, as will be appreciated from previous chapters, Malta has only enjoyed a significant entrepôt trade during peculiar conditions in the nineteenth century. Trade of this type in the eighteenth century was not of great significance and in any case the trade patterns of that time are hardly likely to repeat themselves now.

Perhaps a more rewarding course of action would be to declare the whole island a duty-free area, but this involves technical difficulties since a high proportion of the administration's revenue comes from customs dues. At present it is proposed to turn part of Malta, around Marsaxlokk, into a duty-free zone and this might well encourage the establishment of certain types of manufacturing processes and tourist attractions in the area. However, it is proposed in the second plan to spend £2·5 million on providing a breakwater, quay and warehouses at Marsaxlokk for the scheme. It is highly unlikely that the number of ships calling will justify this expenditure and it is doubtful if the islands have a foreseeable need for elaborate port facilities in the Grand Harbour and Marsaxlokk.[1]

The second plan envisaged the spending of £38·4 million over a period of five years and this figure has given rise to controversy. To help with the production of the second plan a United Nations technical assistance team, headed by Wolfgang F. Stolper, came to Malta in 1962. Stolper is a man of wide experience, who before coming to Malta had spent two years in Lagos working on Nigeria's first development plan.

There was a measure of disagreement between the Maltese civil servants drafting the second plan and the United Nations team. The mission felt that a total expenditure programme of £26·2 million over five years was all the islands could reasonably undertake. The mission argued that the local economy could not be expanded rapidly enough to sustain investment at the higher rate. Their figure of £26·2 million would probably have led to a marked drop in living standards. Obviously such a course of action would have been unpopular politically and the authors of the second plan opted for an attempt to implement a programme large enough to sustain living standards. They argued that there was plenty of room in the Maltese economy and executive machine for expansion and improved efficiency. This is, of course, true but whether the necessary transformation of attitudes could be made within the space of a few years was doubted by the U.N. mission. Conservative attitudes were one of the major obstacles to development commented upon by Stolper in his report.

In order to avoid the worst effects of a fall in living standards the U.N. team suggested that 10,000 Maltese per annum should be induced to emigrate throughout the period of the plan. There are two points to be noted here. First, an emigration target of 10,000 per annum is high and may not be attainable. Secondly, as the

---

[1] Since the publication of the second five year plan, according to newspaper reports, the free port scheme has been pressed by a number of groups and it has been suggested that Malta might become an entrepôt centre and bulk breaking point for Mediterranean trade. To bring about such a development would require a massive investment, for what is involved is the alteration of existing patterns of trade. It is difficult, at present, to see that a sufficient volume of suitable goods is moving in the Mediterranean to justify such an investment.

authors of the plan quickly pointed out, in the early nineteen-sixties 20 per cent of all emigrants had been skilled workers and if the mission had its way the island would lose nearly 10,000 trained men in five years; two and a half times the number of skilled men that would be trained during the period. The second plan suggests an average rate of emigration of 7,500 per annum. If this target is attained the number of Maltese living in the islands will decline to just over 300,000 by 1969.

The islands are at present in what should be their worst post-war period from an economic point of view. The run-down of British service spending is still continuing and not enough new jobs have been created to replace those that have been lost. The islands still have an apparently huge balance of payments problem. In 1966 imports cost £38·9 million. Exports, which were up on the previous years due to the impact of the new industries, earned £7·8 million.[1] In the past the gap has been closed by British service spending and by the earnings of overseas investments. In the future the export industries and the tourist trade will have to earn more foreign exchange but as can be seen the trade gap is very large and it is still widening.

On paper the islands appear to be in a very difficult position economically, and yet the situation has not been fully reflected in everyday life on Malta. Unemployment has not risen to the expected figure; there are few signs of poverty or even of curtailed consumer spending. The reasons for this are various but basically the islands have hidden reserves of wealth which are drawn on in periods of recession; an adaptation by the islanders to their economic environment. A Maltese gentleman released by the Egyptians after serving a prison sentence of several years as the result of an accusation of spying for Britain during the Suez crisis, was interviewed on television in England and asked how he was going to manage financially. He replied simply that 'everyone has something saved for a rainy day.' Many Maltese have and it is savings which tide them over difficult periods. Additionally large numbers of Maltese have more than one job. For instance there are thousands of part-time farmers. The second job may not provide a comfortable living but it is often sufficient, with savings, to see a family through a difficult phase. These devices, and a number of others, have developed in response

[1] The trade figures for 1966 are provisional.

to uncertain conditions in the past, for the islands have for centuries been subject to depressions brought on by one cause or another.

The present economic problems of the islands are not simply a product of having relied for a century and a half on British defence spending. It is incorrect to state, as the economist Thomas Balogh has done, that the local economy has been warped by Britain's strategic needs. The causes of the present situation are many. The islands lack resources. There is even a shortage of water which precludes many industrial processes immediately. The population of the islands is so small that it provides an insufficient market for the local production of many goods. Industries in Malta in the past tended to be precarious affairs and high-cost producers.

The Order of St. John encouraged various schemes in the hope of providing more local employment. The Order was particularly active in the textile industry during the eighteenth century but when money was invested it was frequently lost. For instance, a large investment was made in a silk industry which failed. Significantly the British tried to start a similar project in the nineteenth century, being unaware of the earlier attempt, and this too was a failure. There are several other instances in the nineteenth century of industries being set up, often with government help, and subsequently failing. During the twentieth century the 1911 Royal Commission recommended some industrial development and in the nineteen-twenties efforts were made to encourage industry and tourism. These attempts came to very little. The fact is diversification, industrial growth and more jobs were not suddenly thought necessary for Malta at the end of the Second World War; various groups had been attempting these things for centuries, but the basic geographic and economic facts cannot be avoided. The islands lack many resources, the home market is small and if you produced anything in Malta it was likely to be at a relatively high cost. Social and political forces have also played their part. During the last century and a half at least there have been a number of built-in disadvantages for economic development in Malta's social and political structure. The middle classes have been overwhelmingly composed of professional people: principally doctors and lawyers. Merchants, manufacturers and entrepreneurs have been poorly represented. The people with capital have been more interested in saving and buying land rather than investing in productive capacity. Professional people, particularly lawyers, have tended to dominate the political scene and as a group they have been more interested in constitutional and legal problems than in economic development. Indeed, economic development has often appeared to be a dirty phrase to the group, for to start economic developments a government must have capital and this involves new sources of revenue. Any mention of increased tariffs, the raising of loans or the introduction of income tax was usually accorded a hostile reception. Income tax was not introduced into Malta until 1948. What is more this group, and Maltese society in general, have been strongly conservative. Even in 1964 Stolper could write of 'the unwillingness to make decisions that will disturb the *status quo* and the desire to have other parties make the necessary decisions and changes'.

One of the greatest disadvantages the islands suffered, from an economic point of view, under British rule was the problem of divided responsibility. Too much political energy was wasted railing about reserved matters and too little time spent on running Malta and planning its future. For long periods, even in the nineteenth century, the Maltese had a very large degree of responsibility for financial and economic affairs but this tended to be forgotten as more emotional and nationalistic matters claimed prominence. Here was a great disadvantage. The Maltese always believed, and rightly, that the British held ultimate power and never really accepted a lot of responsibility which was there for the taking. Additionally it was difficult to obtain a consistent policy because power tended to shuttlecock between the Maltese and the United Kingdom administrators as one constitution after another was rejected and the islands returned to spells of full colonial rule. Even since the Second World War, there have been so many changes of administration that it took years longer than it should have done to get economic diversification going.

There is, then, no simple answer as to why Malta failed to develop industries of its own. The answer is a compound of the lack of resources in the islands and their social and political history.

In the 1966 elections the Nationalist Party led by Dr. Georgio Borg Olivier was once more returned to power. The major opposition party remained the Malta Labour Party while the smaller parties failed to retain any seats in the legislature. 1966 was an important year from an economic viewpoint; due to the financial troubles of the United Kingdom the British Government was obliged to place limits on the amount of currency holidaymakers from Britain could spend outside the sterling area. As a result holiday resorts within the sterling area will become increasingly attractive to people living in the United Kingdom and the tourist industry at Malta should receive a very considerable boost. Here, yet again, is another characteristic of Maltese history manifesting itself, namely events taking place far from the island, and completely beyond the control of the Maltese, having an important effect upon the economic life of the community.[1] Maltese leaders will always have a very restricted ability to influence the basic trends in the local economy. Similarly the courses of action open to them are limited by the small area of the islands, the comparatively small population and the lack of resources. The basic geography of the archipelago places considerable bounds on what can be attempted economically in the islands. The bounds can be ignored to a degree but to do so immediately adds to costs.

Much of the individuality of Malta finds its roots in the basic limitations of the island group. Relative isolation from Europe and North Africa has allowed the Maltese to develop distinct cultural traits and, although the islands have frequently been dominated by peoples from other lands, the islanders have been able to preserve a character of their own, at the same time absorbing ideas and techniques from the overlords. The difficulty of reaching the islands, their lack of wealth and high density of population have made them unattractive to settlers in large numbers, at least in the last thousand years. In addition the Maltese have usually been prepared to work with the overlords (economics made this a sensible course of action) and it has been unnecessary for the latter to encourage large-scale settlement of their nationals or to station big garrisons on the archi-

[1] The crisis in British-Maltese relations which developed early in 1967 serves to underline this point. Britain, pressed by heavy defence commitments and economic problems, felt it necessary to further run-down the forces maintained in Malta. This was, of course, a heavy blow to the Maltese and the Prime Minister, Dr. Borg Olivier, had great difficulty in convincing the British Government that additional financial aid was of little value, that the islands needed to retain every possible job and that alternative employment could not be generated overnight. Eventually a compromise was worked out and the islands given a longer period of time to develop new employment opportunities.

pelago. Perhaps the Maltese concern with constitutional rights, the preservation of privileges and of saving money all basically spring, historically, from feelings of isolation, insecurity, lack of natural wealth and, paradoxically, contact with dominating powers interested in the strategic position of the islands? Possibly isolation is one of the root causes of the intense feeling for religion which most Maltese possess? Is it entirely coincidence that the Copper Age inhabitants of Malta developed relatively huge religious monuments and that in modern historical time Maltese villagers have built churches which, comparatively, look vast in relation to the settlements they serve?

The lack of natural resources in the islands has probably helped to develop the strong tradition for craft industries which Malta possessed for a long time. The islanders were forced to adapt the few readily available materials for a large number of tasks and became highly adept at skilled work. The plentiful and easily worked Globigerina limestone was used for a large number of functions and because timber was not readily available it became the basis of a traditional style of building which was constructed entirely of stone and did not require wooden beams to support the roof.

To point out the influence of the physical environment on the development of Maltese society is not to suggest that its form has been completely determined by these factors. Such an assertion would be absurd as it is obvious, for instance, that the modern history of Malta and the form of Maltese society would have been very different had Charles V never granted the archipelago to the Order of St. John or had the Siege of 1565 been lost. Nevertheless, whatever type of community occupies the islands the physical background forms a framework for action which can only be ignored at a cost. To take a rather extreme example: it would be possible to build certain chemical plants in Malta but production costs would inevitably be increased by the need to distil water from the sea as existing supplies would be insufficient.

In recent years, as efforts have been made to diversify the local economy, the basic facts of geography have occasionally been ignored as rather wild and grandiose development schemes have been mooted. Basically the islands are unsuited to the role of manufacturing and trading centre, except on a very limited scale. During its modern history Malta has thrived when special situations

have overriden the lack of local resources. The knights of St. John
and the British were prepared to ignore the high costs of using
Malta as a military base because strategically the islands occupied
an advantageous position. Over the last few years strategic importance has declined but a new special situation has developed. With
rising living standards more and more Europeans are taking holidays
abroad and the Mediterranean, due to its fine summer climate,
has become an increasingly important resort area. Malta is in a
position to gain from the situation for the business of selling holidays
is not simply a question of attaining relatively low costs. However,
even in this field of economic activity the basic geographic limitations are not far away, and if the Maltese fail to control development
very carefully in the few areas of their small islands which are
capable of becoming resorts Malta will soon become blighted and
lose its tourist attraction.

Appendix

List of Grand Masters of the Order of St. John During Its Stay in Malta

Philippe Villiers de L'Isle-Adam (France)	1530–1534
Pietro del Ponte (Italy)	1534–1535
Didiers de Saint Jaille (France)	1535–1536
Juan d'Omedes (Aragon)	1536–1553
Claude de la Sengle (France)	1553–1557
Jean de la Valette (Provence)	1557–1568
Pietro del Monte San Savino (Italy)	1568–1572
Jean l'Evêque de la Cassière (Auvergne)	1572–1581
Huges de Loubenx Verdalle (Provence)	1581–1595
Martin Garzes (Aragon)	1595–1601
Alof de Wignacourt (France)	1601–1622
Louis Mendes de Vasconcellos (Castile, Leon and Portugal)	1622–1623
Antoine de Paule (Provence)	1623–1636
Jean-Paul de Lascaris Castellar (Provence)	1636–1657
Martin de Redin (Aragon)	1657–1660
Annet de Clermont de Chattes-Gessan (Auvergne)	— 1660
Rafael Cotoner (Aragon)	1660–1663
Niccolo Cotoner (Aragon)	1663–1680
Gregorio Carafa (Italy)	1680–1690
Adrien de Wignacourt (France)	1690–1697
Ramon Perrellos y Rocaful (Aragon)	1697–1720
Marcantonio Zondadari (Italy)	1720–1722
Anton Manoel de Vilhena (Castile, Leon and Portugal)	1722–1736
Ramon Despuig (Aragon)	1736–1741
Manoel Pinto de Fonsca (Castile, Leon and Portugal)	1741–1773
Francisco Ximenes de Texada (Aragon)	1773–1775
Emanuel-Marie de Rohan-Polduc (France)	1775–1797
Ferdinand von Hompesch (Germany)	1797–1798

Selected Bibliography

There is a vast body of literature concerning the Maltese islands and, naturally, it is not possible to include a complete bibliography here. The books and articles mentioned below will provide a wider background of knowledge and give a lead into other sources. I owe acknowledgement to most of the authors cited for material I have drawn from their work and included in the present volume.

General

Malta: Background for Development, H. Bowen-Jones, J. C. Dewdney, W. B. Fisher, University of Durham, 1960.
Malta, an Account and an Appreciation, Sir Harry Luke, 1949.
Malta, the Islands and their History, T. Zammit, Malta, 1929.
Malta, Brian Blouet, Progress Press, Malta, 1966.
Gozo, Brian Blouet, Progress Press, Malta, 1965.

Chapter I

The Maltese islands with special Reference to their Geological Structure, John Murray, SCOTTISH GEOGRAPHICAL MAGAZINE, 1890.
Malta, A Geographical Monograph, M. W. Bruce, Progress Press, Malta, 1965.
There is a great deal of information in *Malta: Background for Development*, on Malta's geographical setting.
The Directorate of Overseas Surveys has published a topographical map of Malta in three sheets at a scale of two and a half inches to the mile. Maps of the islands are also available at other scales and a geological map has been published.

Chapter II

Much has been published on the islands in prehistoric times and it is not possible to give a definitive list of works here. The following is a selection of the more recent publications. In 1959 Professor J. D. Evans's *Malta* appeared and this work contained a comprehensive reassessment of the islands in the Neolithic and Bronze Ages. Evans's conclusions were searchingly questioned in a brilliant review by L. Bernabò Brea in ANTIQUITY, Vol. 34, 1960. A reply by Evans is contained in the same volume. D. H. Trump's article in ANTIQUITY, Vol. 35, 1961, contains important new evidence and revises the cultural sequence suggested by Evans. The same author adds further information in ANTIQUITY, Vol. 36, 1962, and Vol. 37, 1963. More recently Trump has produced an extensive account of some of his Malta excavations in a monograph entitled *Skorba*, published by the Society Antiquaries in 1966. A *corpus* on Maltese prehistory by Professor J. D. Evans is pending. Evans (1959) op. cit. contains a useful bibliography. However short a bibliography, it is impossible to leave out Sir Temi Zammit who undertook the first major work on the megalith temples. Zammit's *Prehistoric Malta: the Tarxien Temple*, 1930, is but one example of his fine pioneer work.

H. S. Gracie's *The Ancient Cart-Tracks of Malta*, ANTIQUITY, Vol. 28, 1954, is the best review of the subject we possess so far.[1]

Chapter III

Our lack of knowledge relating to the period between prehistory and the late Middle Ages is reflected in the paucity of the literature. A preliminary report on the most recent work on the Punic, Roman and Byzantine ages is contained in *Missione archeologica a Malta*, Sabatino Moscati, Cagiano de Azevado et alii, Rome, 1964. T. H. Ashby's *Roman Malta*, JOURNAL OF ROMAN STUDIES, 1915, is still a very useful source of information.

The standard work on the Maltese language is Professor J. Aquilina's *The Structure of Maltese*, Royal University of Malta, 1959. *Teach Yourself Maltese*, by the same author, (1965) is a more general introduction to the subject. Professor Aquilina's *Papers in Maltese Linguistics*, Royal University of Malta, 1961, contains the results of many year's research into a great diversity of topics associated with the Maltese language. P. P. Saydon's article *Pre-Arabic Latin*

---

[1] Bernabò Brea's *Sicily before the Greeks*, 2nd edition, 1966, contains a great deal of general information on the central Mediterranean region in prehistory.

Element in Maltese Toponymy, ORBIS, Tom. V, No. I., 1956, argues that the Maltese spoke Low Latin at the Arab conquest.

Two works by Michele Amari, although primarily concerned with Sicily, do contain some information on Arab Malta: *Storia del Musulmani di Sicilia*, 2nd ed., Catania, 1933–39, and *Biblioteca Arabo-Sicula*, Turin and Rome, 1880.

A very useful series of articles on medieval Malta by R. Valentini is to be found in ARCHIVIO STORICO DI MALTA, Rome, 1929 et seq. Valentini draws on archive material found in the Royal Malta Library, the Mdina Cathedral and southern Italy. Many of the relevant documents are reproduced. E. R. Leopardi has published a long series of articles in MELITA HISTORICA, Malta, 1952 et seq. Again many documents are printed. The same author's *Malta before the coming of the Knights*, MALTA YEAR BOOK, 1961, gives a useful summary of the period. ARCHIVIUM MELITENSE, Valletta, 1910 et seq., contains a number of articles of varying quality by A. Mifsud on medieval Malta and the period of the Order. Two articles by Anthony Luttrell provide valuable information: *Venetians at Medieval Malta*, MELITA HISTORICA, Vol. 3, No. 1, 1960, and *Malta and the Aragonese Crown: 1282–1530*, JOURNAL OF THE FACULTY OF ARTS, Royal University of Malta, Vol. III, No. 1, 1965.

Chapter IV

A large number of works have been written on the Order of St. John of Jerusalem. They vary immensely in validity and utility; unfortunately many of the most useful works are not easily available. The standard work on the history of the Order up to 1571 is Giacomo Bosio's *Dell' Istoria della Sacra Religione et Illma. Militia di San Giovanni Gierosolimitano*, Rome, 1602. Many subsequent writers have found this work a most profitable source. B. del Pozzo continues the history of the knights from the point at which Bosio ceased in *Historia della sacra religione militare di S. Giovanni Gerosolimitano, della di Malta*, Verona, 1703. R. Vertot's, *Histoire des Chevaliers Hospitaliers de St. Jean de Jérusalem*, 4 Vols, Paris, 1726, is available in English as *History of the Knights of Malta*, London, 1728. Vertot is a somewhat variegated source of information. Louis de Boisgelin's *Ancient and Modern Malta*, 2 vols., London, 1805, is a valuable book. Two books by Whitworth Porter are more easily available and generally reliable. *A History of the Knights of Malta*, 2 vols., London, 1858, and

Malta and its Knights, London 1871. Claire Eliane Engel's *L'Ordre de Malte en la Méditerranée,* 1530–1798, Monaco, 1957, is useful but not easily consulted.

Chapter V

There are innumerable descriptions of the Siege of Malta. Convenient accounts are to be found in *History of the Reign of Philip the Second,* W. H. Prescott, and *The Great Siege,* Ernle Bradford. Both these writers very largely retell the story of the Siege as recorded by sixteenth-century chroniclers, particularly Bosio and Francesco Balbi de Correggio. The latter was a foot soldier in Malta throughout the Siege and maintained a diary. In recent years two editions of Balbi's account have appeared in English: *The Siege of Malta,* trans. by Henry Alexander Balbi, Copenhagen, 1961, and *The Siege of Malta,* trans. by Ernle Bradford and published by the Folio Society, London, 1965.

The difficulties of Don Garcia de Toledo's position are indicated in *The Government of Sicily under Philip II,* Helmut Koenigsberger, 1951, and in R. B. Merriman's *The Rise of the Spanish Empire,* Vol. IV, 1934. Merriman drew principally on Spanish sources and, as a result, probably gives too much credit to Toledo and de Bazán in his account of the Siege. However, Merriman makes it clear that Toledo was acting resourcefully and was severely handicapped by the indecision of Philip II. Useful documents on the Siege are to be found in *Colleccion de Documentos Inéditos Para la Historia de España,* Vol. 29 (1856), and Vol. 30 (1857), Madrid.

Chapter VI

The major source of information on Malta during this period is the Archives of the Order, which are housed in the Royal Malta Library, Valletta. Other collections of documents, mostly uncatalogued, exist in the Valletta law-courts, the notarial archives, and the Archbishop's palace. The Rev. Can. A. Zammit Gabarretta and Rev. Giuseppe Mizzi have published a *Catalogue of the Records of the Order of St. John of Jerusalem in the Royal Malta Library,* Malta, 1964.

The standard works on the Order contain a great deal on this period but naturally look at events from the point of view of the knights. *Malta of the Knights,* Elizabeth Schermahorn, 1929, contains much information. *The Last of the Crusaders*, Roderick Cavaliero, 1960, is a very useful source on Malta in the eighteenth century. *The changing Landscape of Malta during the rule of the Order of St. John of Jerusalem, 1530–1798*, B. W. Blouet, Ph.D. thesis, University of Hull, 1964, contains more detail on the development of the islands than is presented here. Some interesting comments on Malta in the sixteenth century are to be found in an article by D. L. Farley Hills entitled *Was Marlowe's 'Malta' Malta?*, JOURNAL OF THE FACULTY OF ARTS, Royal University of Malta, Vol. III, No. 1, 1965.

The growth of population. *Malta: Background for Development*, contains remarks on population growth during the period as does *Aspects of the Demography of Malta*, M. Richardson, Ph.D. thesis, University of Durham, 1960. Cassar Pullicino's article *Social Aspects of an Apostolic Visit*, MELITA HISTORICA, Vol. II, No. 1, 1956, gives some information on population in 1575. The most important documentary sources are to be found in the Royal Malta Library. Information on individual settlements is to be found in parish archives which are normally retained by the parish priest.

The development of towns and villages. The thesis of M. Richardson, mentioned above, contains some discussion of these matters. *Town Planning in Malta 1530–1798*, B. W. Blouet, TOWN PLANNING REVIEW, Vol. XXXV, 1964, outlines the growth of the harbourside towns during the period. *The Officio delle Case and The Housing Laws of the earlier Grand Masters, 1531–69*, S. R. Borg Cardona, LAW JOURNAL, Malta, 1951, contains details of some of the Order's town-planning regulations. *The Building of Malta, 1530–1798*, Quentin Hughes, 1956, is the standard work on the architecture of Malta during the Order's rule. A series of short books by Dr. Edward Sammut—*The Co-Cathedral of St. John*, Malta, 1950, *The Palace of the Grand Masters*, Malta, 1951, *The Monuments of Mdina*, Malta, 1960, and *Art in Malta*, Malta, 1954—are all important contributions to the history of art and architecture in the islands. Sir Hannabel Scicluna's *The Church of St. John in Valletta*, Rome, 1955, is a superb book. The same author's *The Buildings and Fortifications of Malta*, in MALTA AND GIBRALTAR ILLUSTRATED, ed., A. MacMillan, London, 1915, contains a valuable account of the development of the island's fortifications. Victor Denaro has contributed a fine series of articles to MELITA HISTORICA which deal with many individual buildings that are to be found in Valletta. *Valletta—An*

Historical Sketch, T. Zammit, Malta, 1929, is an extremely useful source. *Valletta—A report to Accompany the Outline Plan for the Region of Valletta and the Three Cities*, Austen St. B. Harrison and R. Pearse S. Hubbard, Valletta, 1945, contains much interesting historical information.

Trade, Industry and Finance. Boisgelin (op. cit.) contains a great deal of useful information on the Order's finances in the late eighteenth century including accounts. W. H. Thornton's *Memoir on the Finances of the Order*, Malta, 1836, attempts to estimate the contribution which the Order made to the local economy. Boisgelin also contains much on trade as does *The Last of the Crusaders*. E. Rossi's *Storia della marina dell' Ordene di S. Giovanni di Gerusalemme, di Rodi e di Malta*, Rome, 1926, outlines the development of the Order's navy and associated facilities. Roderick Cavaliero's *The decline of the Maltese Corso in the XVIIIth century*, MELITA HISTORICA, Vol. 2, No. 4, 1959, is an interesting study of the island's pillaging industry. A great deal of research work on the history of slavery in Malta has been undertaken by Godfrey Wettinger. Little has been published so far although *Coron captives in Malta, An episode in the history of slave-dealing*, MELITA HISTORICA, Vol. 2, No. 4, 1959, and *The galley-convicts and buonavoglia in Malta during the rule of the Order*, JOURNAL OF THE FACULTY OF ARTS, Royal University of Malta, Vol. III, No. 1, 1965, contain a great deal of interest.

On ecclesiastical history *Descrizione storica delle Chiese de Malta e Gozo*, Malta, 1866, is the standard work. *The Rising of the Priests* by P. Callus, Malta, 1961, and Professor A. Vella's *The Tribunal of Inquisition in Malta*, Royal University of Malta, 1964, contain much useful information.

In conclusion two general accounts of the islands published during the Order's rule should be mentioned. Giovanni Francesco Abela's *Della Descrizione di Malta*, Malta, 1647, contains a very fine description of Malta at the time. Nearly a century and a half later Abela's work was revised by Gio. Antonio Ciantar and published as *Malta Illustrata*, Malta, 1780.

Chapter VII and Chapter VIII

Roderick Cavaliero, op. cit., 1960, has many interesting things to say on the Order in decline. The standard works on the French period are: Scicluna, H.P., *Documents relating to the French Occupation of Malta in 1798–1800*, Malta, 1923; Hardman, W., *A History of Malta during the French and British Occupations 1798–1815*, London, 1909. More recently Victor F. Denaro has produced an excellent study entitled *The French in Malta*, which has been published in the quarterly magazine SCIENTIA, Malta, 1963.

There are a large number of official sources relating to the British period, which are stored in record offices in London and Malta. It is unnecessary to list these sources here for C. A. Price's *Malta and the Maltese. A study in Nineteenth Century Migration*, Melbourne, 1954, contains an extensive bibliography of the period. *British Malta* by A. V. Laferla, Malta, 1947, is a fine study of the period. *An Outline of The Constitutional Development of Malta under British Rule*, J. J. Cremona, Royal University of Malta, 1963, is a good, compact treatment of the subject. Hilda J. Lee has contributed to MELITA HISTORICA several articles on British policy towards the Maltese.

Chapter IX

The official war histories outline the military situation at Malta. The *Debates of the Council of Government* for the relevant period contain a great deal of information on the hardships which the population suffered. *The Battle for the Mediterranean*, Donald Macintyre, gives full weight to the part Malta played in this theatre of the Second World War. *Briefed to Attack*, Air Marshal Sir Hugh Lloyd's story of air operations at Malta during the period of his command, besides being an excellent general account, contains much on the technical problems associated with air operations from the Malta bases. Many who served in Malta have recorded their impressions of events; I found *A Sailor's Odyssey*, Viscount Cunningham of Hyndhope, 1951, and *Malta Strikes Back*, Major R. T. Gilchrist, 1945, particularly useful. The diaries of Ciano provide a great deal of information on Axis plans to invade Malta. *The Maltese Economy During World War II*, Salvino Busuttil, MALTA YEAR BOOK, 1965, is one of the very few studies we have of economic matters during the period. Unfortunately few accounts of life in the islands have been published by Maltese who lived through the war.

Chapter X

A large number of reports have been published on social, economic, and constitutional problems. Most of these works are referred to in *Malta: Background for Development*. Later work of importance includes: *Review of the Development Plan for the Maltese Islands 1959–64*, Malta, 1961; and *Development Plan for the Maltese Islands 1964–69*, Malta, 1964. Stolper's discussion of the second plan is contained in *Economic Adaptation and Development in Malta*, Wolfgang F. Stolper, United Nations Commissioner for Technical Assistance, Department of Economic and Social Affairs, 1964. An account of the dockyard troubles will be found in *Report on Bailey (Malta) Ltd.* (H.C. 131), J. R. Muirie, 1963. The provisions for British aid to Malta are outlined in *Proposed Agreement on Mutual Defence and Assistance*, (Cmnd. 2423).

Recent constitutional developments are basically covered by *Report of the Malta Constitutional Commission, 1960*, (Cmnd. 1261), and *Malta: Independence Conference, 1963*, (Cmnd. 2121).

Index